A History of Shorthand

Also from Westphalia Press
westphaliapress.org

The Idea of the Digital University

Criminology Confronts Cultural Change

Eight Decades in Syria

Avant-Garde Politician

Socrates: An Oration

Strategies for Online Education

Conflicts in Health Policy

Material History and Ritual Objects

Jiu-Jitsu Combat Tricks

Opportunity and Horatio Alger

Careers in the Face of Challenge

Bookplates of the Kings

Collecting American Presidential Autographs

Misunderstood Children

Original Cables from the Pearl Harbor Attack

Social Satire and the Modern Novel

The Amenities of Book Collecting

Trademark Power

A Definitive Commentary on Bookplates

James Martineau and Rebuilding Theology

Royalty in All Ages

The Middle East: New Order or Disorder?

The Man Who Killed President Garfield

Chinese Nights Entertainments: Stories from Old China

Understanding Art

Homeopathy

The Signpost of Learning

Collecting Old Books

The Boy Chums Cruising in Florida Waters

The Thomas Starr King Dispute

Salt Water Game Fishing

Lariats and Lassos

Mr. Garfield of Ohio

The Wisdom of Thomas Starr King

The French Foreign Legion

War in Syria

Naturism Comes to the United States

Water Resources: Iniatives and Agendas

Designing, Adapting, Strategizing in Online Education

Feeding the Global South

The Design of Life: Development from a Human Perspective

A History of Shorthand

Written in Shorthand

by Isaac Pitman

WESTPHALIA PRESS
An Imprint of Policy Studies Organization

A History of Shorthand, Written in Shorthand

Westphalia Press
An imprint of Policy Studies Organization
1527 New Hampshire Ave., NW
Washington, D.C. 20036
info@ipsonet.org

ISBN-13: 978-1-63391-536-7
ISBN-10: 1-63391-536-0

Cover design by Jeffrey Barnes:
jbarnesbook.design

Daniel Gutierrez-Sandoval, Executive Director
PSO and Westphalia Press

Updated material and comments on this edition
can be found at the Westphalia Press website:
www.westphaliapress.org

A HISTORY OF SHORTHAND.

BY

ISAAC PITMAN.

Written in Phonography.

LONDON.

FRED PITMAN, PHONETIC DEPOT, 20, PATERNOSTER ROW

1852.

INDEX.

Index.

HISTORY
OF
SHORTHAND.

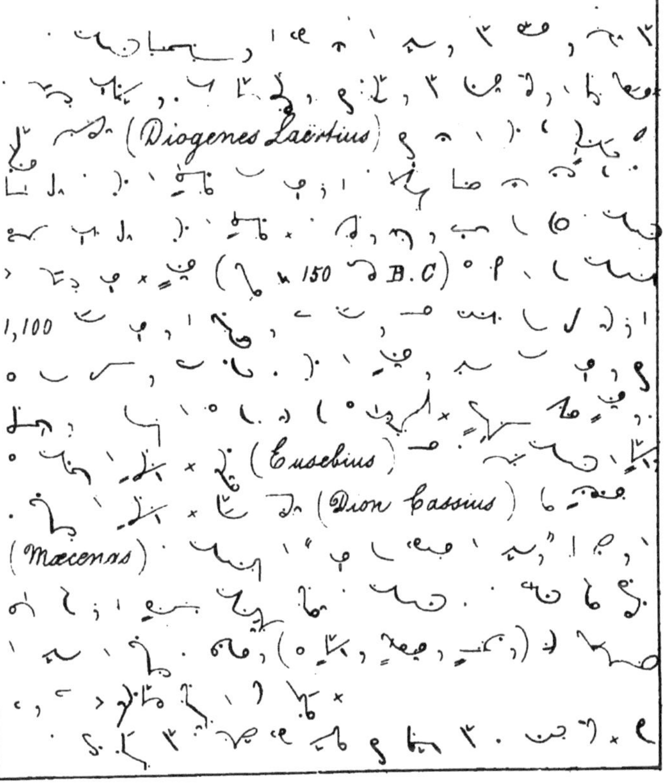

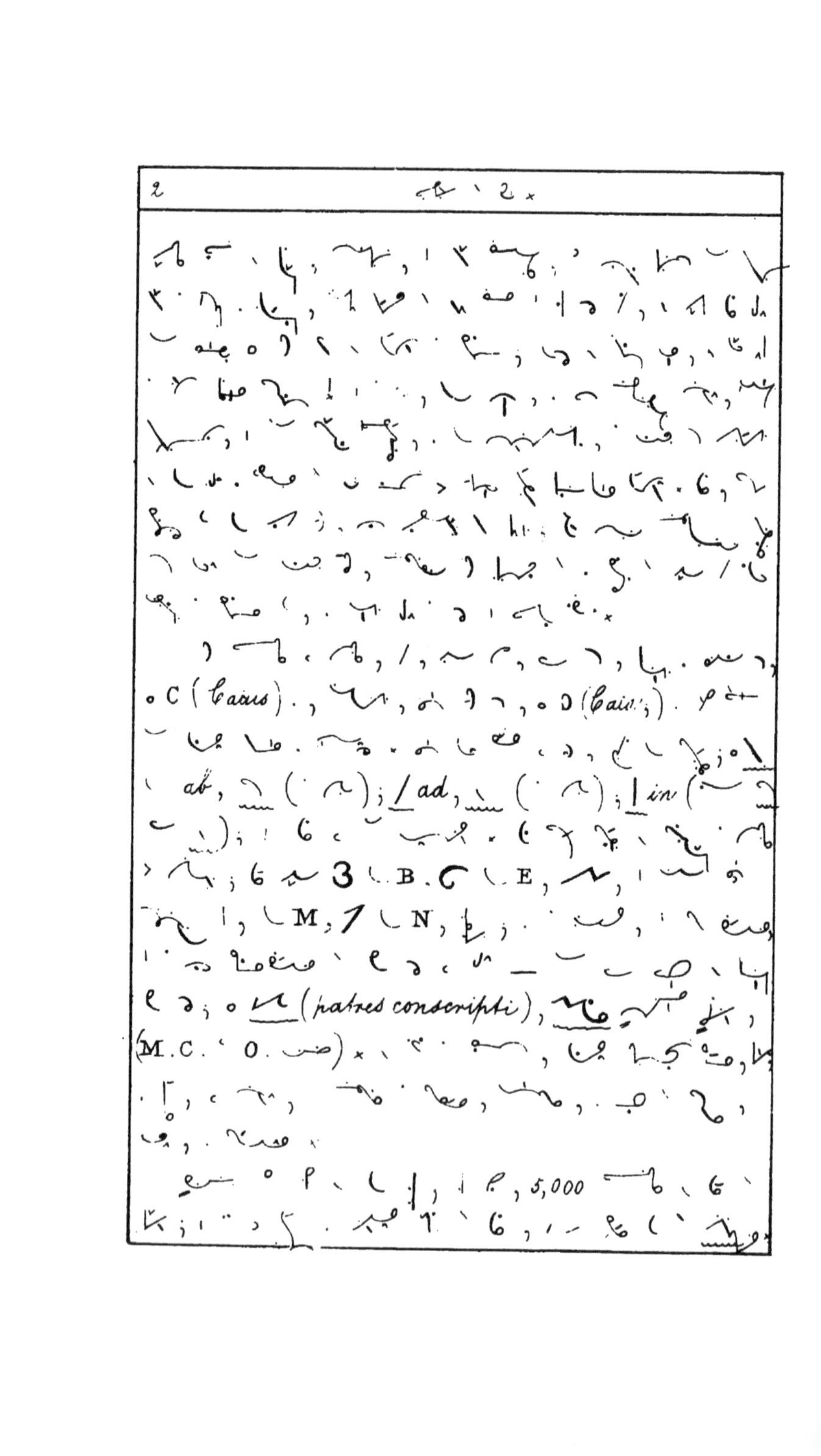

C (Caius) … D (Caius)

ab, … ad, … in

3 … B. … E, … M, … N,

(patres conscripti),

(M. C. … O. …)

5,000

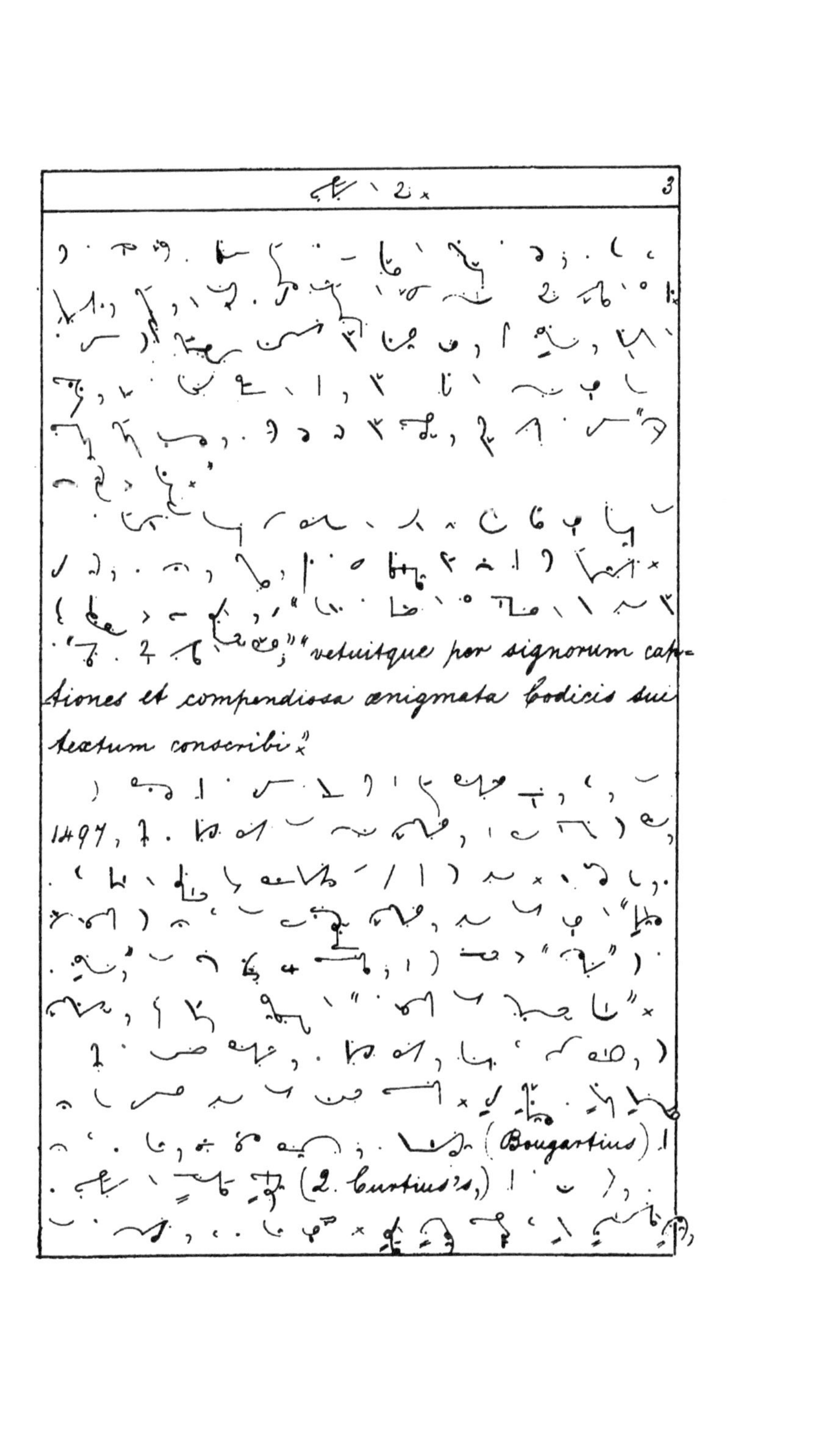

1497,

"vetuitque per signorum captiones et compendiosa ænigmata codicis sui textum conscribi."

(Bougartius)

(2. Curtius's,)

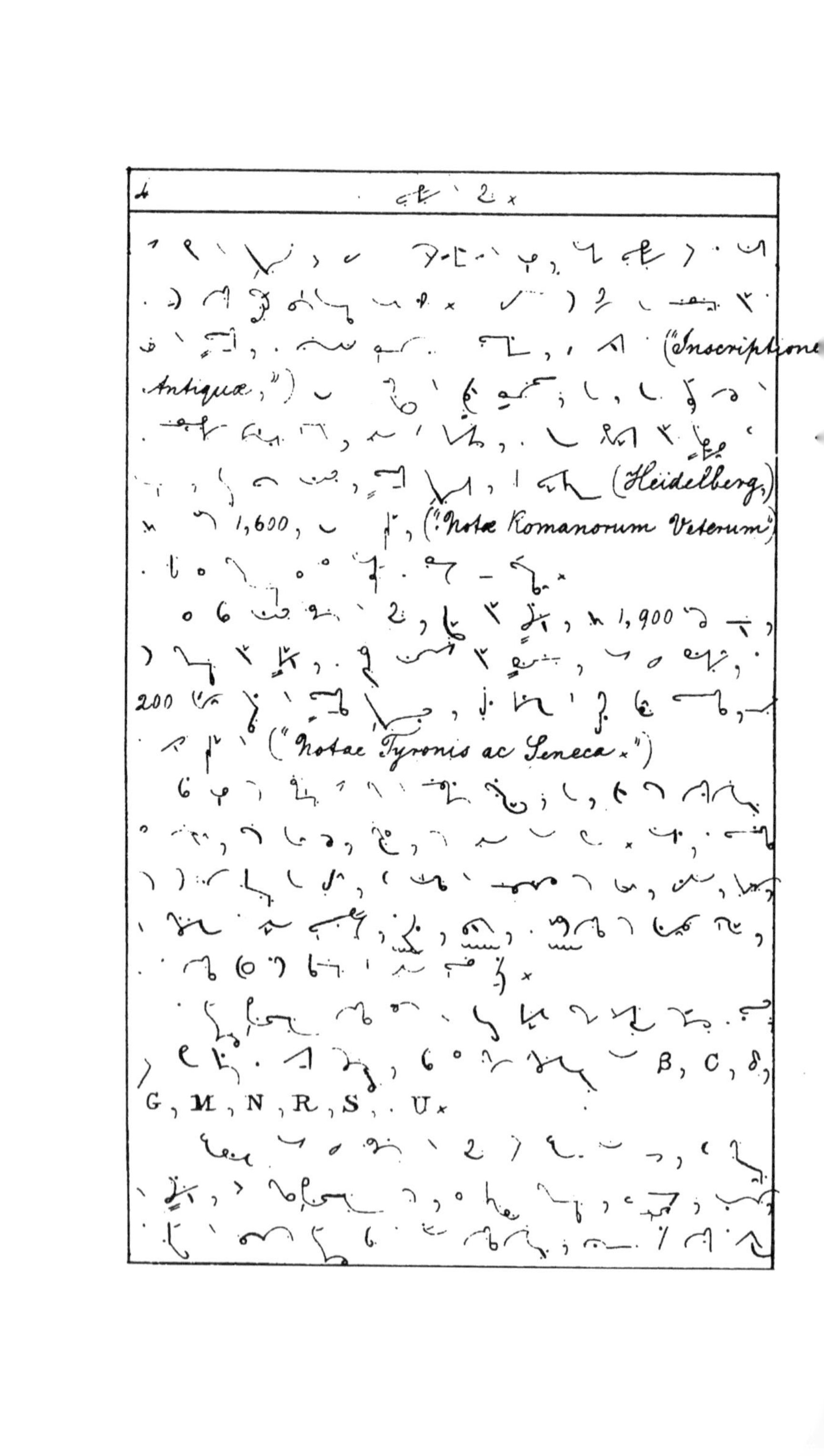

("Inscriptiones Antiquæ,")

(Heidelberg,)

1,600, ("Notæ Romanorum Veterum")

1,900

200

("Notae Tyronis ac Senecæ.")

B, C, D, G, M, N, R, S, . U.

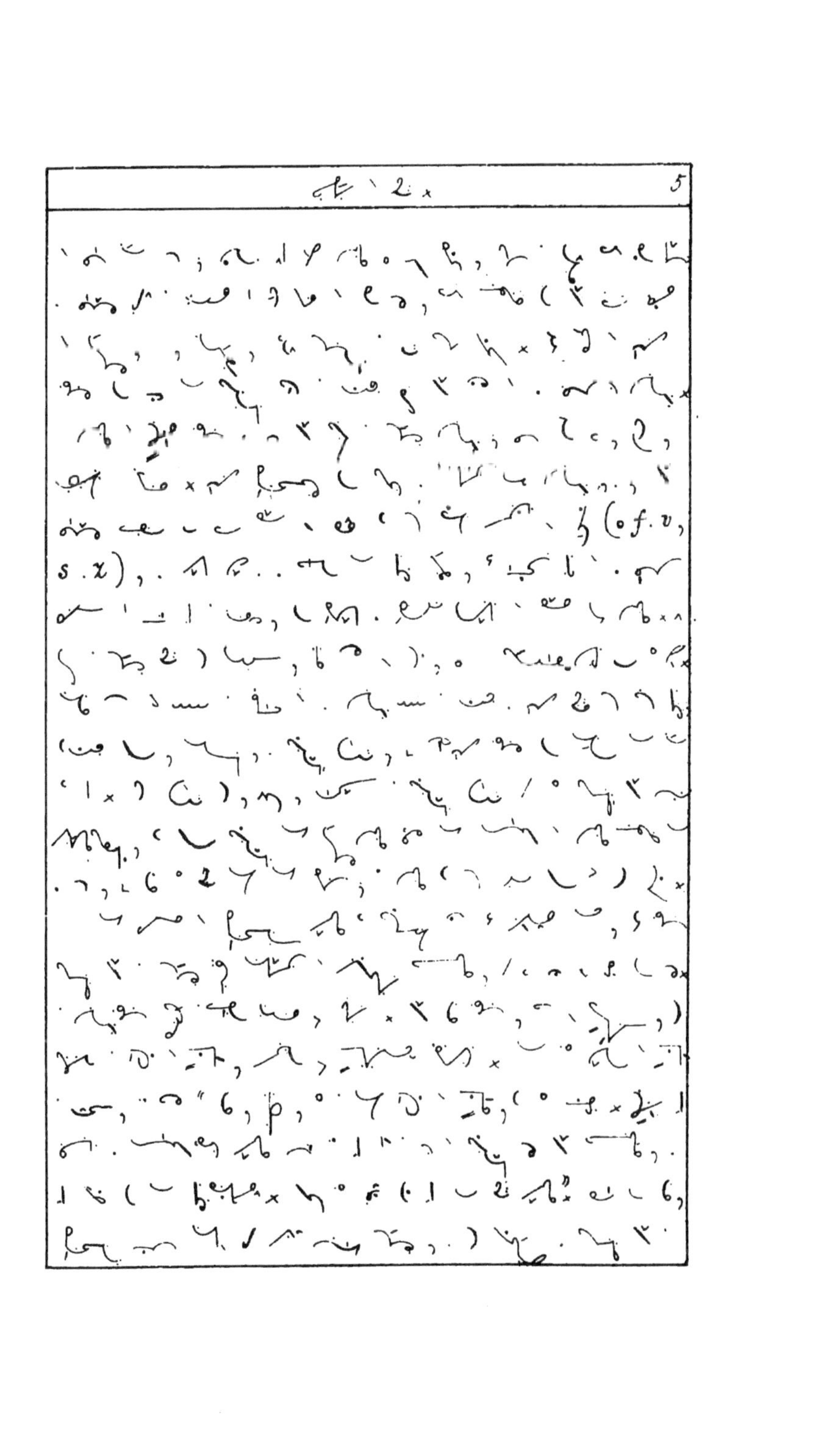

(of. v, s. x)

(1) (Staines's) 98

[illegible] (2)

[illegible]

[illegible], pp. 28—30.

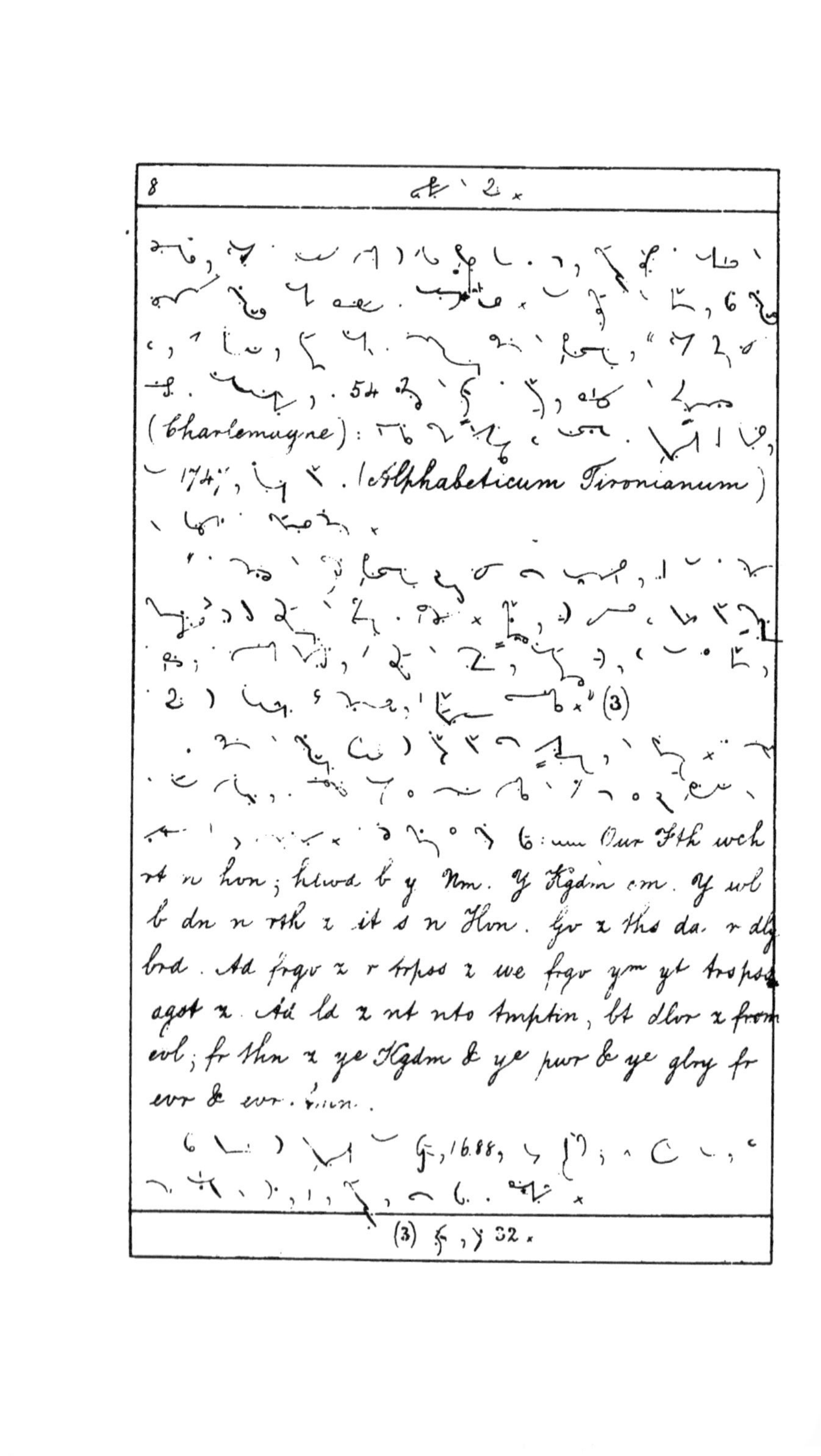

54 (Charlemagne): 174 (Alphabeticum Tironianum)

(3)

Our Fth wch rt n hvn; hlwd b y Nm. Y Kgdm cm. Y wl b dn n rth z it s n Hvn. Gv z ths da. r dly brd. Ad frgv z r trpss z we frgv ym yt trpss agst z. Ad ld z nt nto tmptin, bt dlvr z from evl; fr thn z ye Kgdm & ye pwr & ye glry fr evr & evr. Amn.

1688

(3) 32.

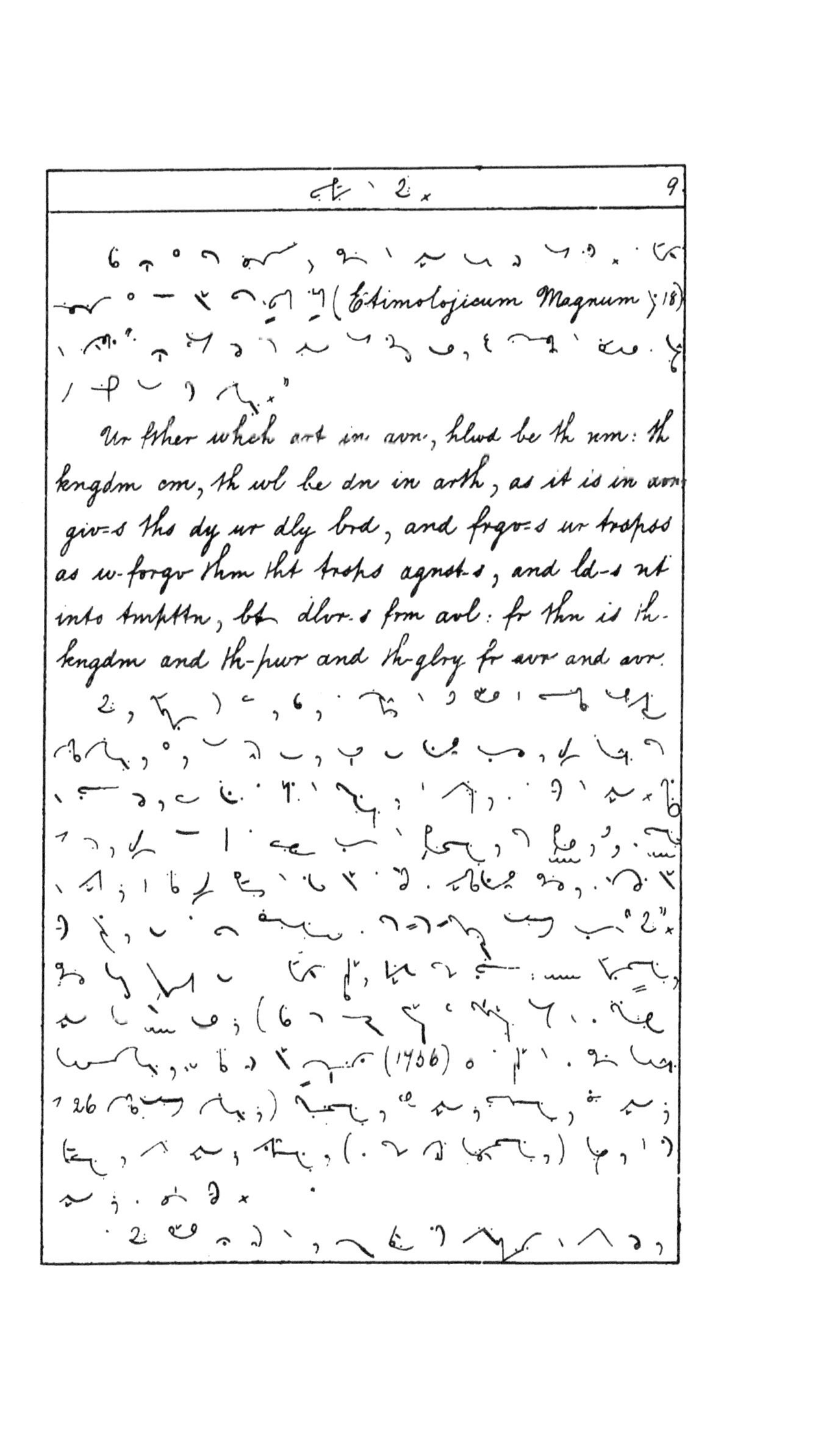

(Etimolojicum Magnum; 18)

Ur fther whch art in avn, hlwd be th nm: th kngdm cm, th wl be dn in arth, as it is in avn: giv-s ths dy ur dly brd, and frgv-s ur trspss as w-forgv thm tht trsps agnst-s, and ld-s nt into tmpttn, bt dlvr-s frm avl: fr thn is th-kngdm and th-pwr and th-glry fr avr and avr.

(1756)

126

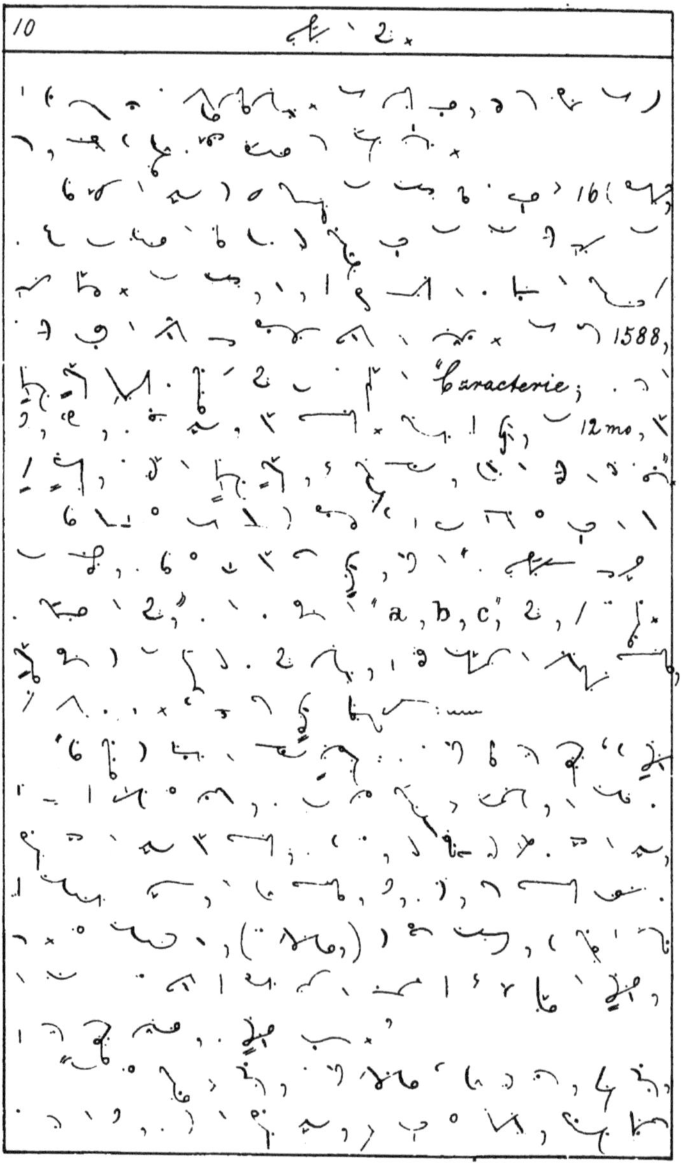
16
1588
Caracterie
12mo
a, b, c

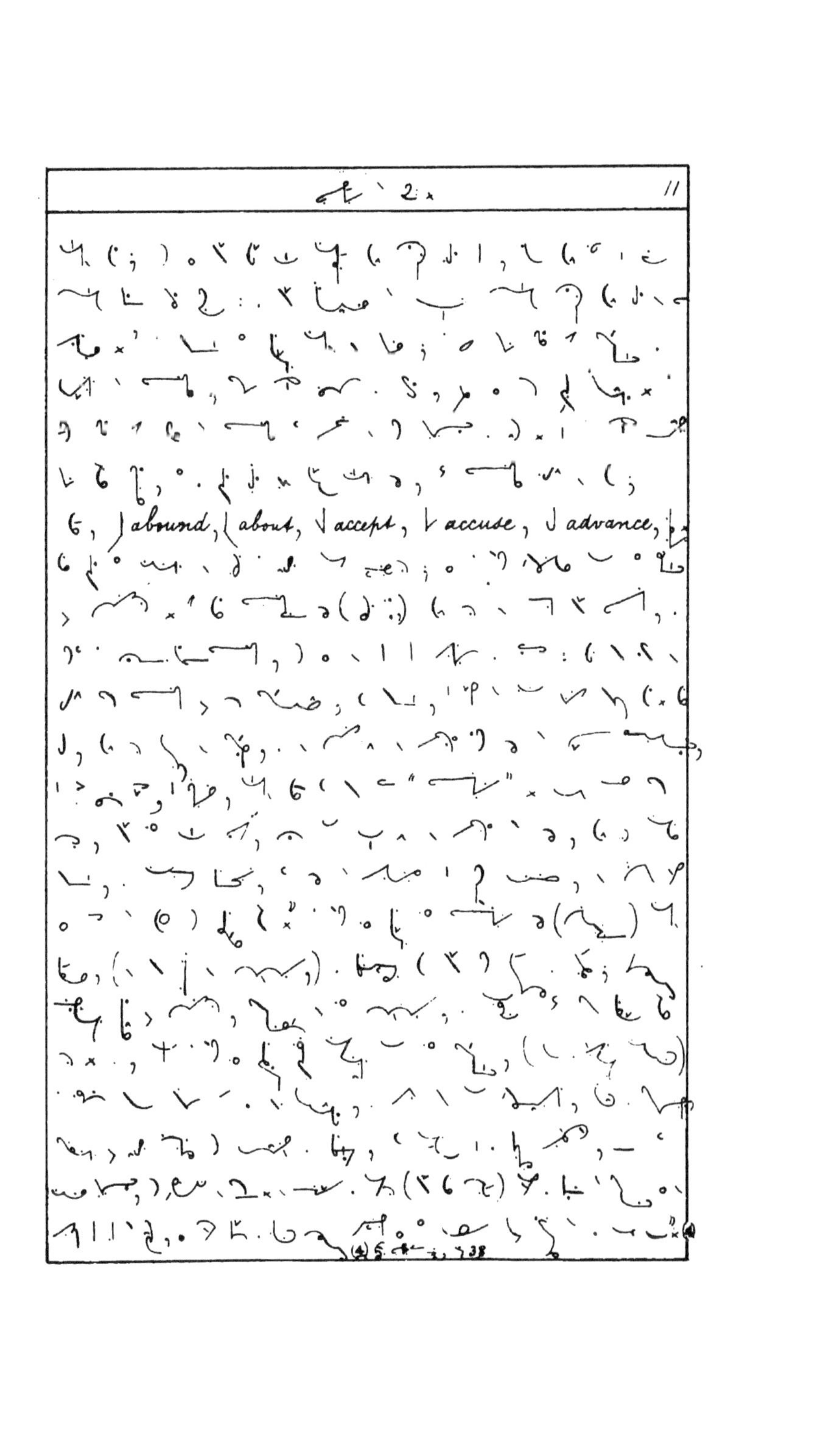

abound, about, accept, accuse, advance,

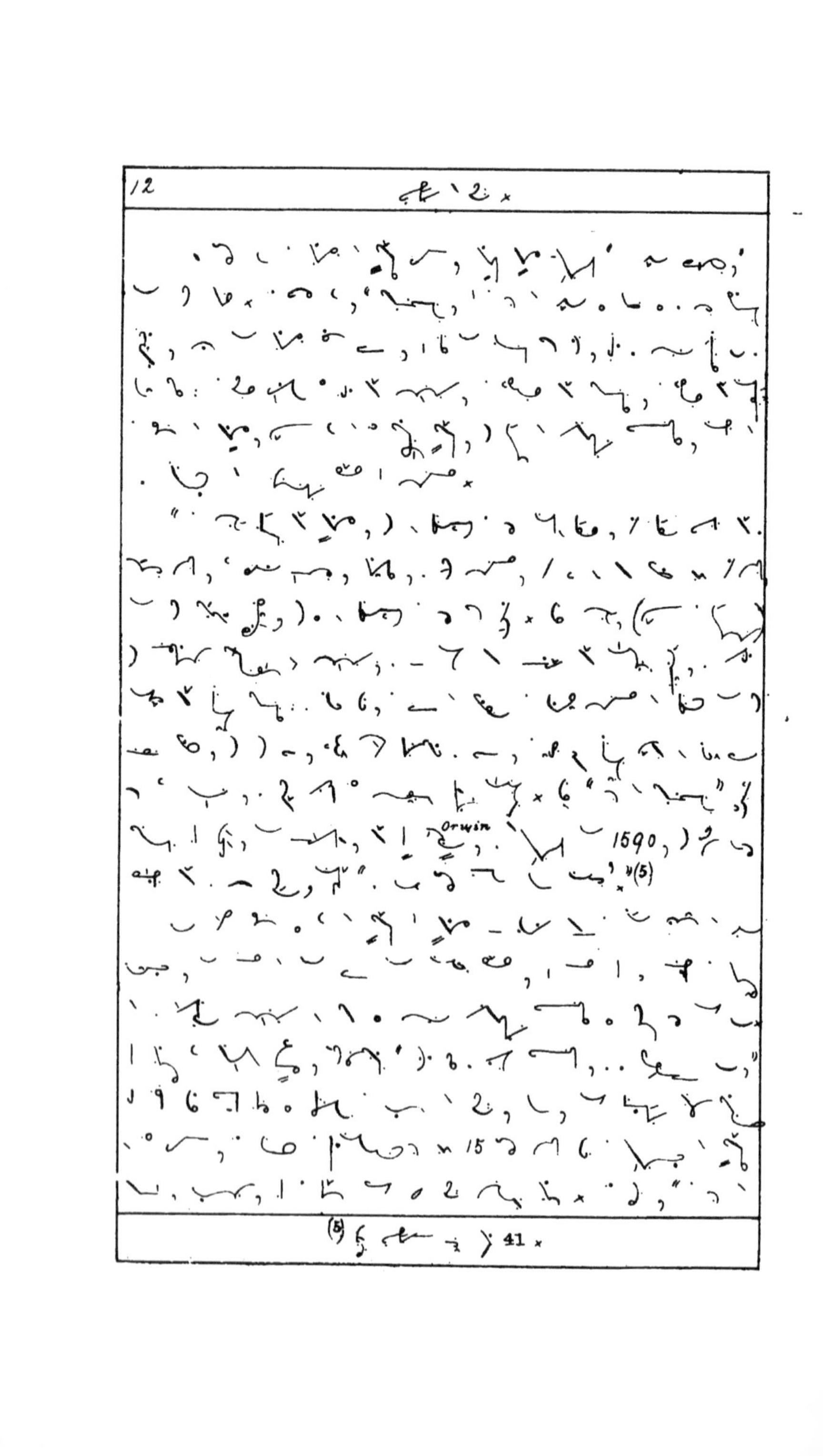

Orwin

1590

(5)

15

(5) 41

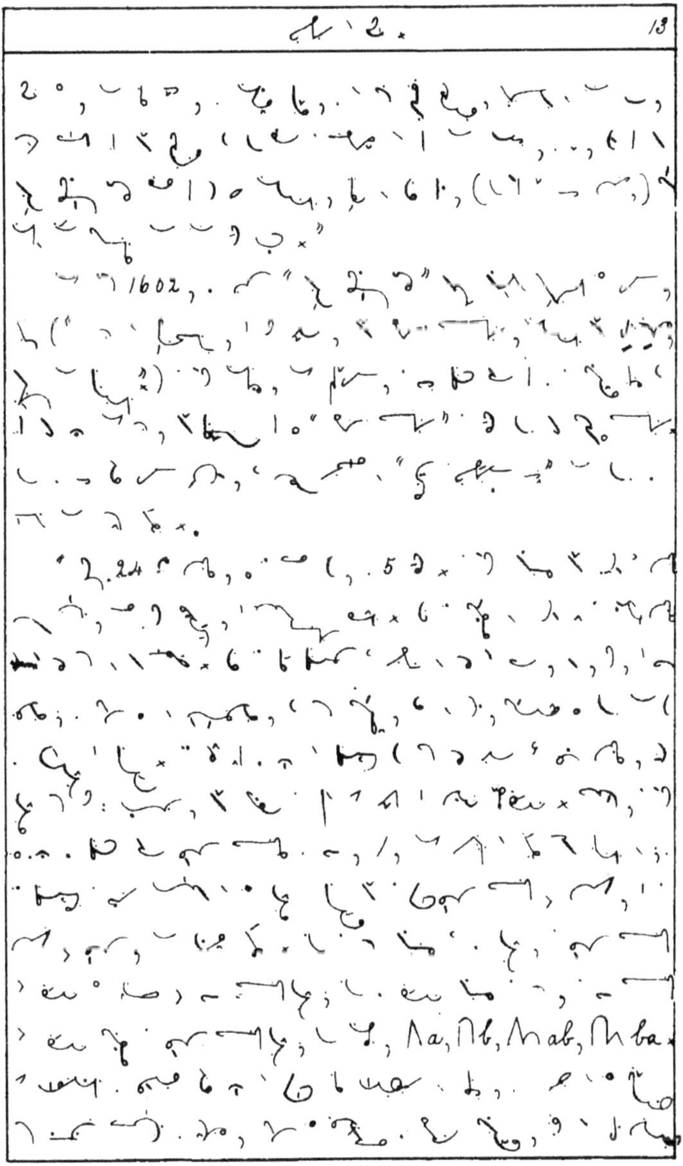
1602
24
5
Λa, Πb, Λab, Πba

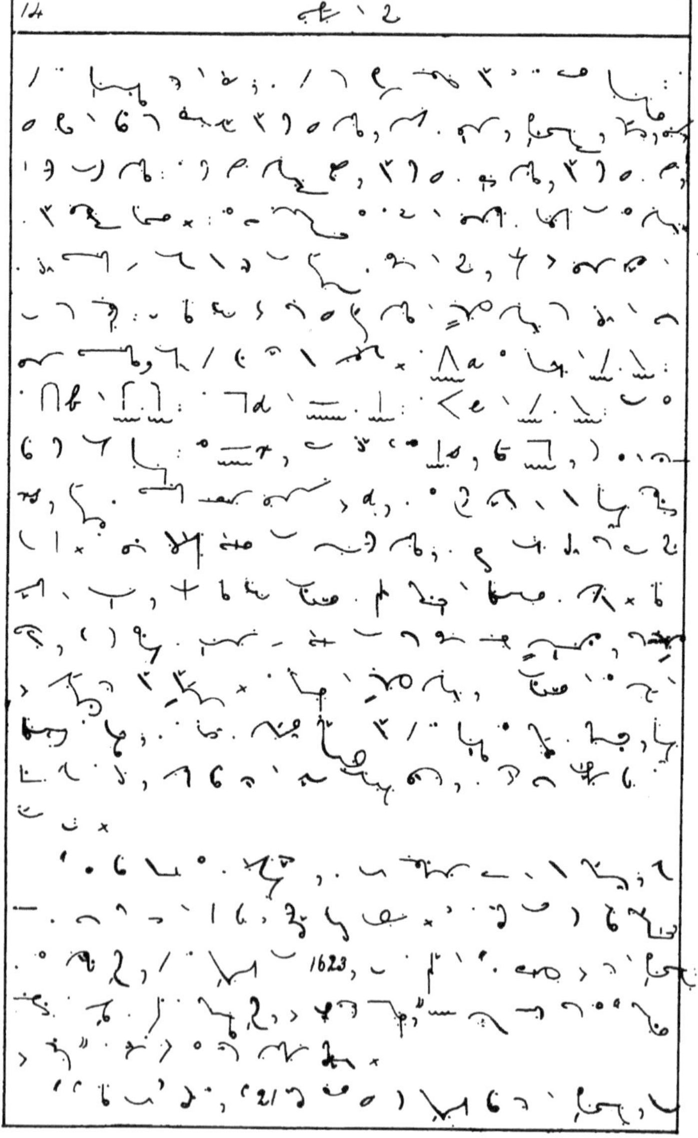
1623

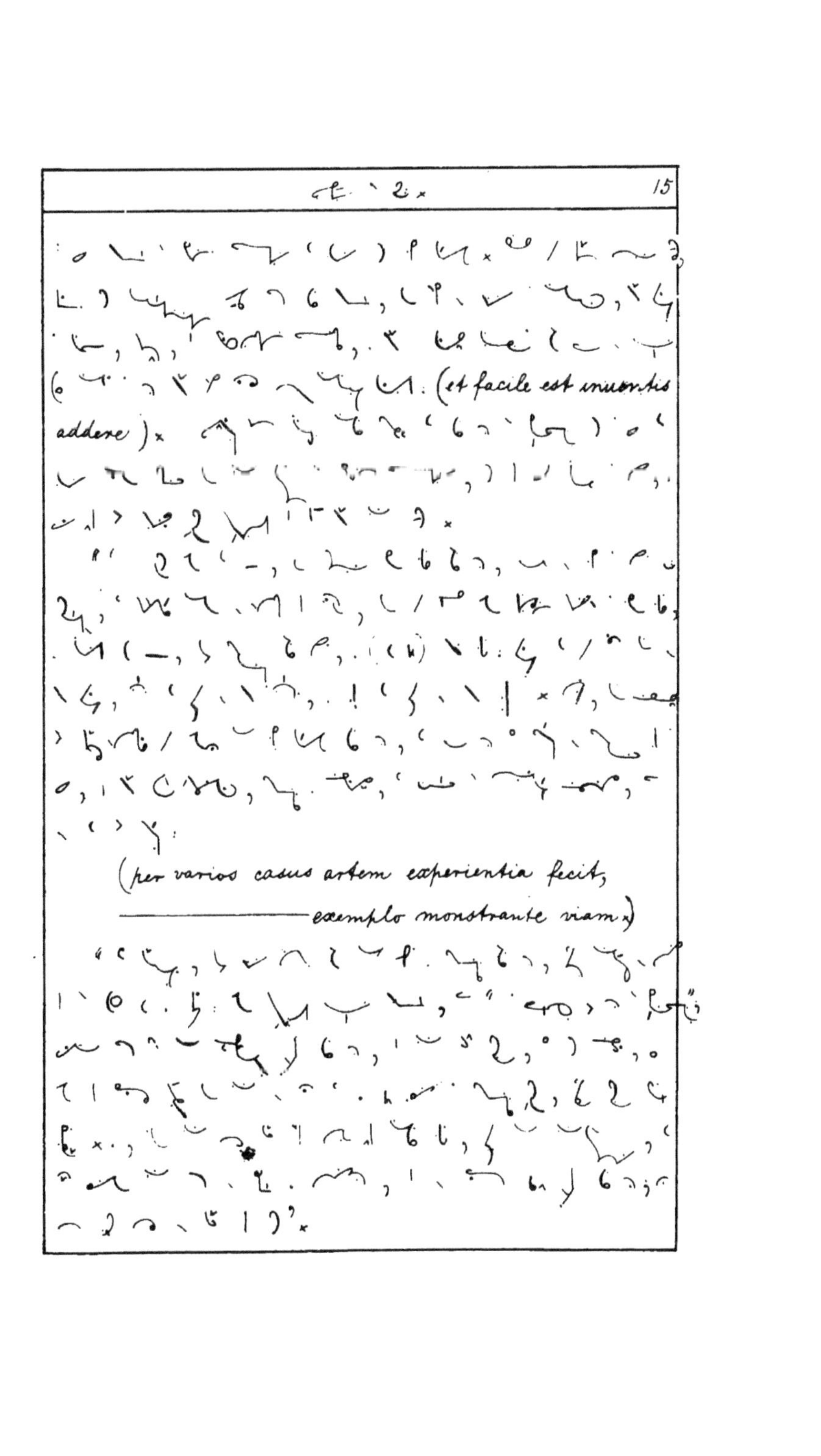

(et facile est inuentis addere)

(per varios casus artem experientia fecit,
———————— exemplo monstrante viam.)

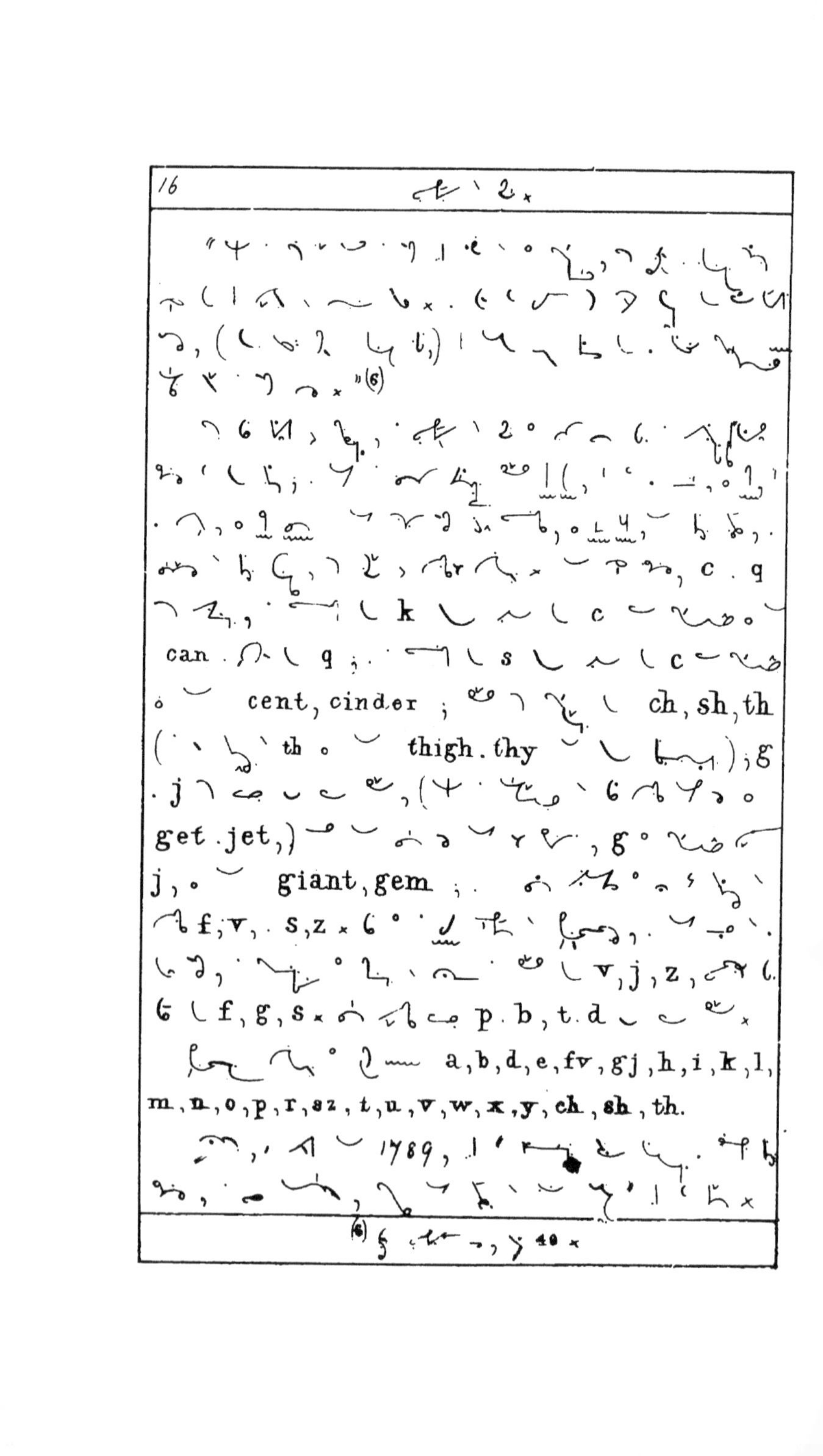

"(6)

c . q

k c

can q ; s c

cent, cinder ; ch, sh, th

th thigh. thy); g

. j

get . jet,) g

j, giant, gem ;

f, v, . s, z

v, j, z,

f, g, s p . b, t . d

a, b, d, e, fv, gj, h, i, k, l,

m, n, o, p, r, sz, t, u, v, w, x, y, ch, sh, th.

1789,

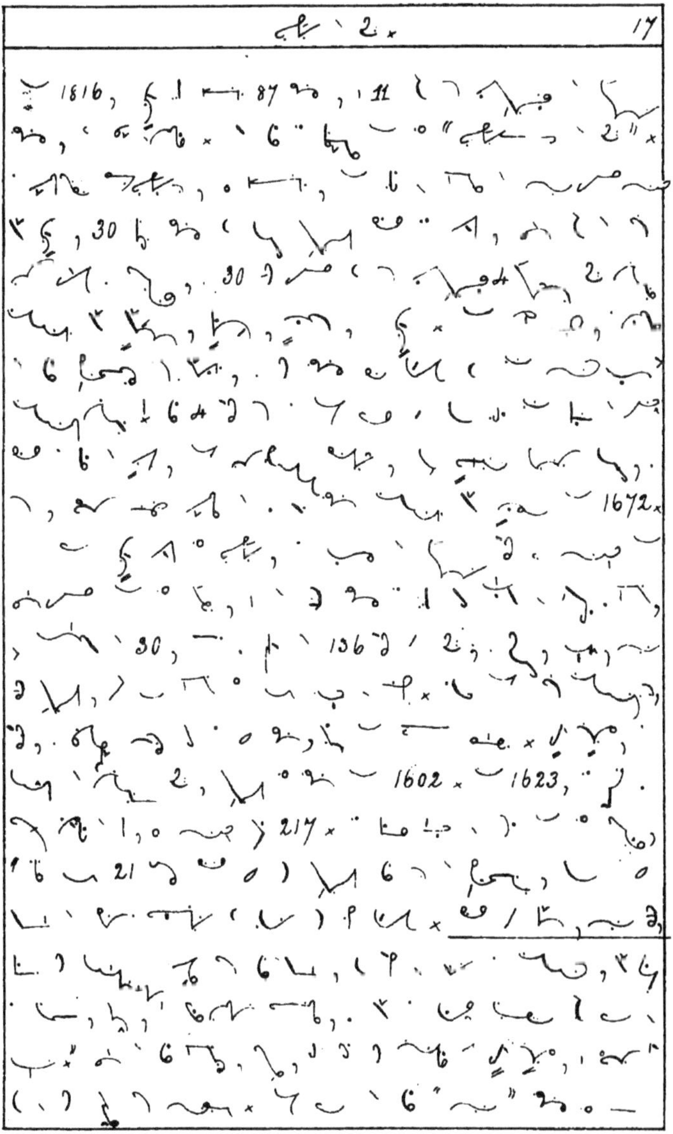

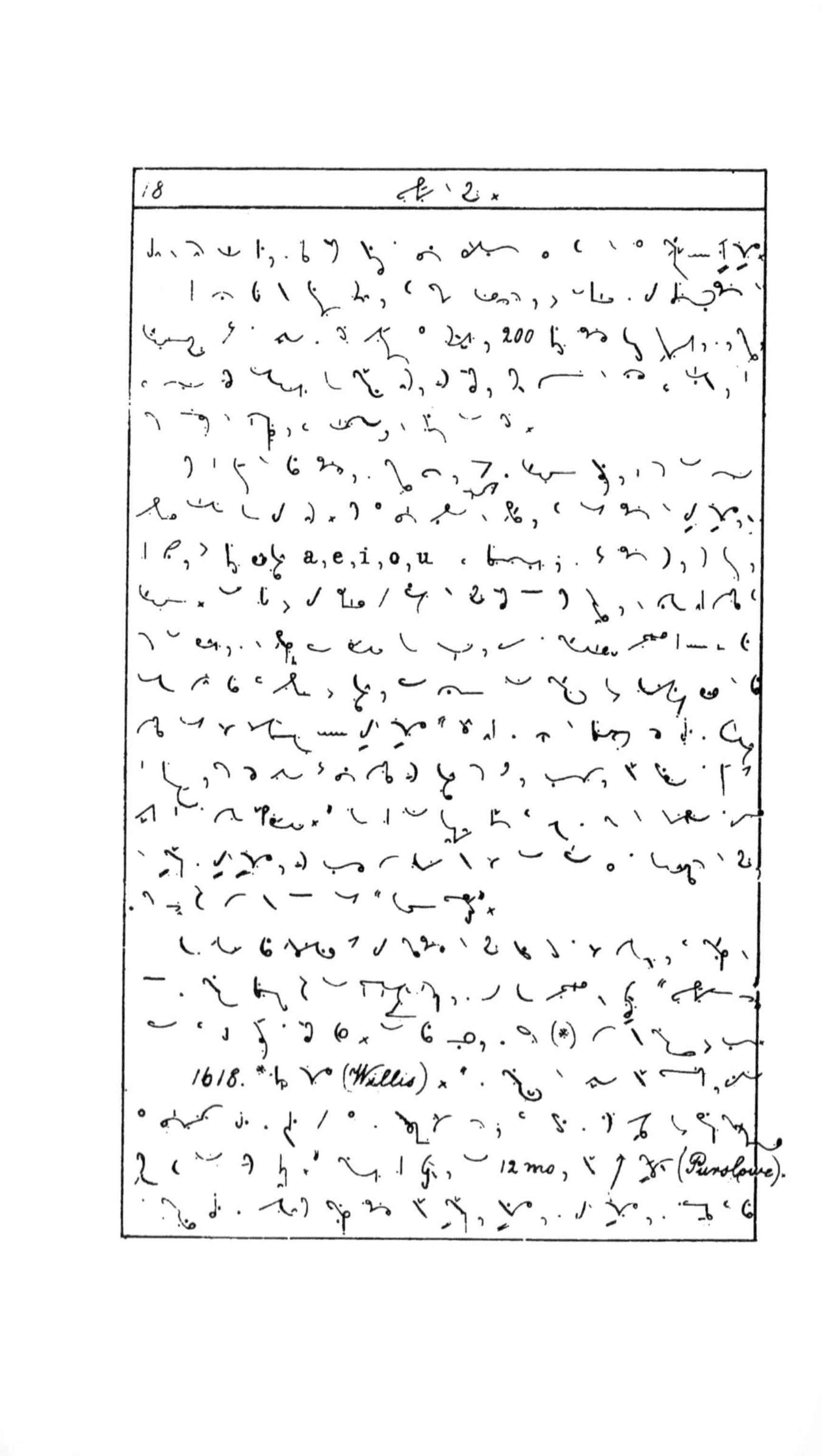

200

a, e, i, o, u

(*)

1618. (Willis)

12mo, (Purslowe).

ai ea

a

ee | e

oi | i

oo | o

u

au ou

200

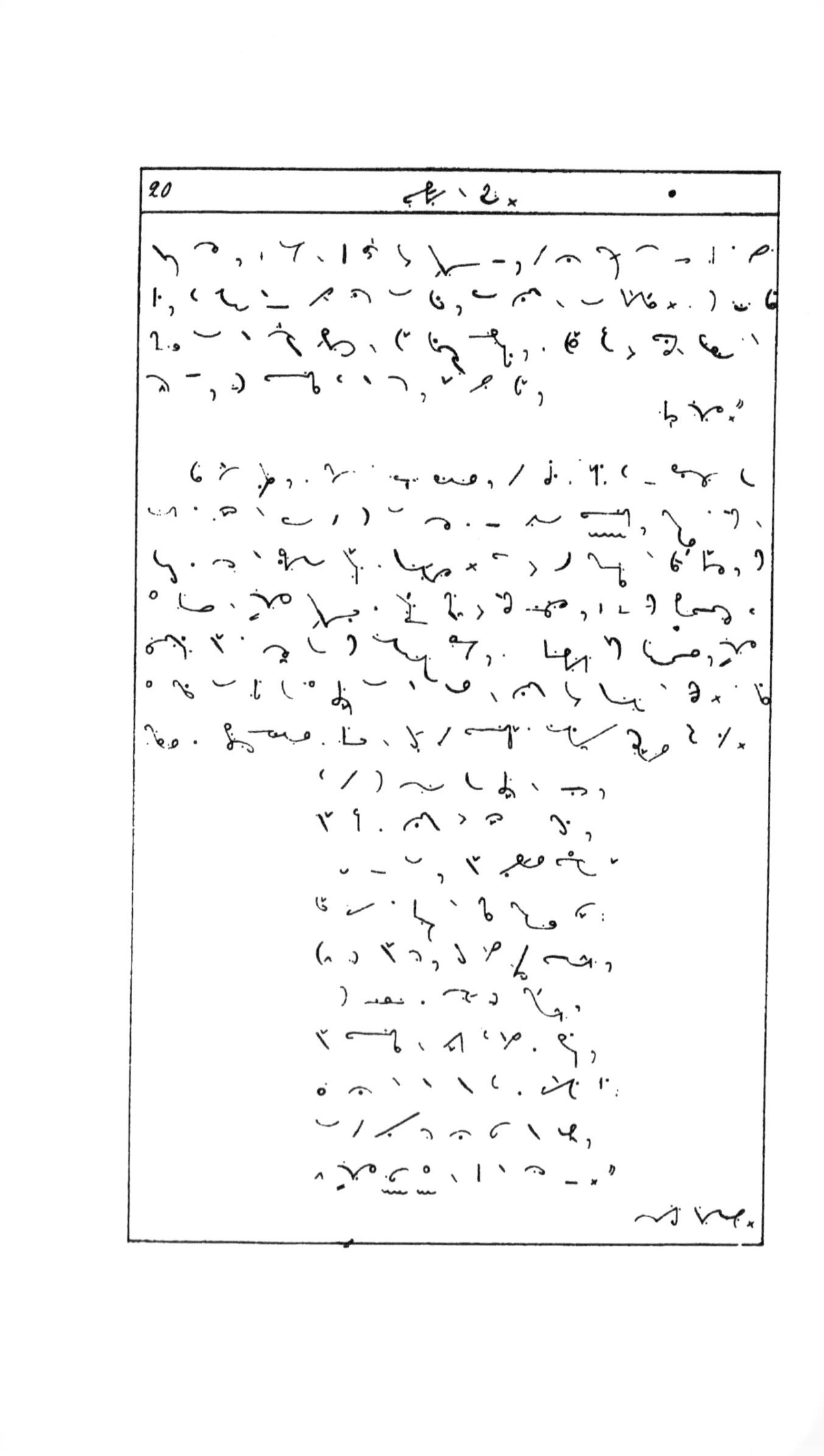

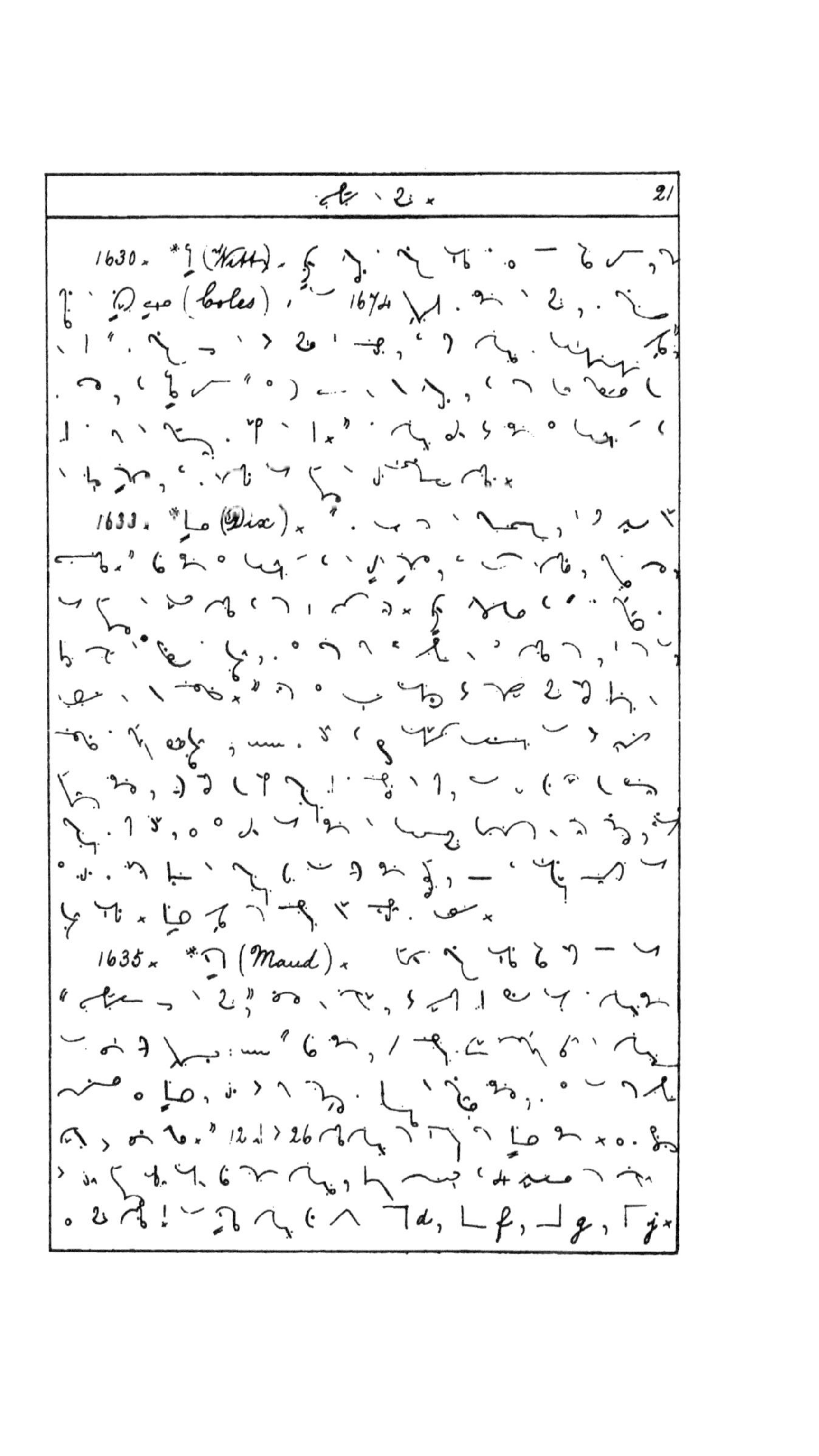

1630. (Kitty) (Coles) 1674

1633. (Dix)

1635. (Maud) 12 26 d, f, g, j.

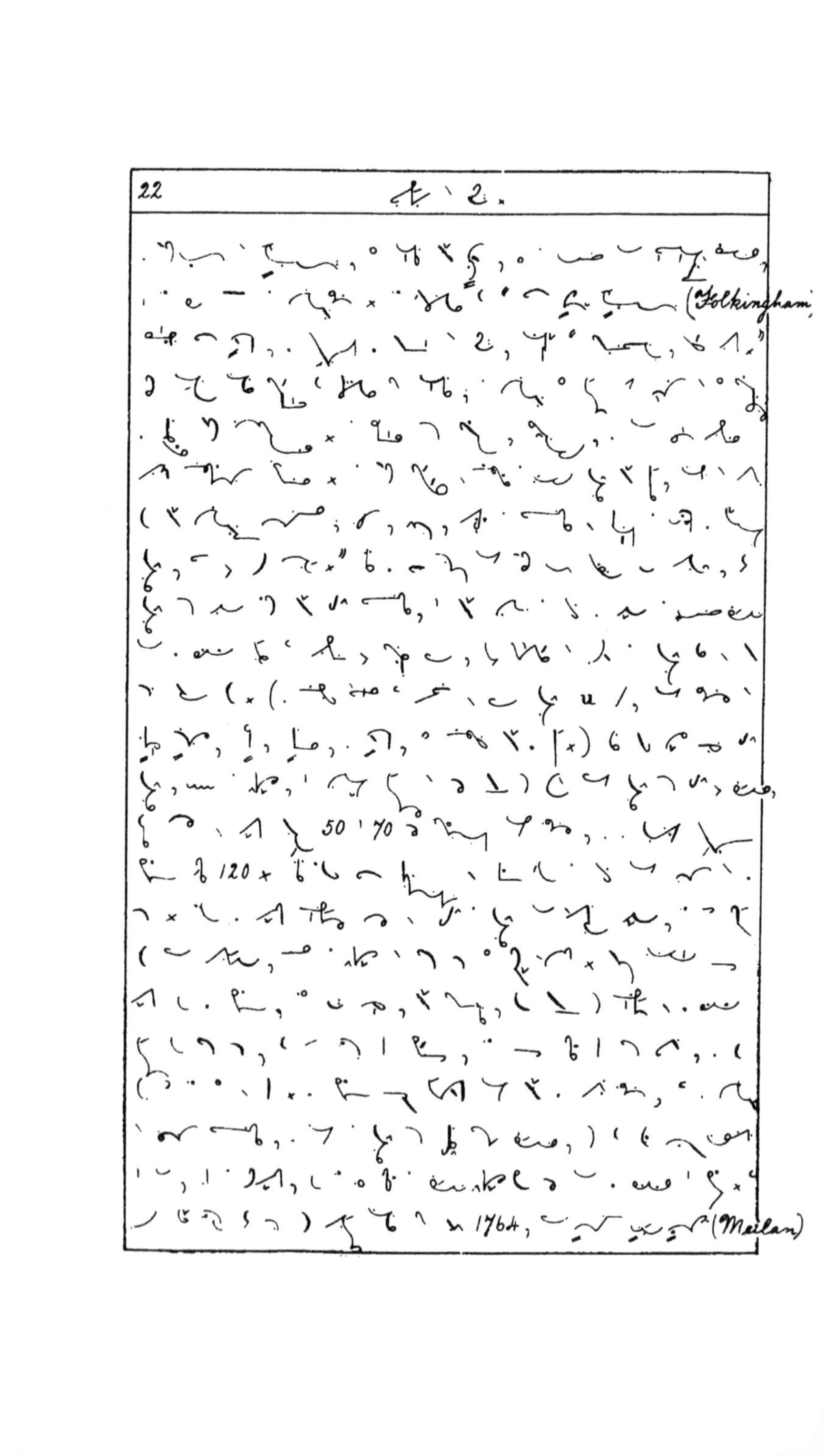

(Folkingham)

50 70

120

1764, (Mailan)

(a, e, i, o, u.)

1763

1767

1641 (Shelton)

1650

1641 q, r, u, x,

(Tracy)

1710 1641

2

a, i

b, n,

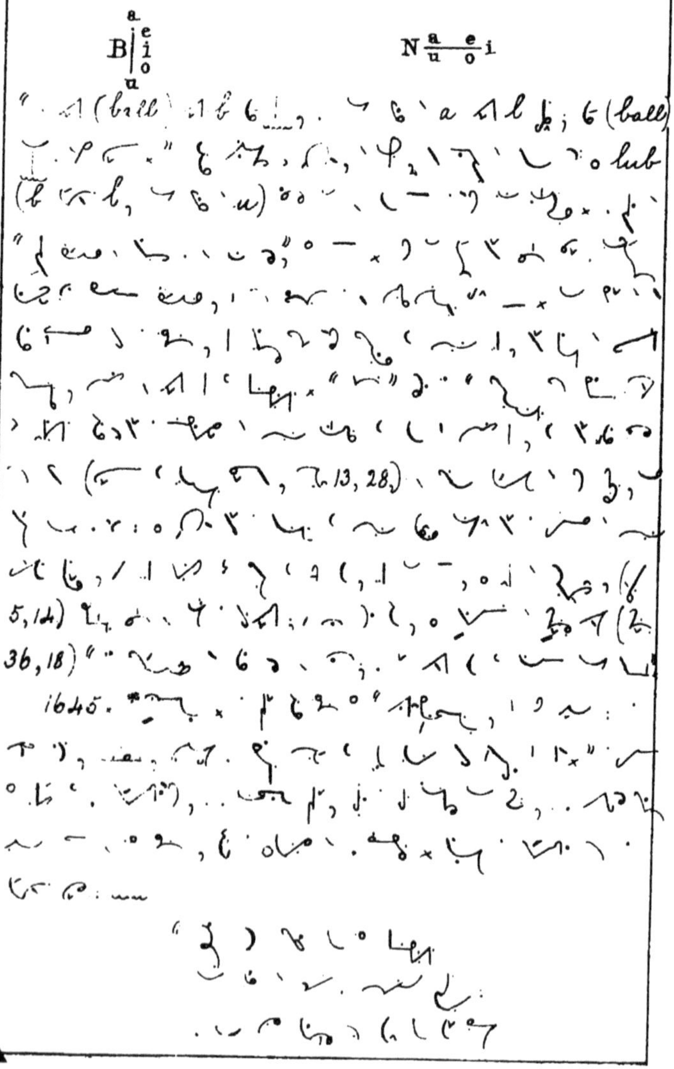
B a e i o u
N a e u o i
(ball)
(ball)
lub
(b u)
13, 28
5, 14
36, 18
1645

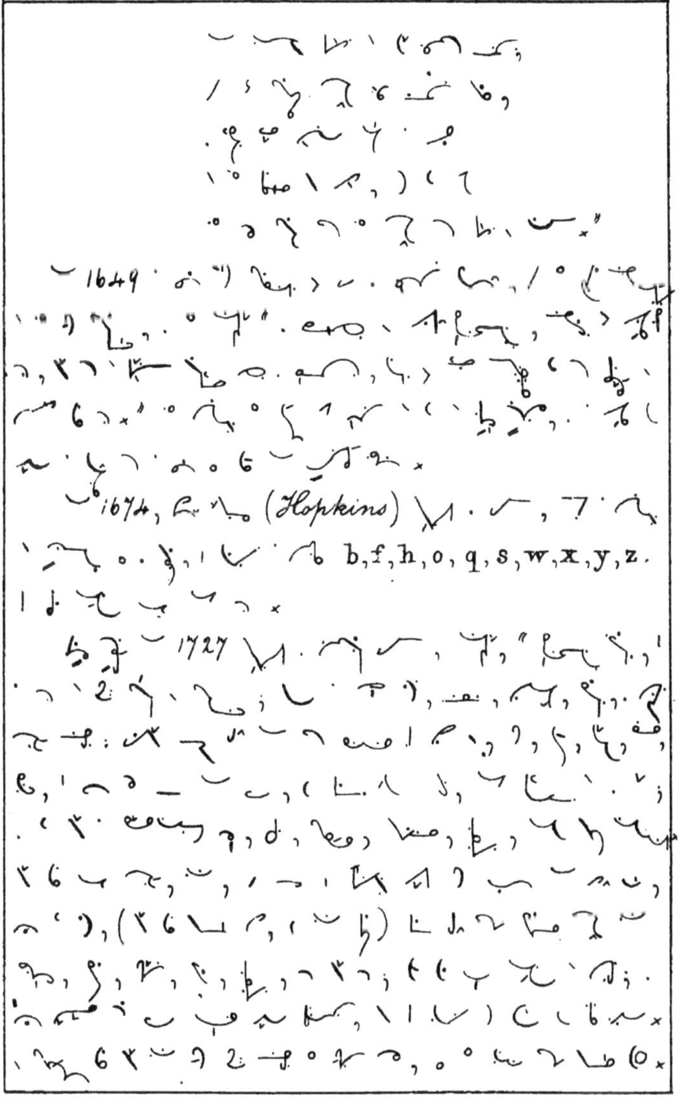
1649
1674, (Hopkins)
b, f, h, o, q, s, w, x, y, z.
1727

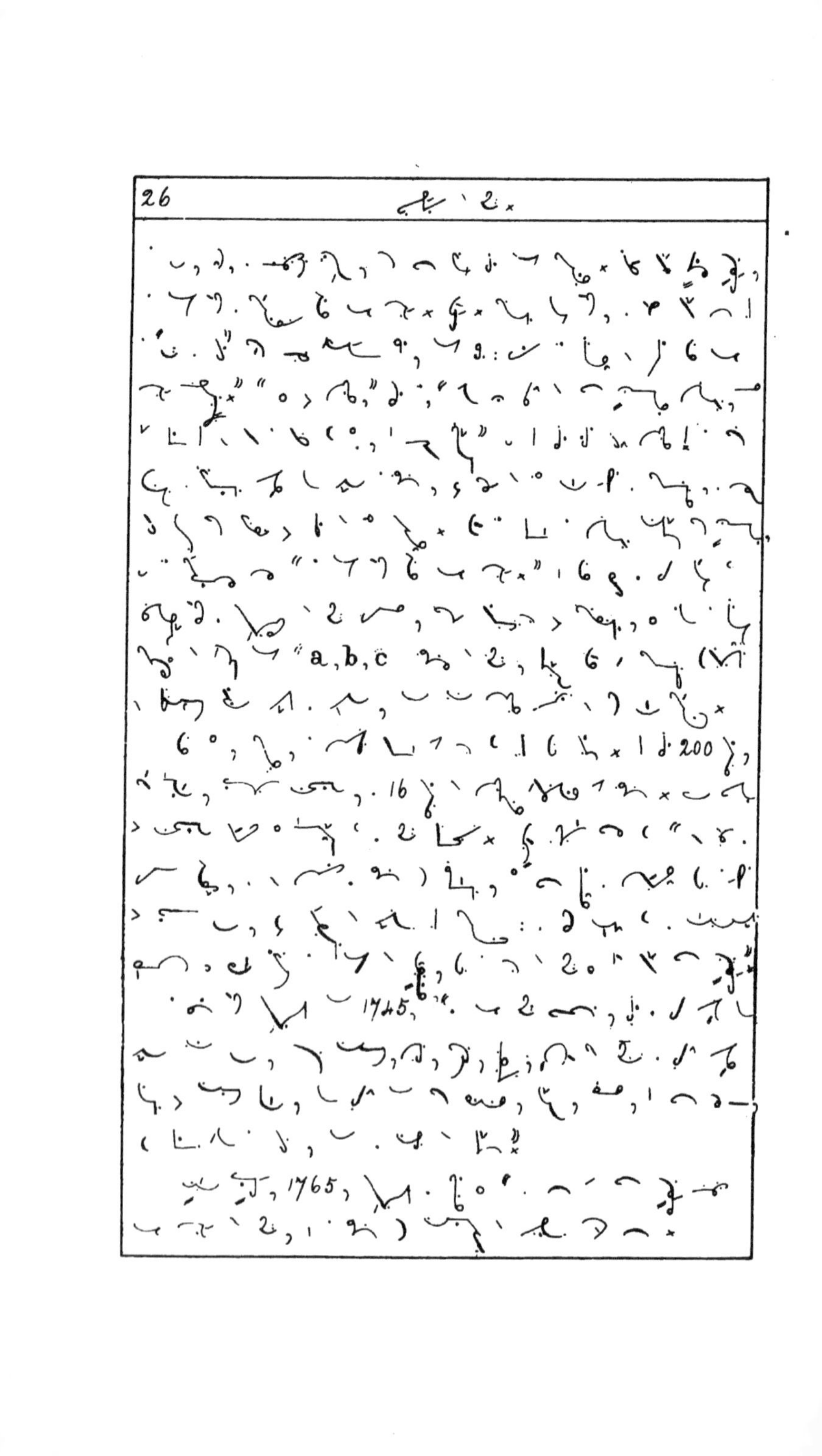

a, b, c

200

16

1745

1765

[illegible] 1782, 3, 4, [illegible] (Mitchell) [illegible] "Ars Scribendi sine penna; [illegible] "Ars Scribendi sine penna, [illegible]

[illegible] 1618; [illegible] 1635 [illegible] 1641; [illegible] 1610, [illegible] 1640, [illegible] 1758, [illegible] 1658 [illegible] 1710; [illegible] 1641 [illegible] 1635, [illegible] 1645, [illegible] 1655 [illegible] 1654 [illegible]

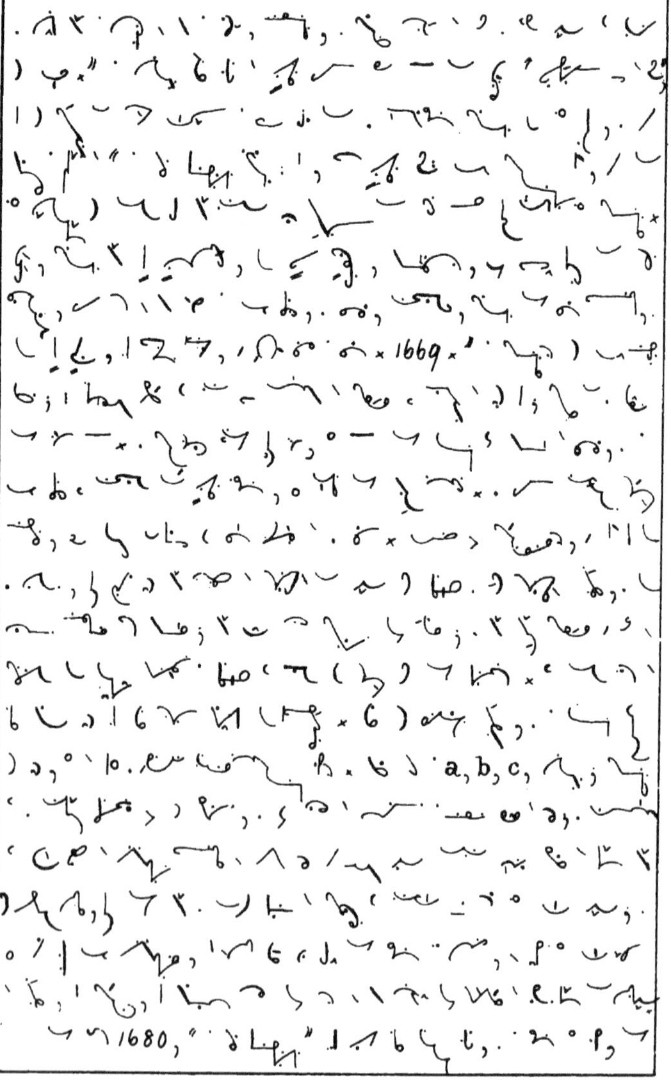
1669
a, b, c,
1680,

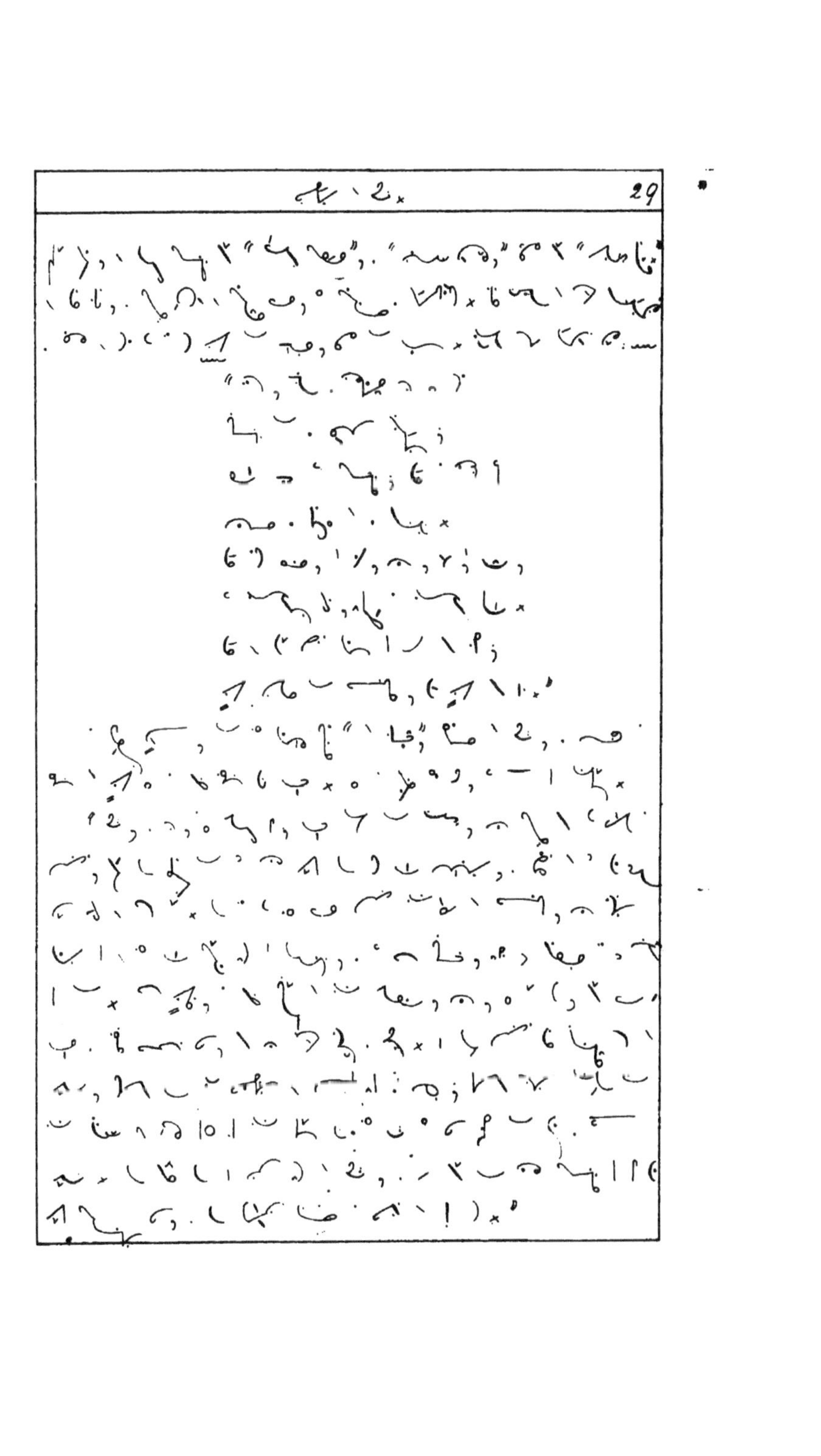

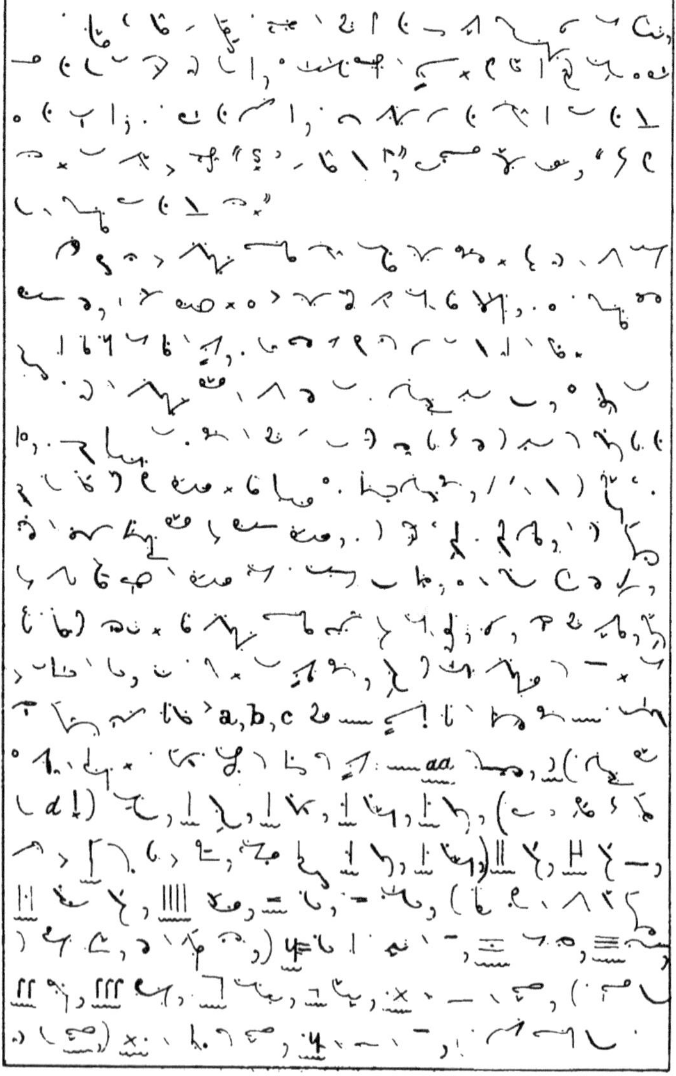
a, b, c
aa
d

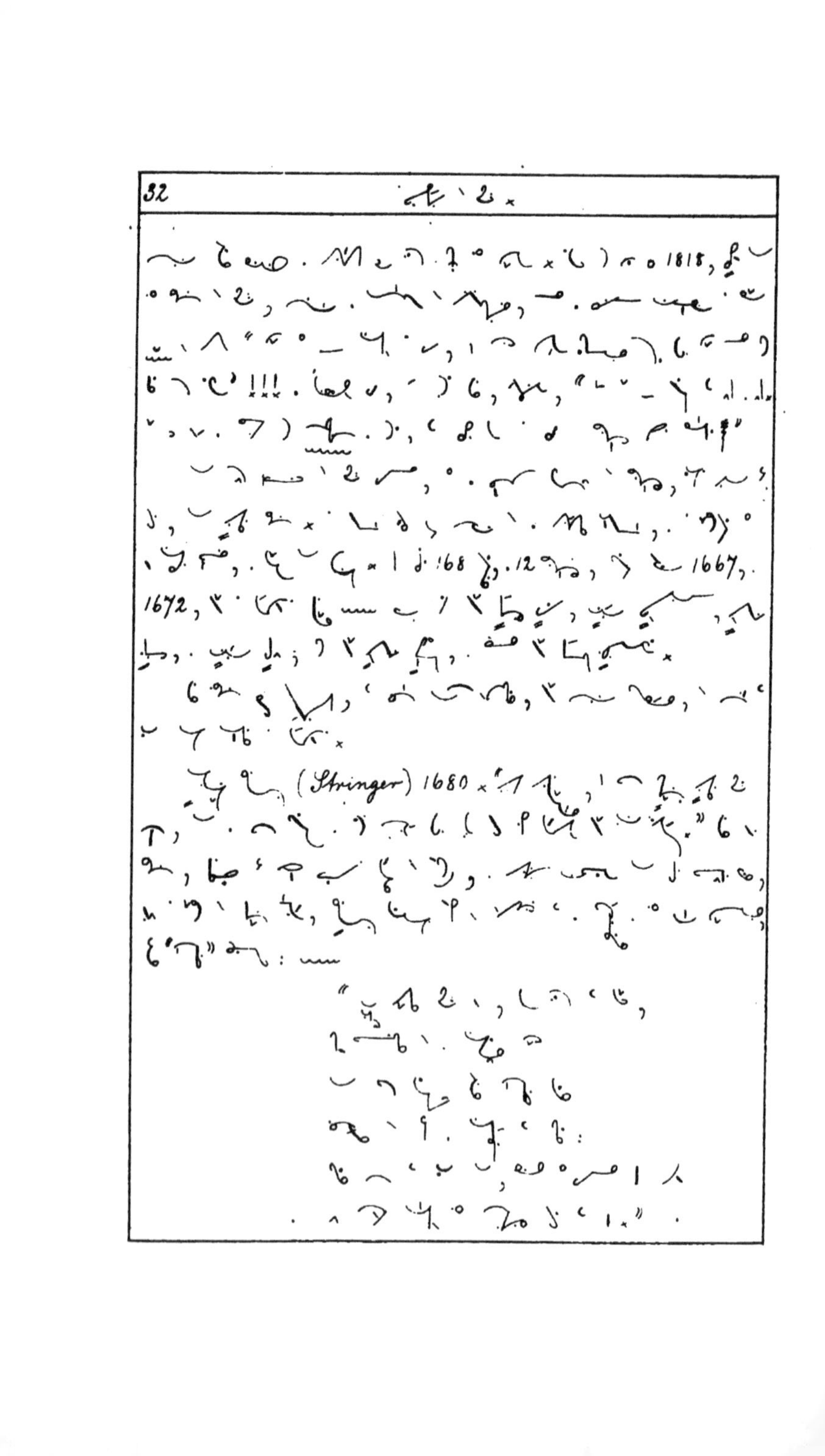

1818,

!!!

168 12 1667, 1672,

(Stringer) 1680

(Addy) 1695 … byg, hh, … byghh … 1805, … 49

1654 …

1656 …

1658 … Everardt … 33 …

1659 … Bridges …

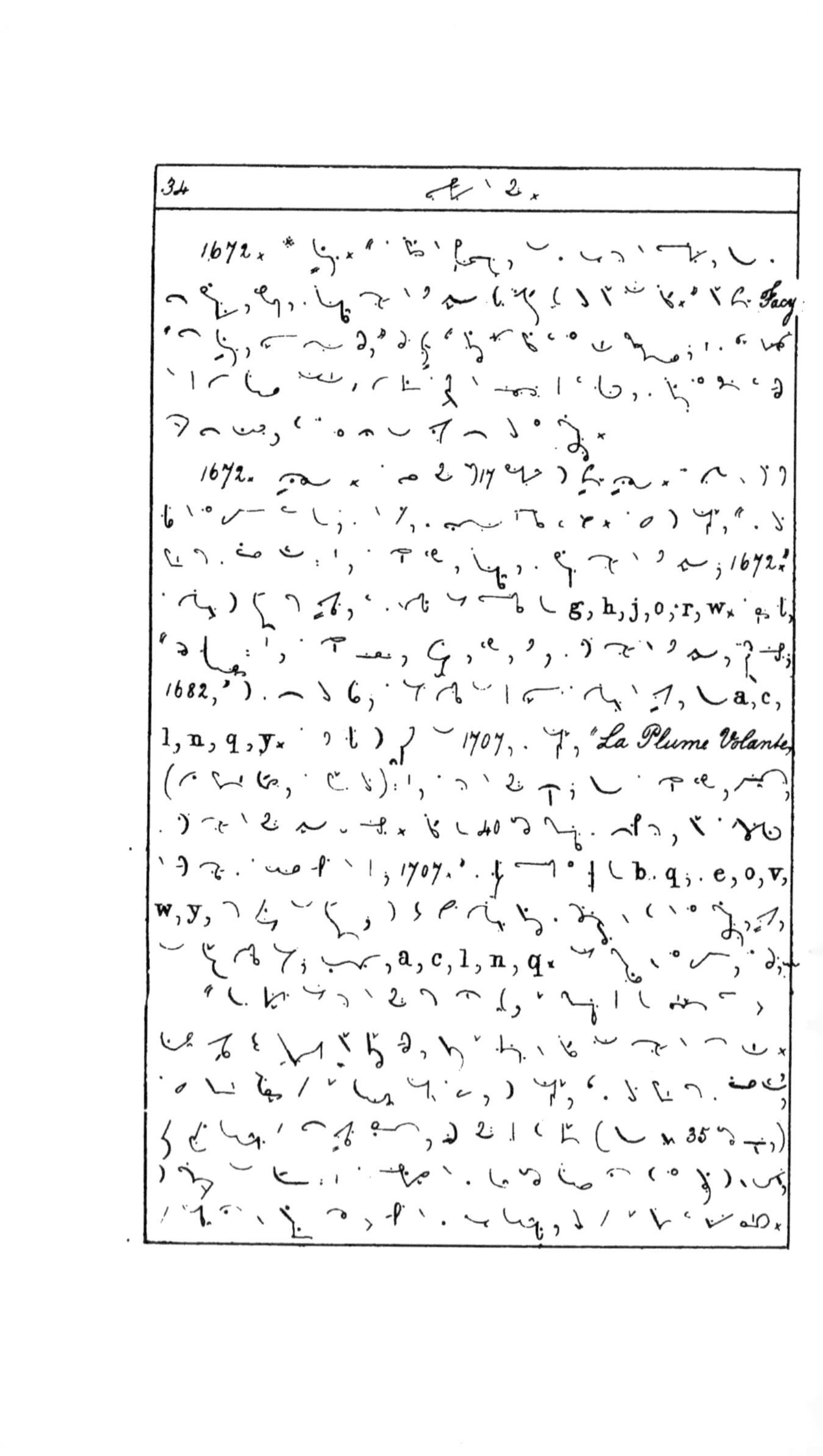

1672. … Facy …

1672. …

… 1672. …

… g, h, j, o, r, w. …

1682, … a, c,

l, n, q, y. … 1707, … "*La Plume Volante*,

… 1707. … b. q, . e, o, v,

w, y, …

… a, c, l, n, q. …

… 35 …

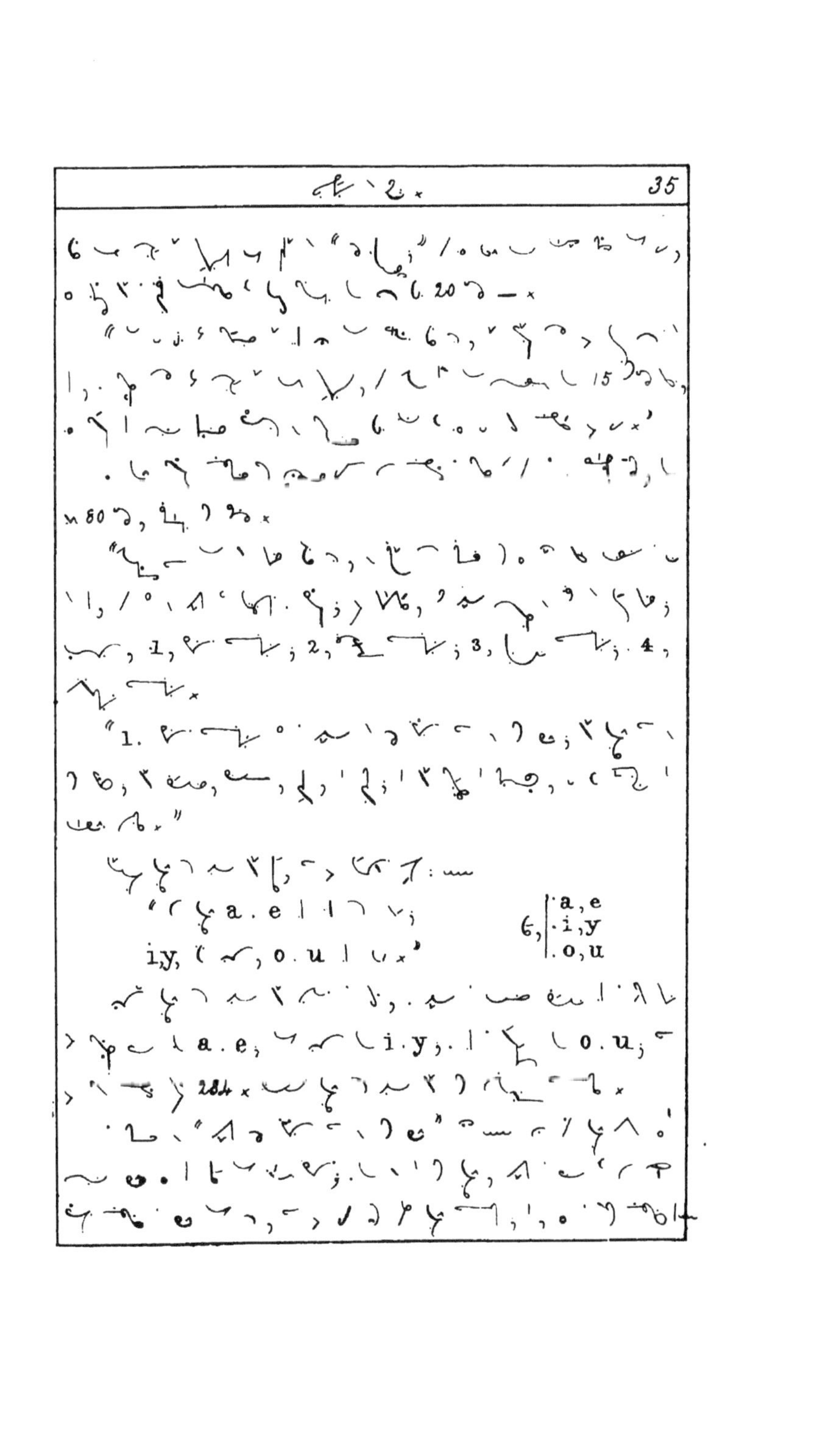

20

15

80

1, 2, 3, 4,

"1.

a . e

i,y, o . u

6,	a , e
	i , y
	o , u

a . e, i . y, o . u;

284

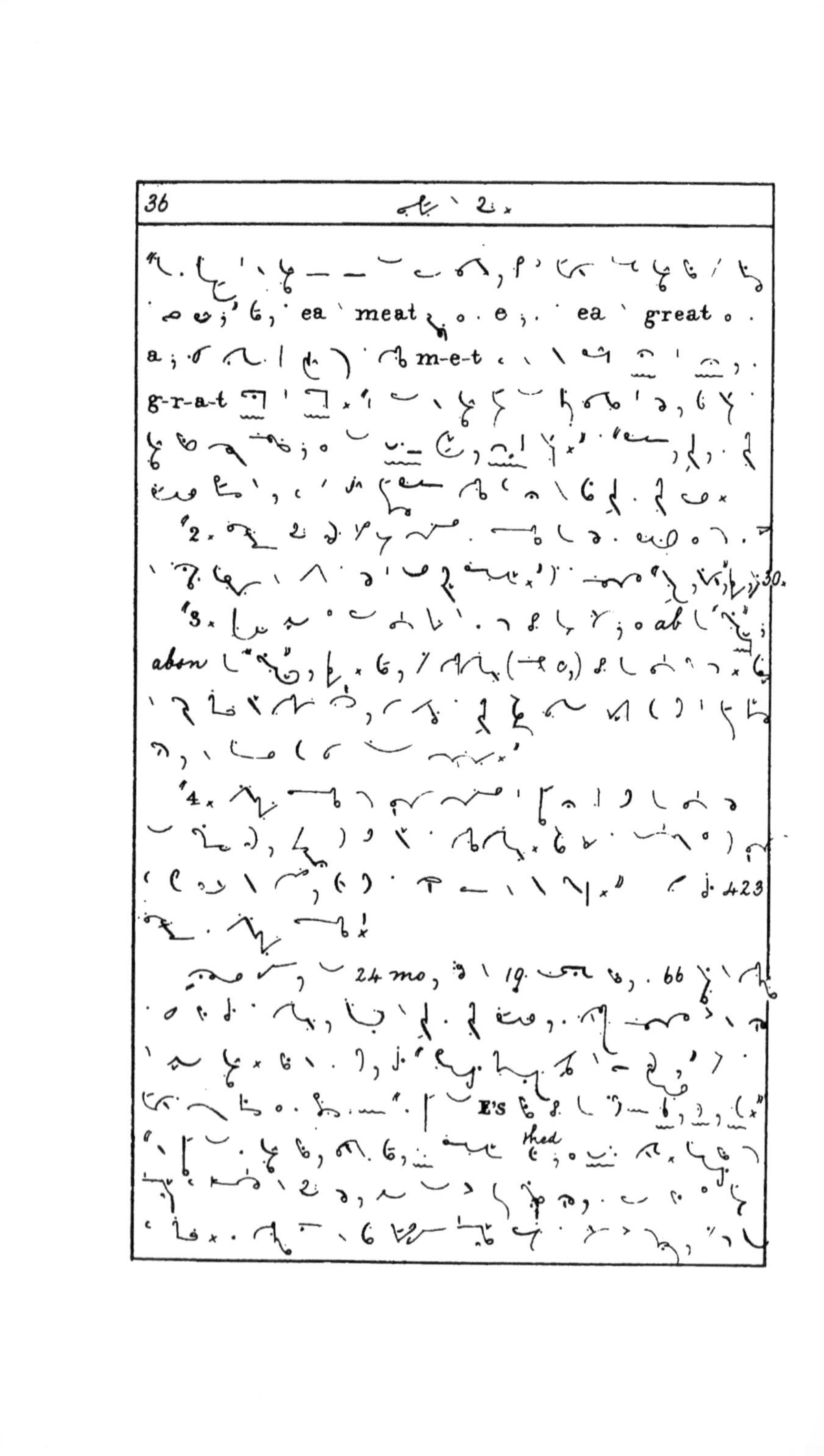

ea meat ea great

a m-e-t

g-r-a-t

2

30

3 ab

abon

4

423

24 mo 19 66

E's

thed

4,800

1602

1690

1751

40

10/6

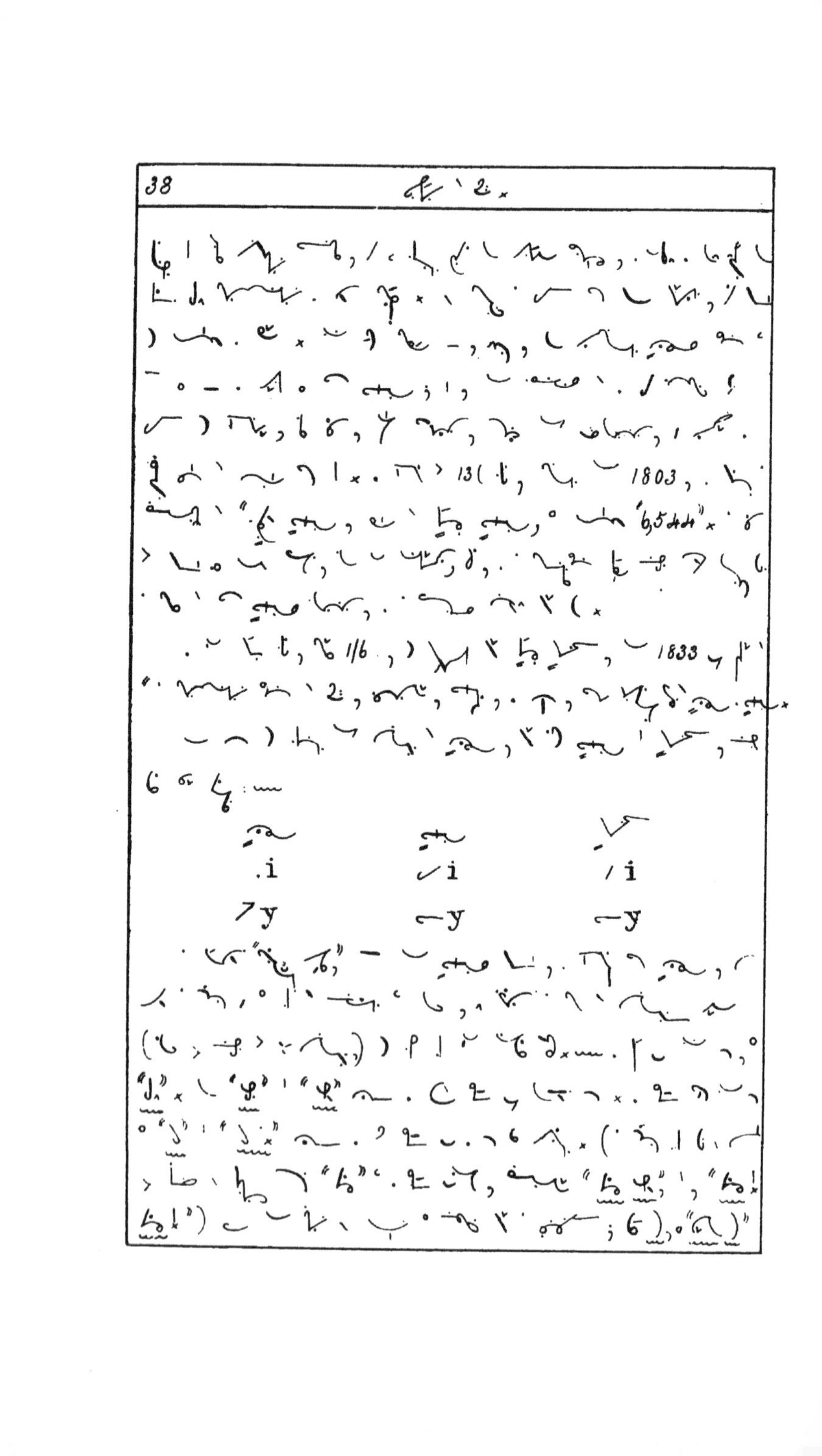

131 1803 6,544 1/6 1833

.i	✓i	/i
7y	⌐y	⌐y

16 … 12 … 13

16 … 11 … 11

1674 …

… boles …

… a e

… i y … o u …

1678 … Steel

1681 …

… *Tacheographie, ou L'Art d'Escrire aussi viste qu'on parle* …

… Ramsay … 1681;

… 200 …

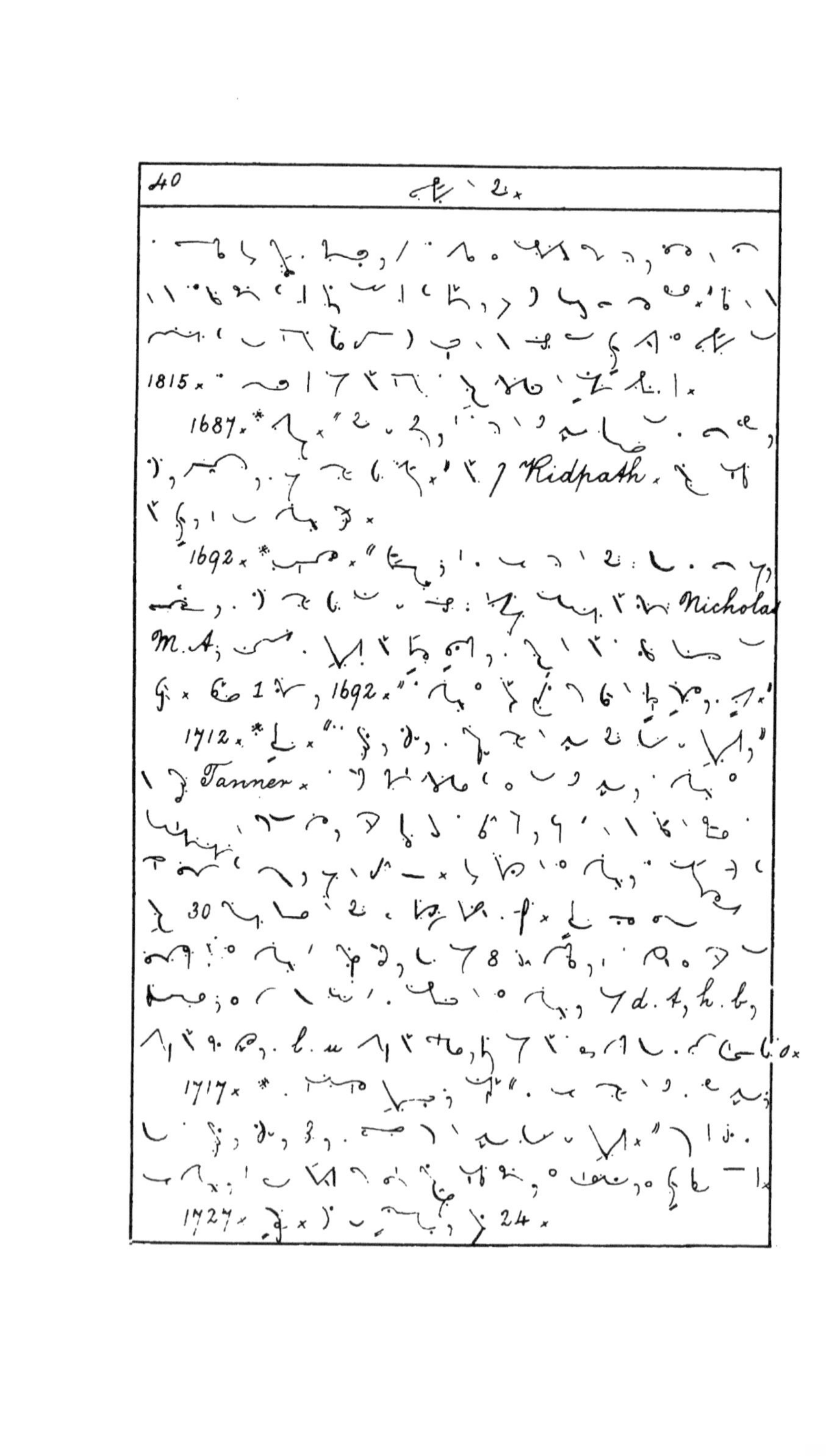

[illegible]

1815 [illegible]

1687 [illegible] Ridpath [illegible]

1692 [illegible] Nicholas M.A. [illegible] 1692 [illegible]

1712 [illegible] Tanner [illegible] 30 [illegible] 78 [illegible] d. t, h. b, [illegible]

1717 [illegible]

1727 [illegible] 24

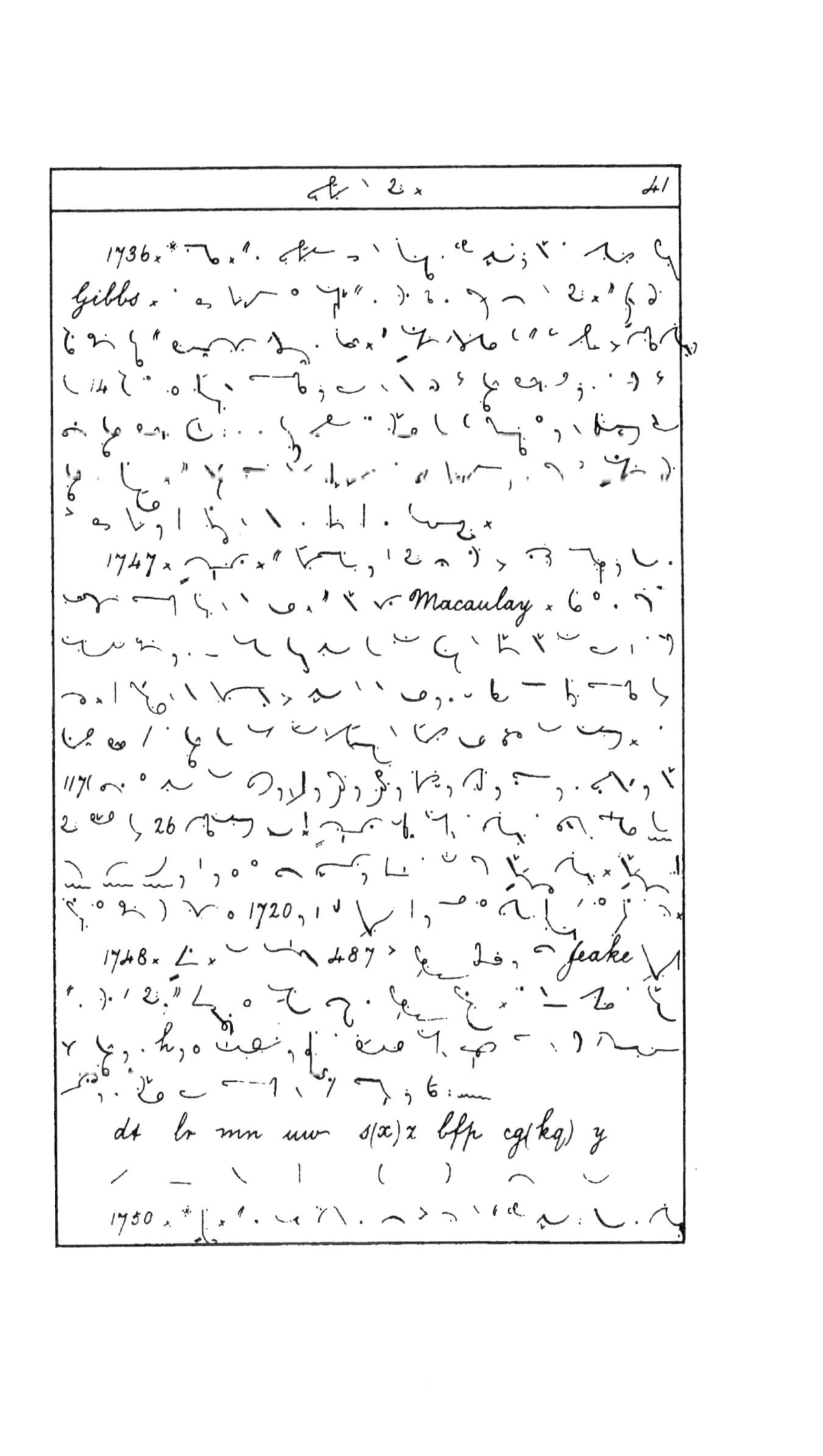

1736 … Gibbs …

1747 … Macaulay … 26 … 1720 …

1748 … 487 … Jeake …

dt lr mn uw s(x)z bfp cg(kq) y

1750 …

[illegible]

1750. [illegible] 1768, [illegible]

[illegible] 1779, [illegible] (Hervey), [illegible] 92 [illegible] 12mo, [illegible] 700 [illegible]

1753. [illegible] 34.

1758. [illegible] 100 [illegible] A. M. [illegible]

1760.

p b, t d, c g, f v, s z;

1760.

n, f, s, st.

1761.

Swaine, Simms.

1762.

Lyle, A.M.

6

in order

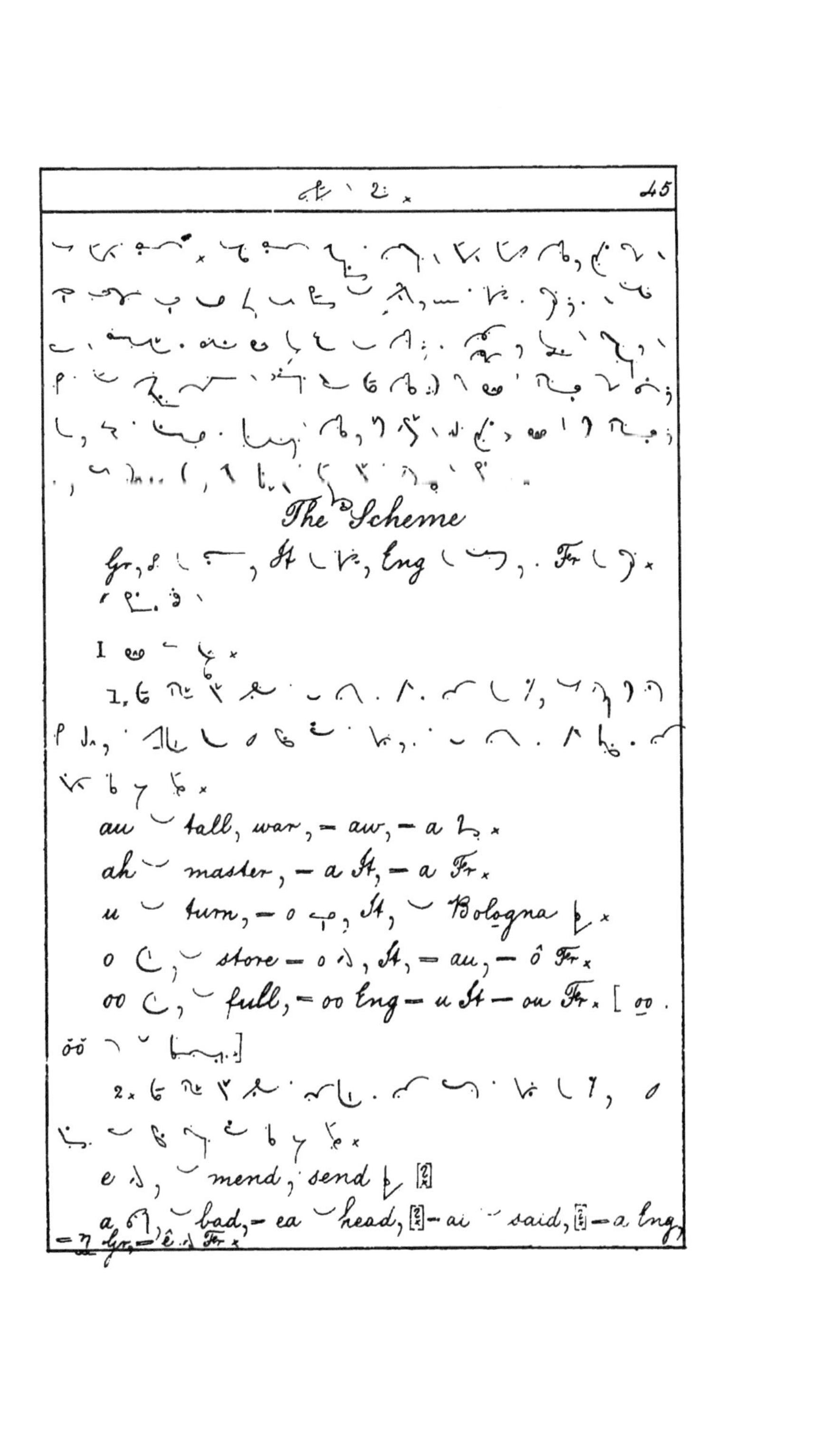

The Scheme

Gr, It, Eng, Fr.

I

au tall, war, — aw, — a

ah master, — a It, — a Fr

u turn, — o It, Bologna

o store — o It, — au, — ô Fr

oo full, — oo Eng — u It — ou Fr [oo. ŏŏ]

2

e mend, send

a bad, — ea head, — ai said, — a Eng, — η Gr, — ê Fr

e . i [illegible] liberal, kin, = e [illegible] Fr.

e [illegible] get = e It, e [illegible] Fr.

ee [illegible] siege – ee Eng. = i It. – y [illegible] i Fr.

II [illegible]

1 [illegible]

1) [illegible]

(1) [illegible]

(a) [illegible]

y = i [illegible] you – iou – eeou.

r. [illegible] rare. [illegible]

l. [illegible] loll.

w = oo [illegible] i [illegible] y [illegible] way, = uay – ouay

(b) [illegible]

ng – n [illegible] Fr. [illegible]

n. [illegible] l. [illegible] nun.

m. [illegible] mum.

(2) [illegible]

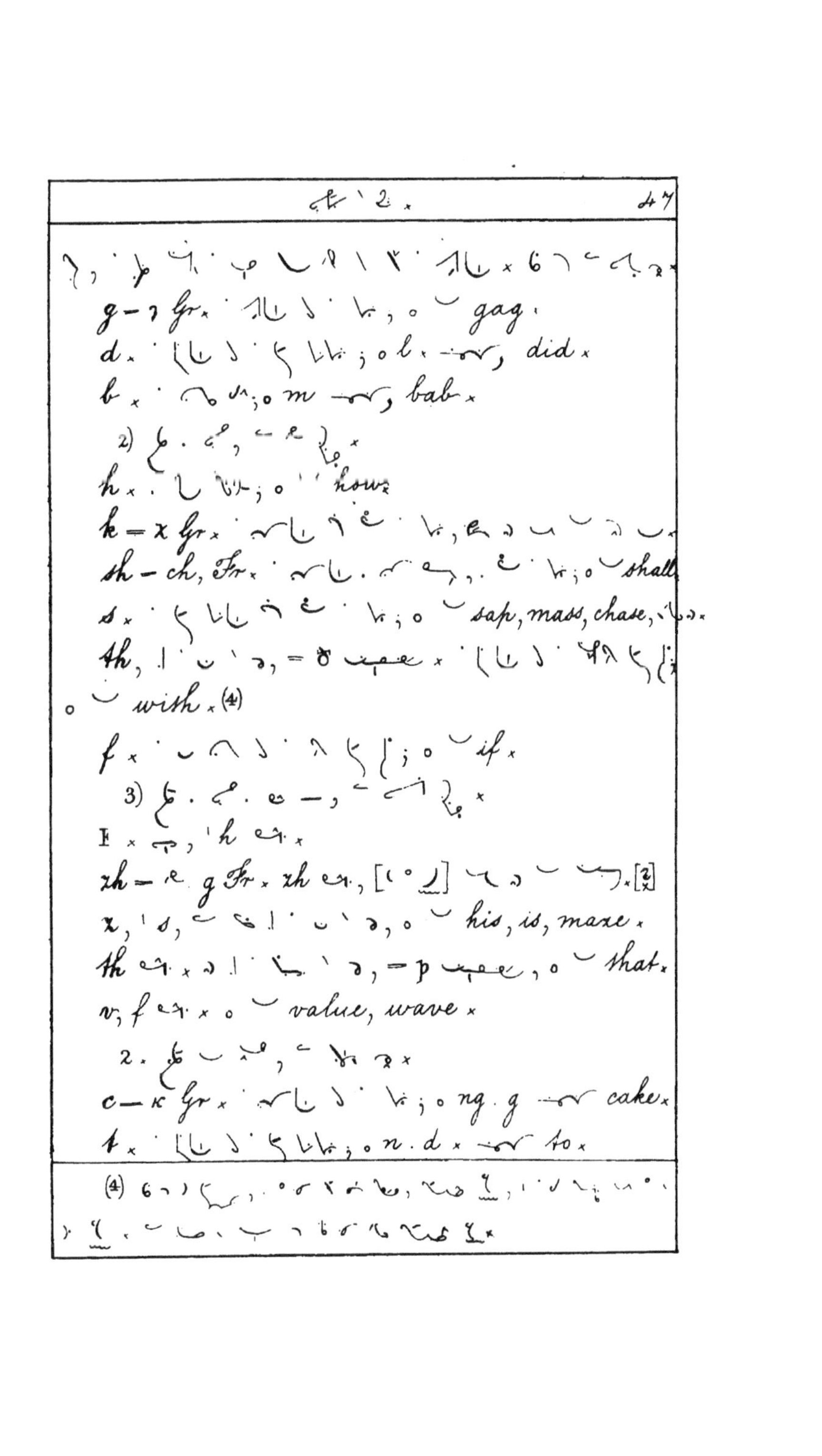

g — Gr. gag.

d. l, did.

b. m, bab.

2)

h. how.

k = x Gr.

sh — ch, Fr. shall

s. sap, mass, chase,

th,

with. (4)

f. if.

3)

F. h

zh — g Fr. zh [2]

z, s, his, is, maze.

th p that.

v, f value, wave.

2.

c — κ Gr. ng. g cake.

t. n. d. to.

(4)

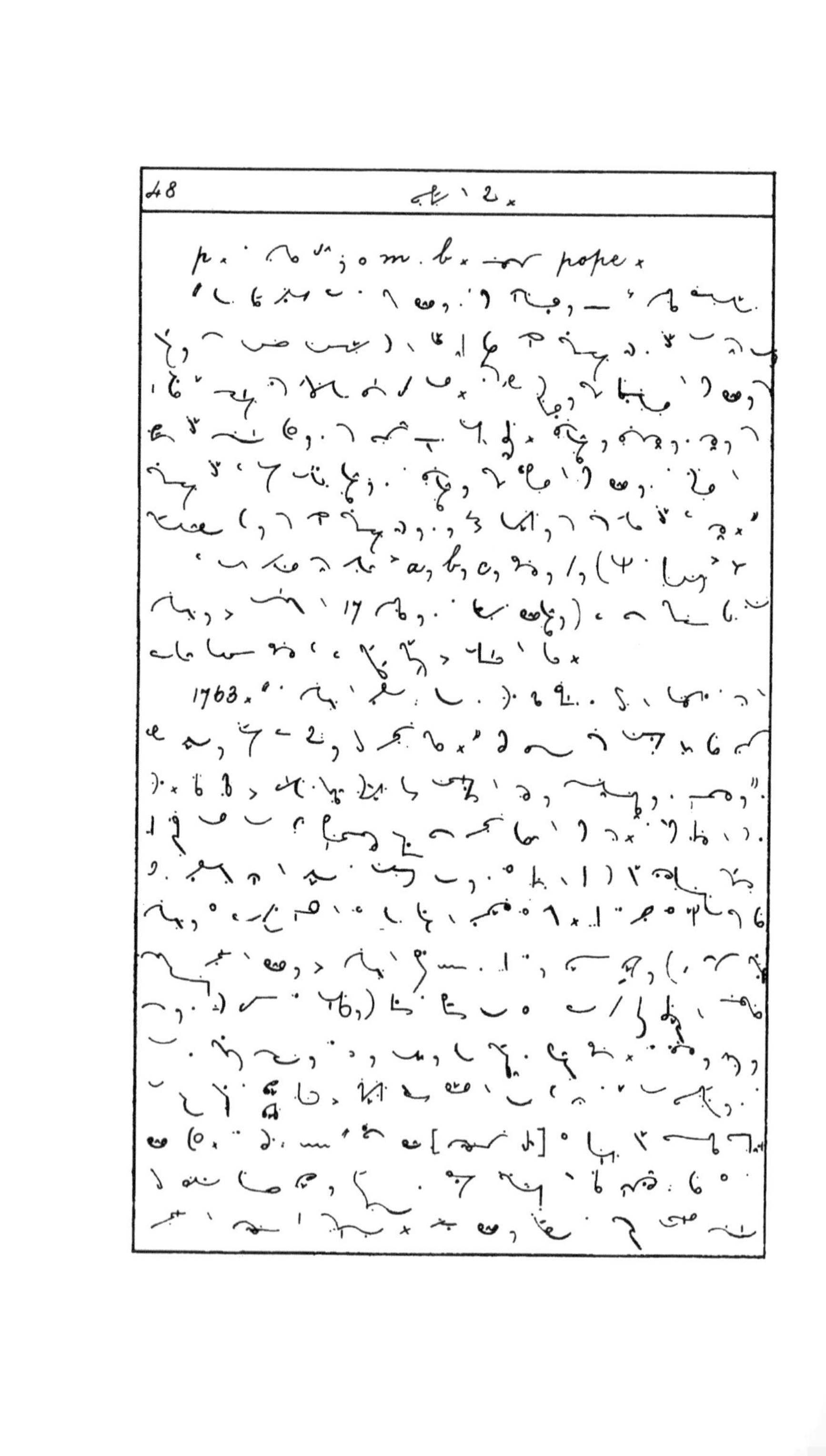

p. o m. b. pope.

a, b, c,

1763.

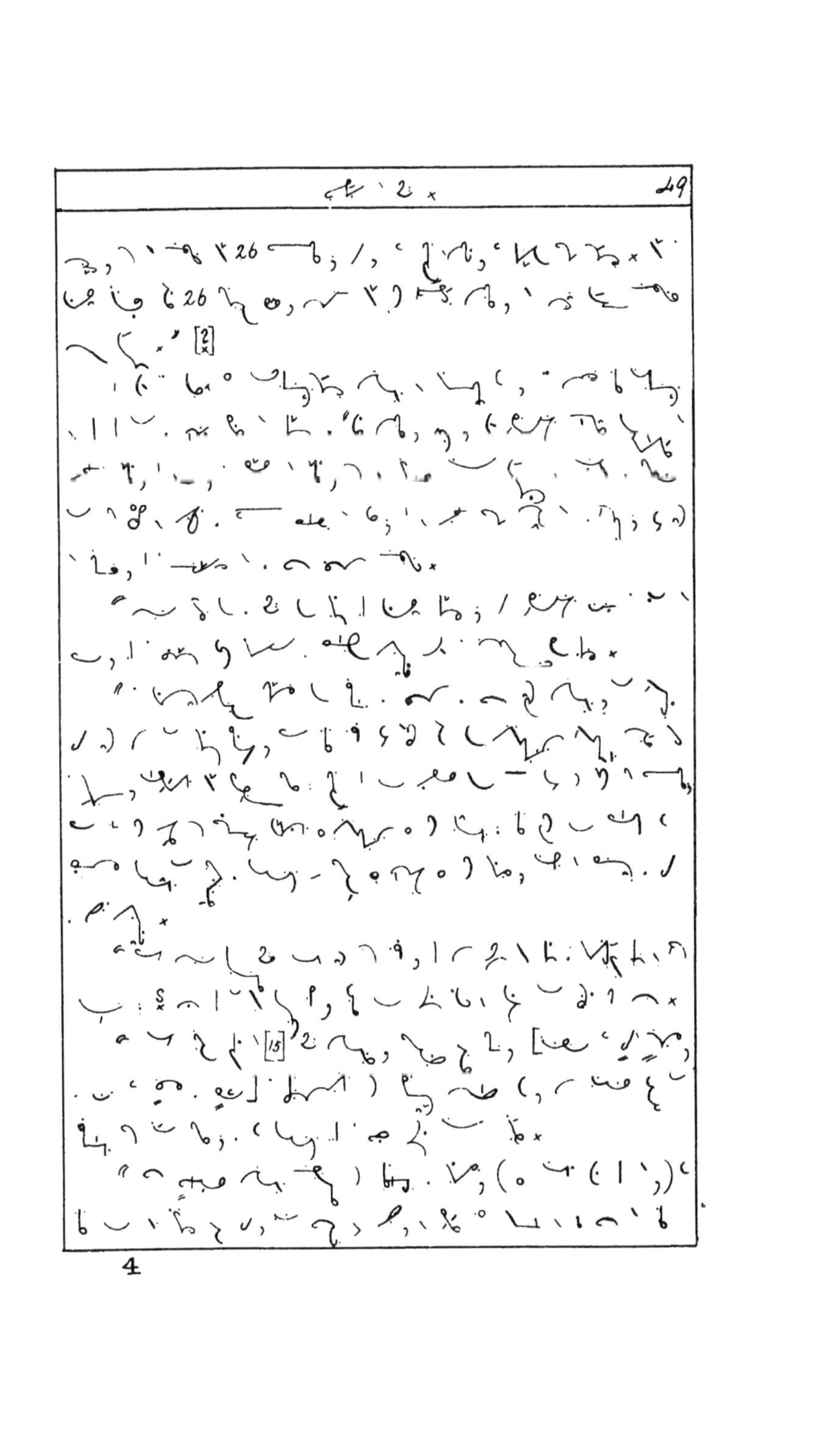

26 26 [2]

[15]

a, b, c
(De Hondt)
1764
Meilan
j, v, w, y,
h
a. e.
o. u
a. e
i, y,
o. u
a o
e. u

[illegible]

1766. [illegible] Hodgson. [illegible] 1780, [illegible]

1766. [illegible] Holdsworth, [illegible] Aldridge, [illegible]

1767. [illegible]

(Byrom), M.A., F.R.S.,

Harrop.

1691,

(Kersall)

1763. (5)

1814.

2,

2;

(5)

[illegible] 1634, [illegible]
[illegible] (Roffe).

[illegible] 1720.

[illegible] 1742, [illegible] 1749, [illegible] 50 [illegible] 403, [illegible]

[illegible] 136,

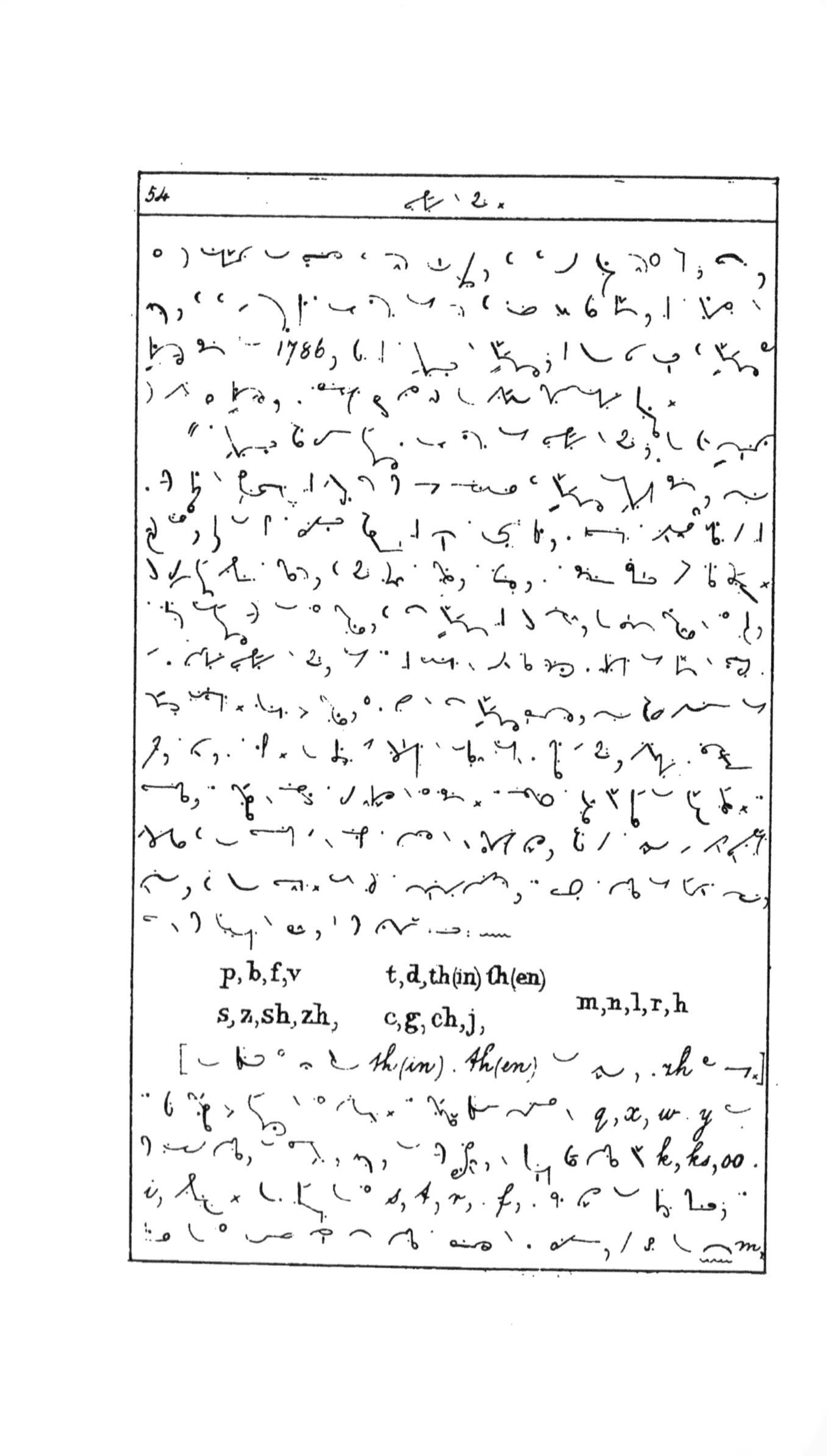

1786,

p, b, f, v   t, d, th(in) th(en)
s, z, sh, zh,   c, g, ch, j,   m, n, l, r, h

[th(in). th(en) zh]

q, x, w, y
k, ks, oo.
i, s, t, r, f,
m,

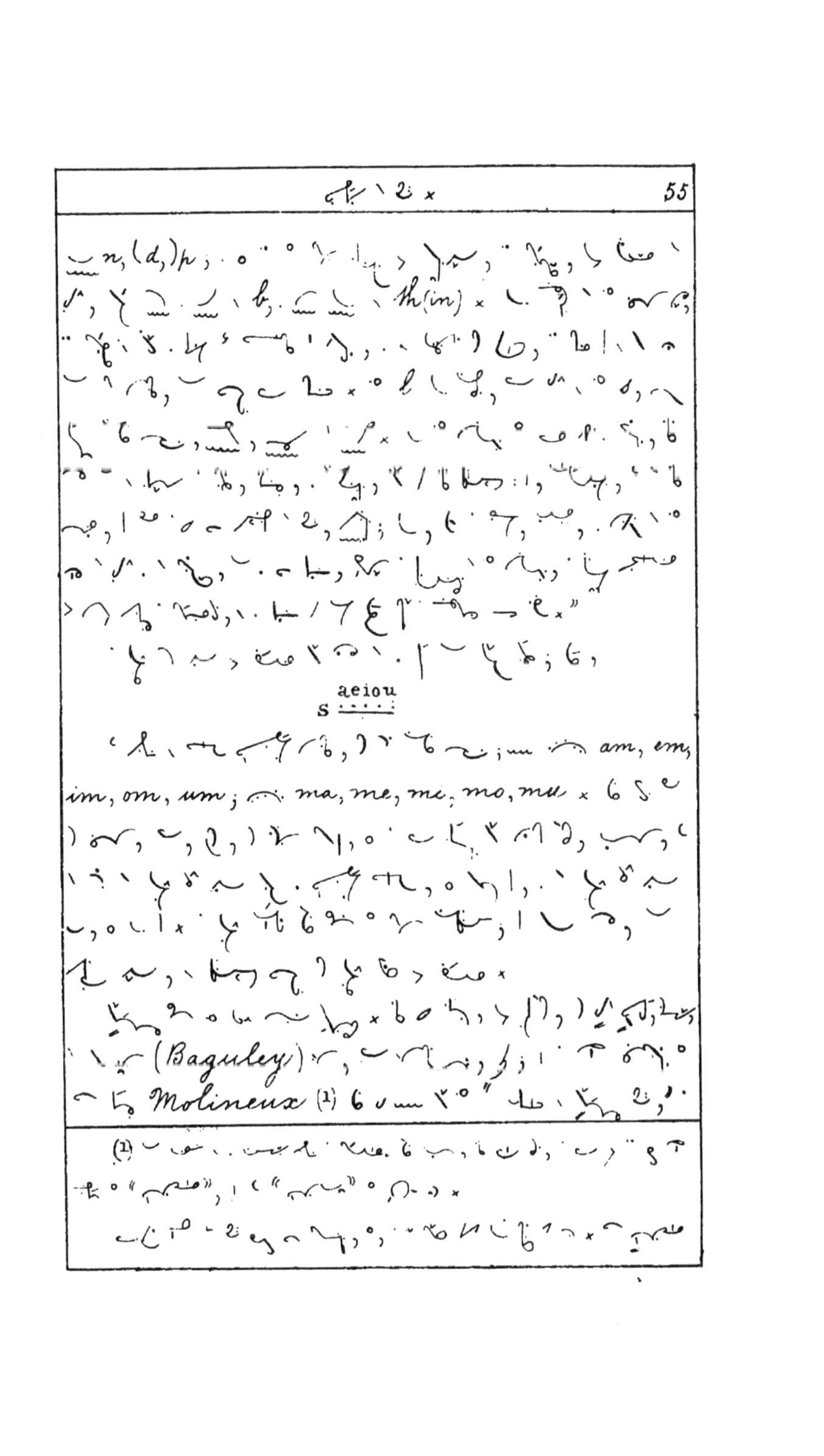

n, (d,) p ; b, th(in)

aeiou
s

am, em, im, om, um ; ma, me, mi, mo, mu

(Baguley)

Molineux (1)

(1)

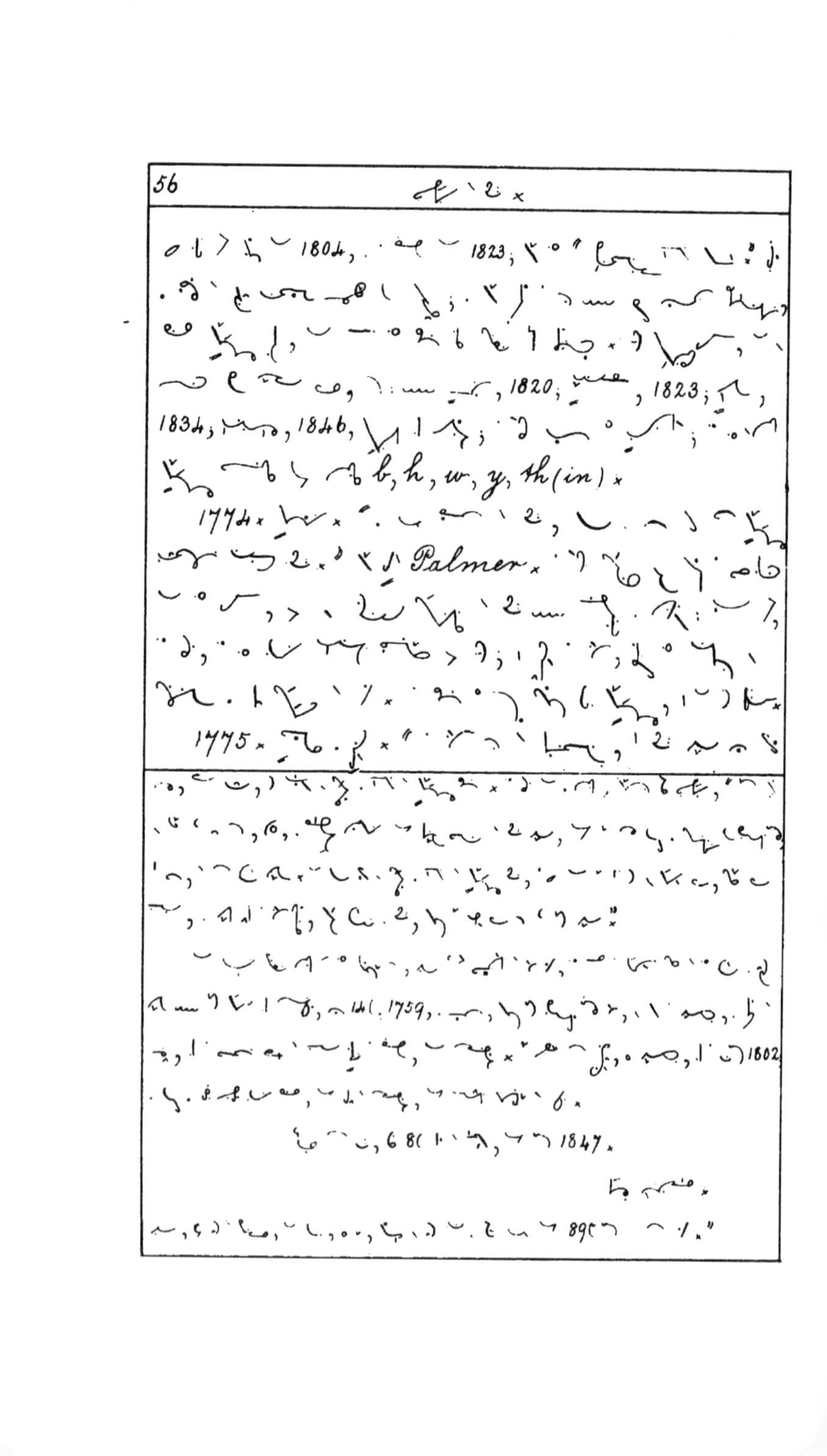

1804, 1823; 1820; 1823; 1834; 1846; b, h, w, y, th(in).

1774. Palmer.

1775.

1759, 1802.

6 8 1847.

89

[illegible] Graves, [illegible] Ashton; [illegible]

1775. [illegible] c, k, r, t, th, ch, [illegible]

[illegible] 130 [illegible]

[illegible] mn, [illegible]

1777. [illegible] 18mo; [illegible] 26 [illegible]

1779. [illegible]

158 … 1779 …

1786 …

b … i … y …

b … i … y …

brn … irn …

youth … booth … a … w …

f … ch …

c … q … g … th …

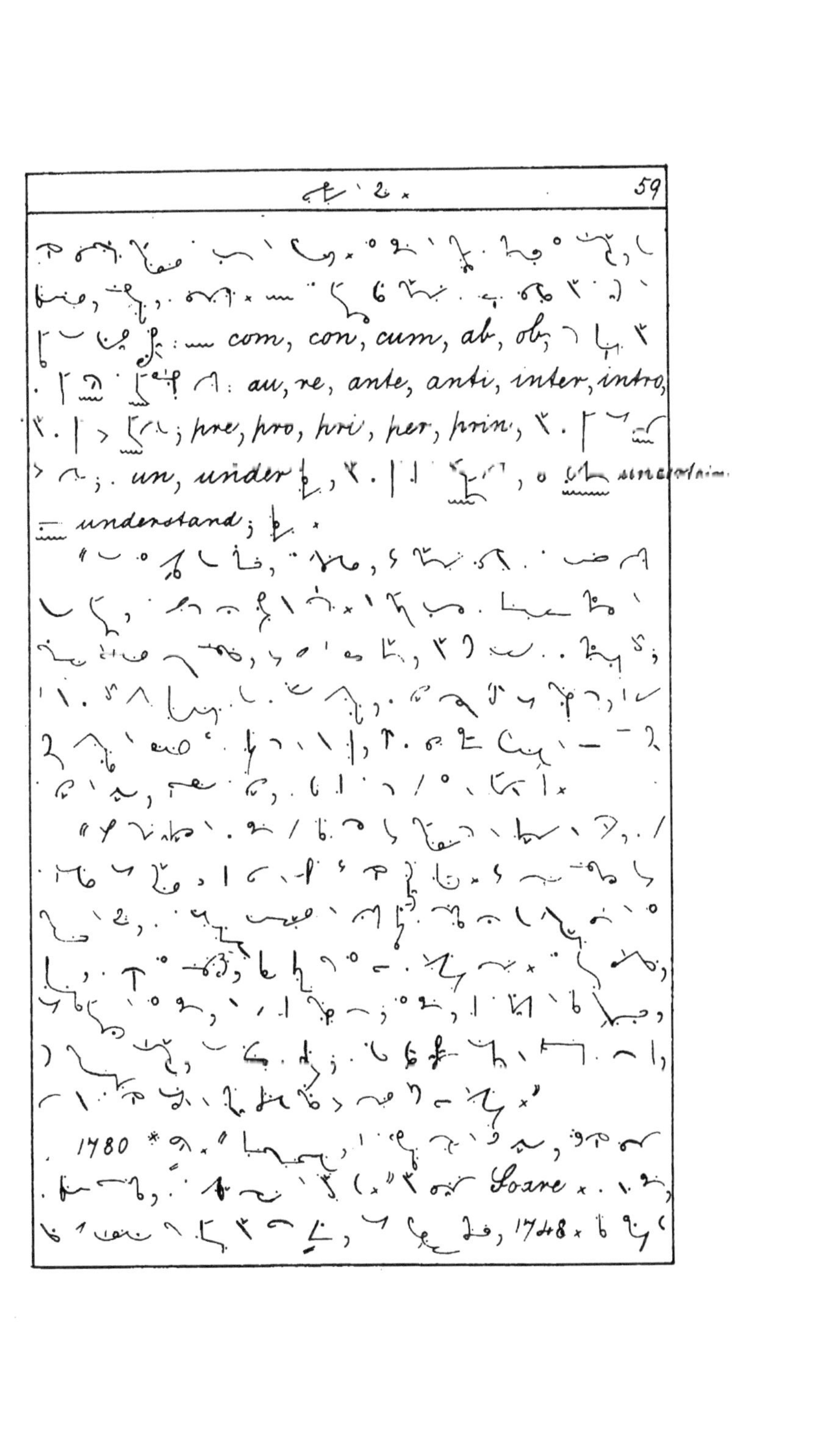

com, con, cum, ab, ob,

au, re, ante, anti, inter, intro,

pre, pro, pri, per, prin,

un, under uncertain

understand;

1780

Soare

1748

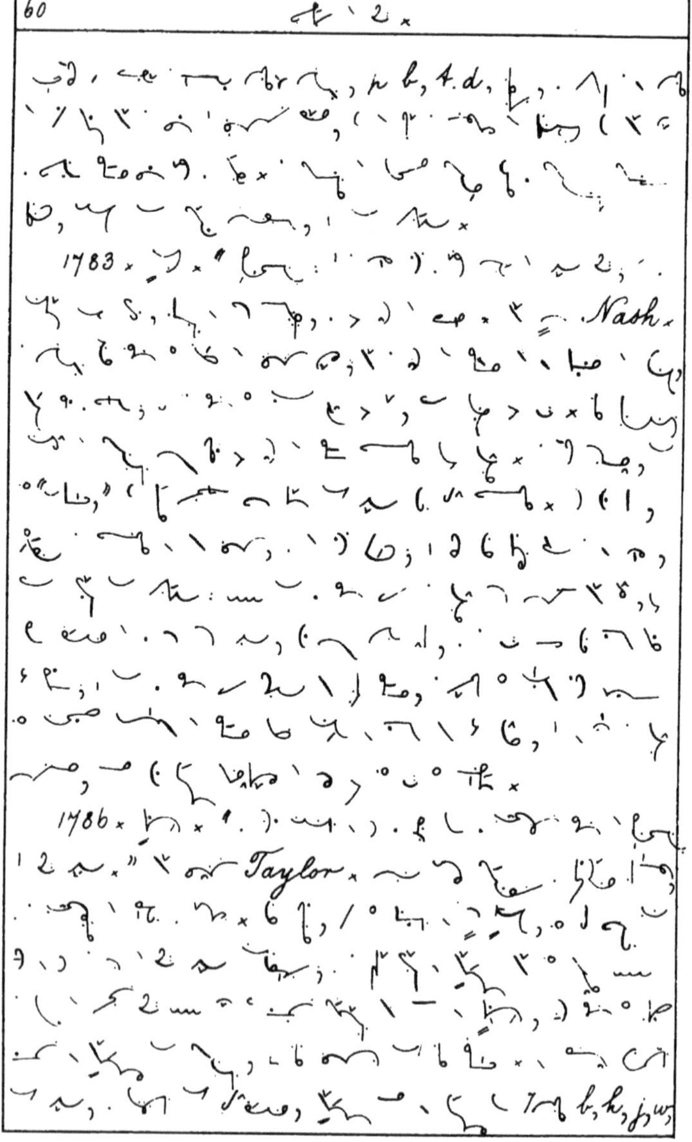

1783
Nash
1786
Taylor

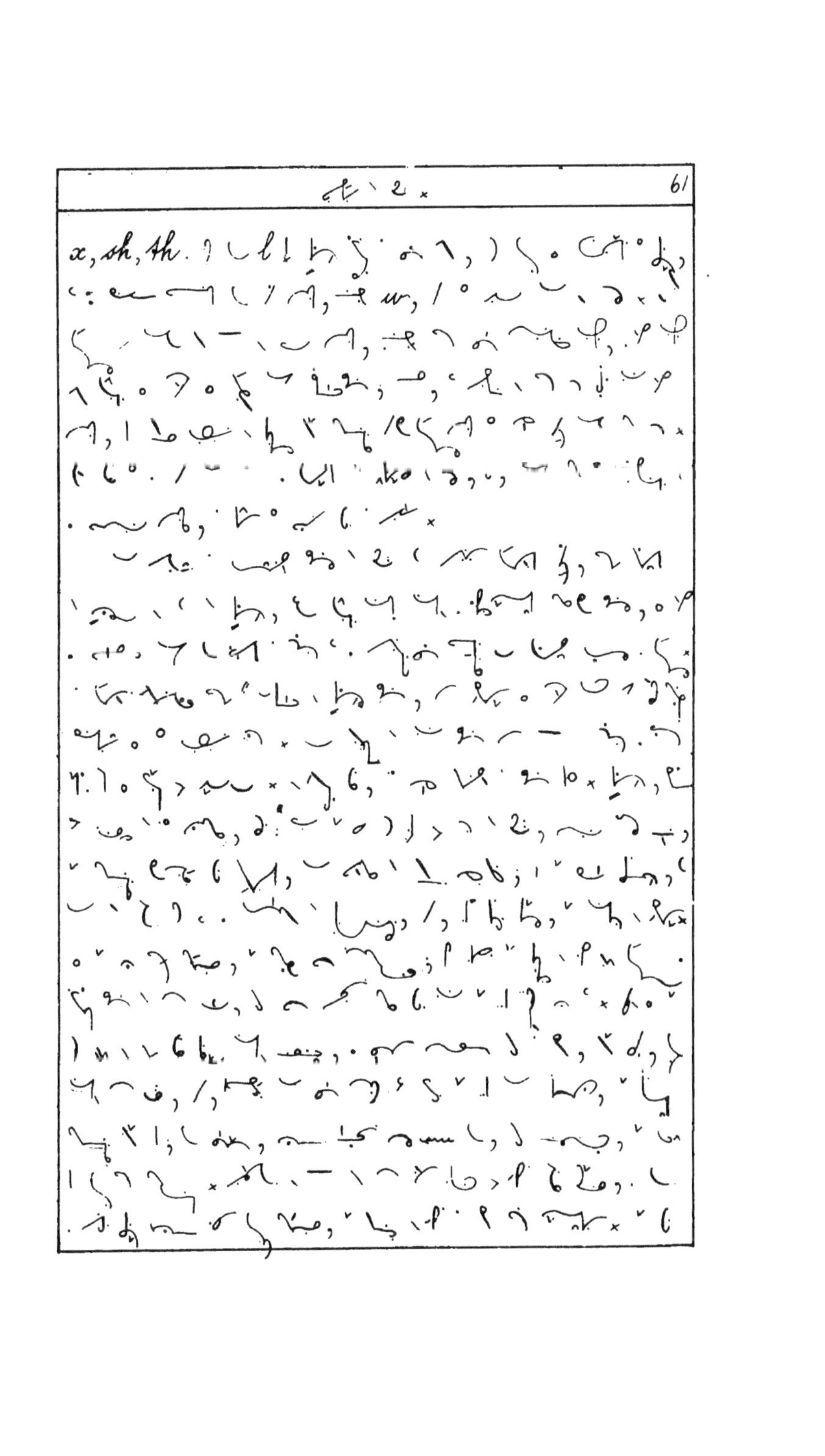

x, sh, th.

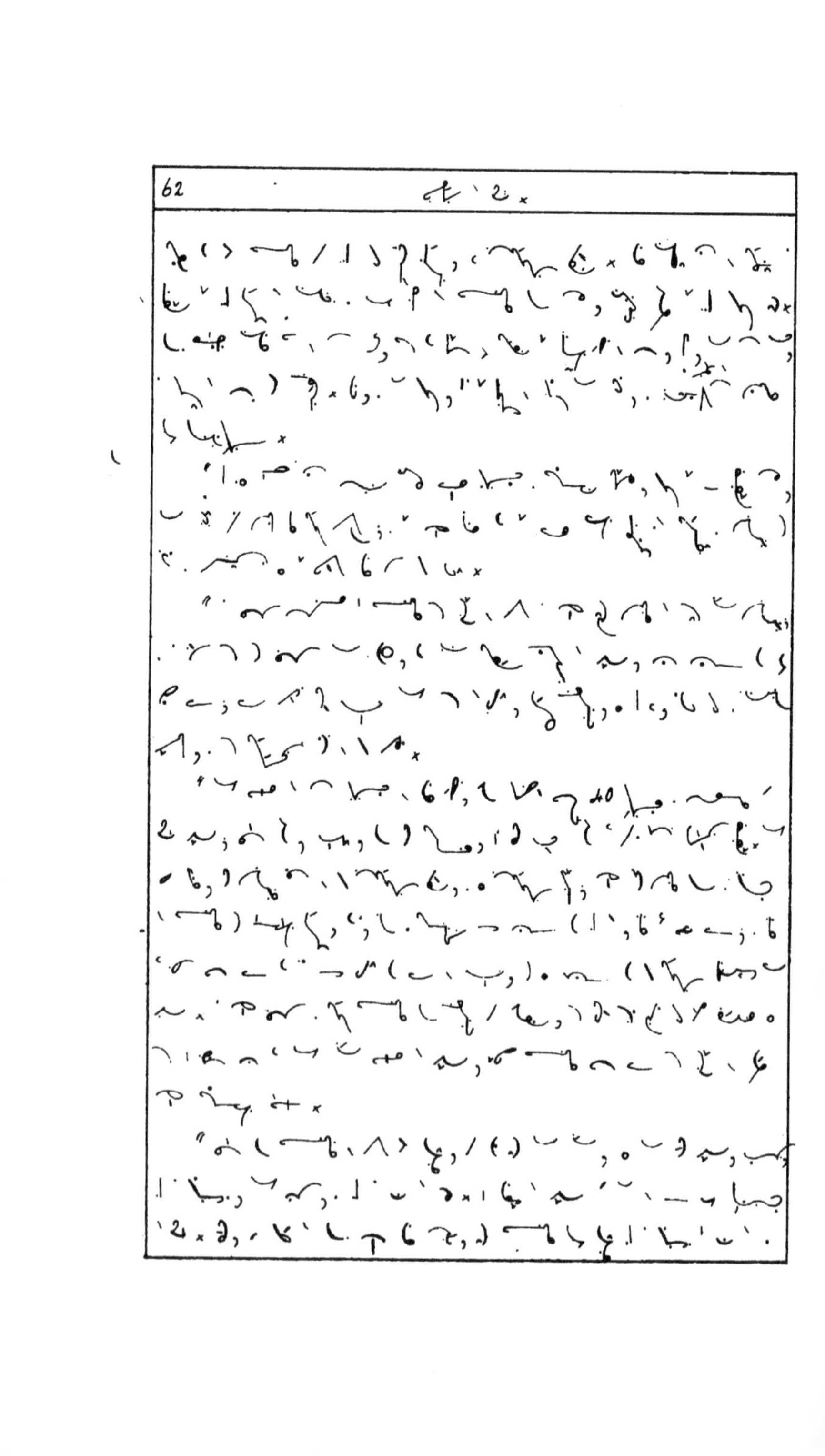

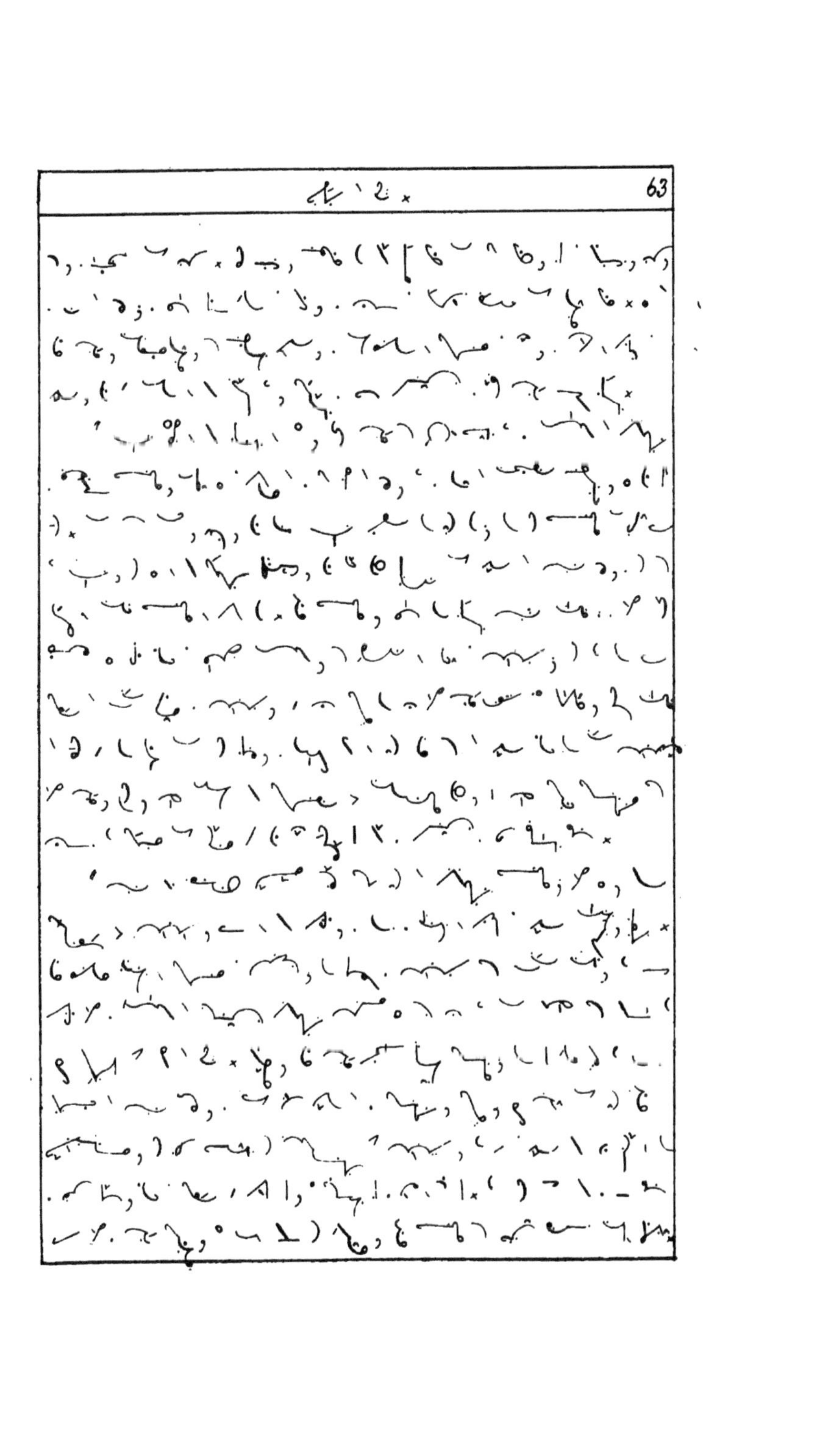

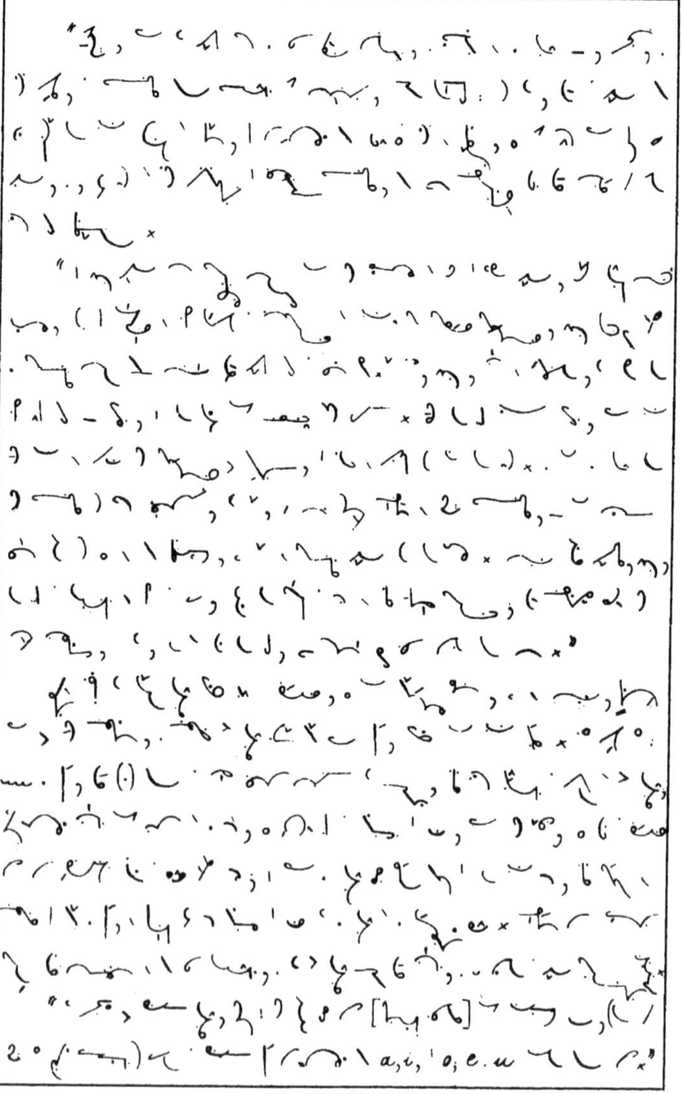

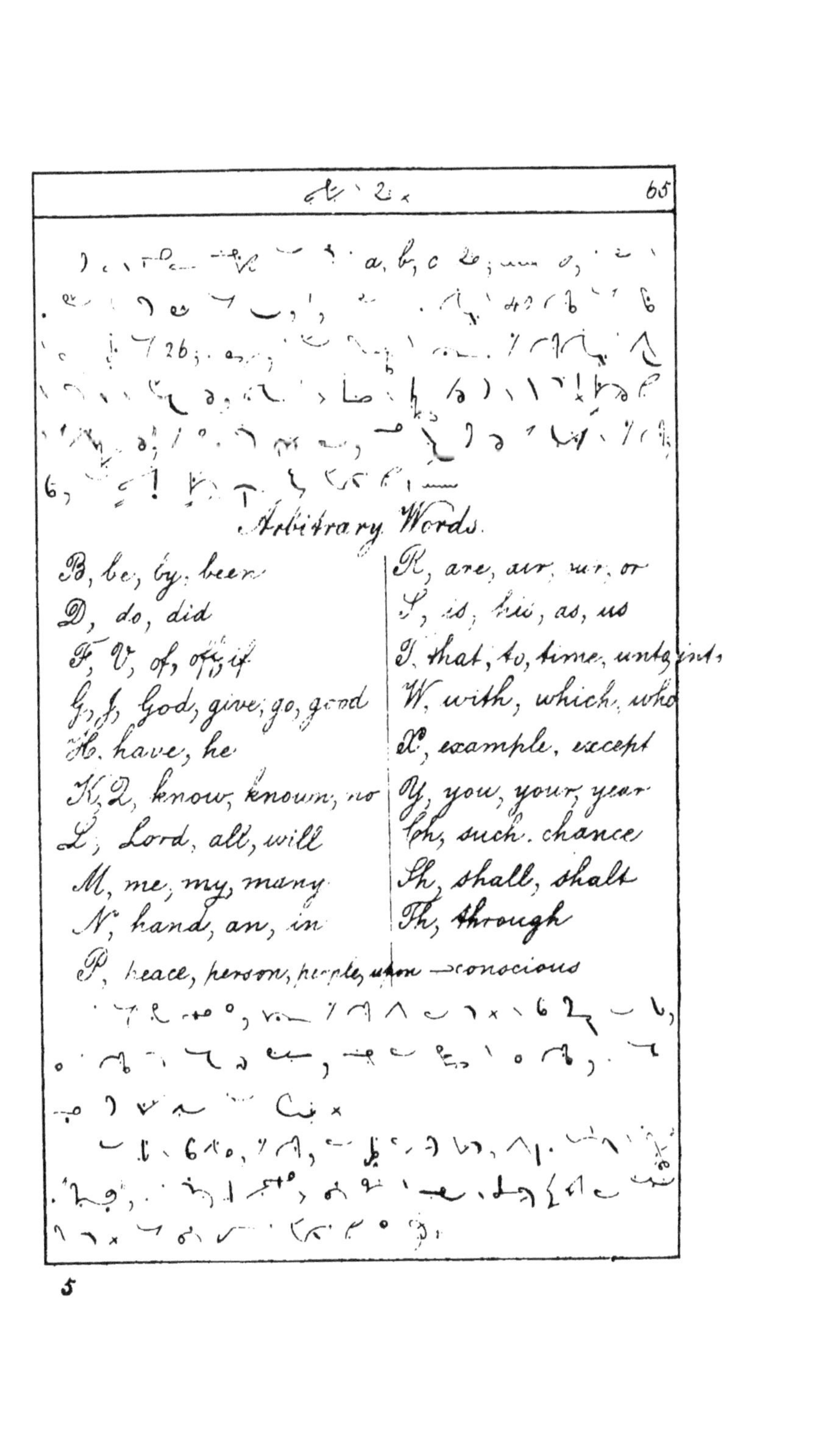

Arbitrary Words.

B, be, by, been	R, are, air, our, or
D, do, did	S, is, his, as, us
F, V, of, off, if	T, that, to, time, unto, into
G, J, God, give, go, good	W, with, which, who
H, have, he	X, example, except
K, Q, know, known, no	Y, you, your, year
L, Lord, all, will	Ch, such, chance
M, me, my, many	Sh, shall, shalt
N, hand, an, in	Th, through
P, peace, person, people, upon — conscious	

Prepositions.

B, ab- abs- ob- obs-
D, de- des-
F, for
G, J, gen-
H, hypo-
K, Q, con- com- accom- con-
L, al-
M, magni- mis-
N, in- inter- intro-
P, par- pre- pro-
R, re- recom-
S, satis- circum- signi- sub- super-
T, tra- tri- trans-
W, where- with-
X, ex- extra-
Sh, sh- short-
Th, th- theo-

Terminations.

B, -ble, -ible, -ibly,
D, -dom, -end, -ened, -ed,
F, V, -ful,
G, J -ong, -ogy,
H -hood
K, Q, -acle, -ic, -ical, -kind
L, -al, -ally, -el, les
M, -ment, -sum
N, -ance, -ant, -ness, -ent
P, -pal, -ple, -part
R, -ar, -ary, -ory
S, -asion, -esion, -ision, osion, -usion, ation, -etion, ition, -otion, -ution
T, -at, -ity, -tude
W, -with
Y, -ify
Ch, -ch, -tian, -cian
Sh, -shall -tial, -ish, -ship
Th, -th, -est, -ist, -eth -eous, -ious

1819, ... 1823;

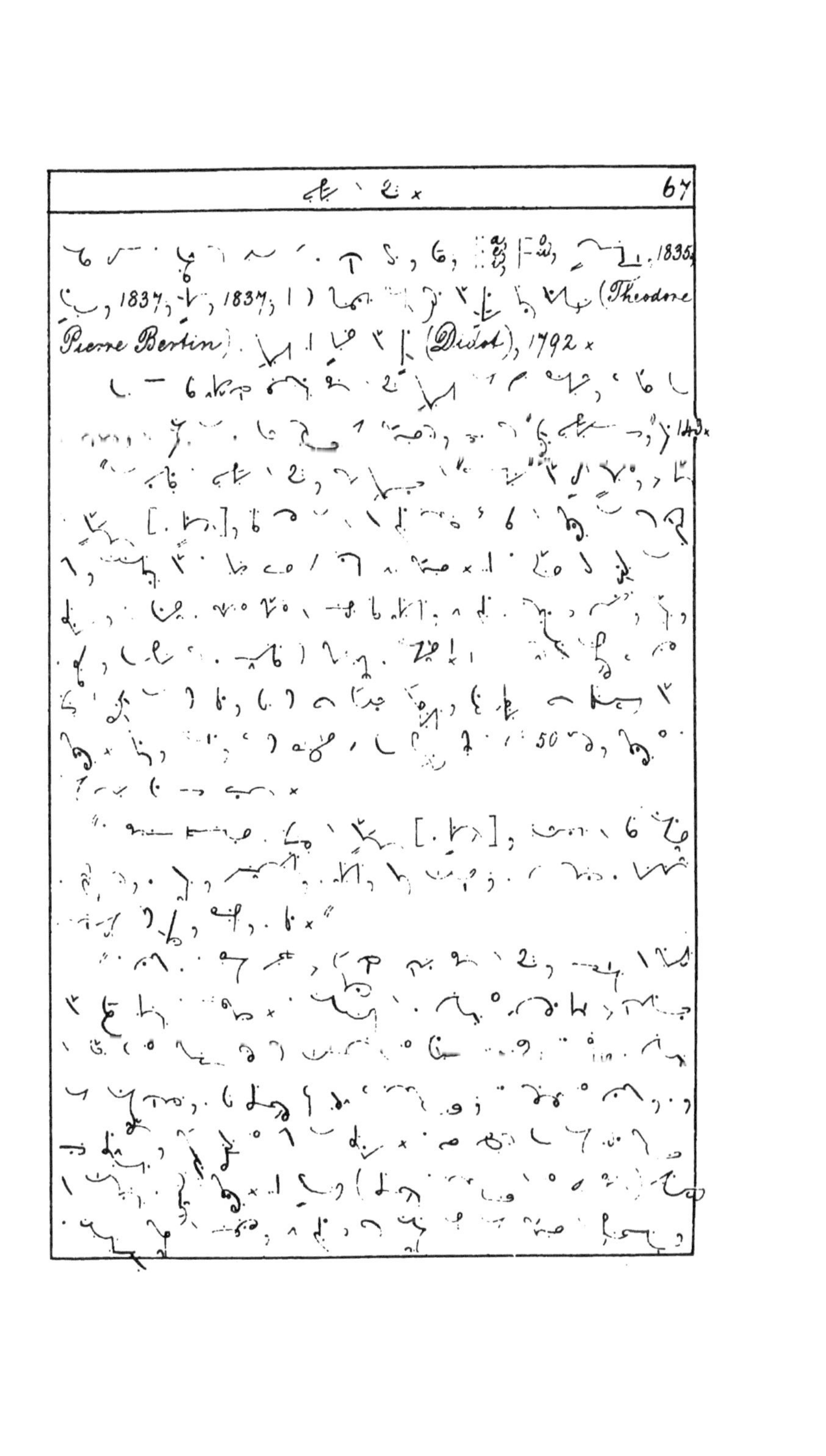

1835; 1837; 1837; (Theodore Pierre Bertin) (Didot), 1792

143

50

1772

1787

Graham

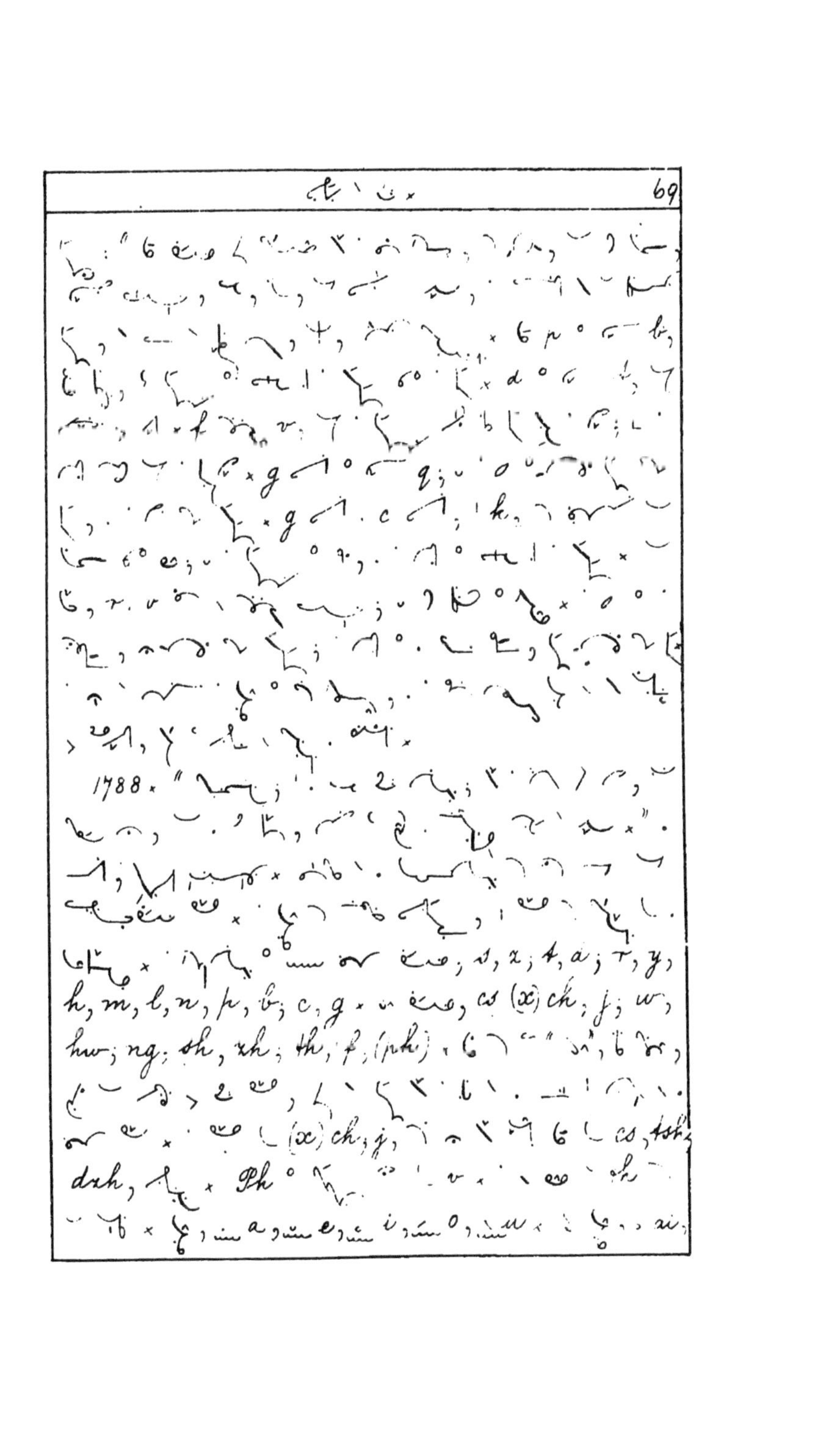

[illegible]

1788. [illegible]

[illegible] s, z; t, d; r, y, h, m, l, n, p, b; c, g. [illegible] cs (x) ch; j; w, hw; ng; sh, zh; th, f, (ph). [illegible]

[illegible] (x) ch; j, [illegible] cs, tsh; dzh, [illegible]. Ph [illegible]

[illegible] a, [illegible] e, [illegible] i, [illegible] o, [illegible] u. [illegible] ai,

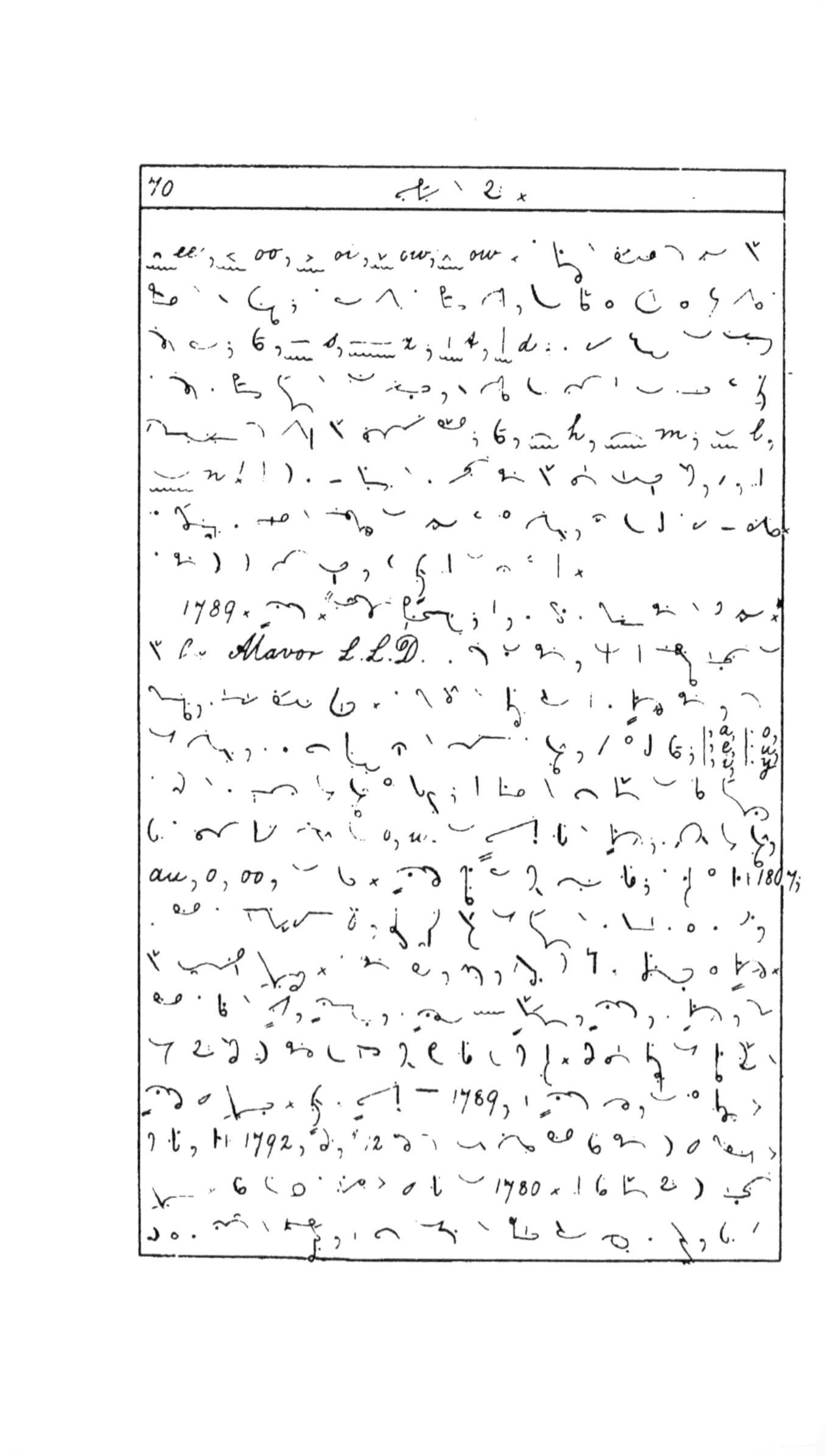

ee, oo, oi, ow, ow.

6, s, z, t, d.

6, h, m, l, n.

1789. Mavor L.L.D.

a, e, i; o, u, y.

o, u.

au, o, oo, 1807;

1789, 1792, 1780.

1780, 1792,

1795

Rees

12

60

a-afore, -a after, h- heretofore
i inferior, =u ultimate "here-abouts,
roundabout, thereabouts, whereabouts,"
h, r, t, w,

a, b, c,

David

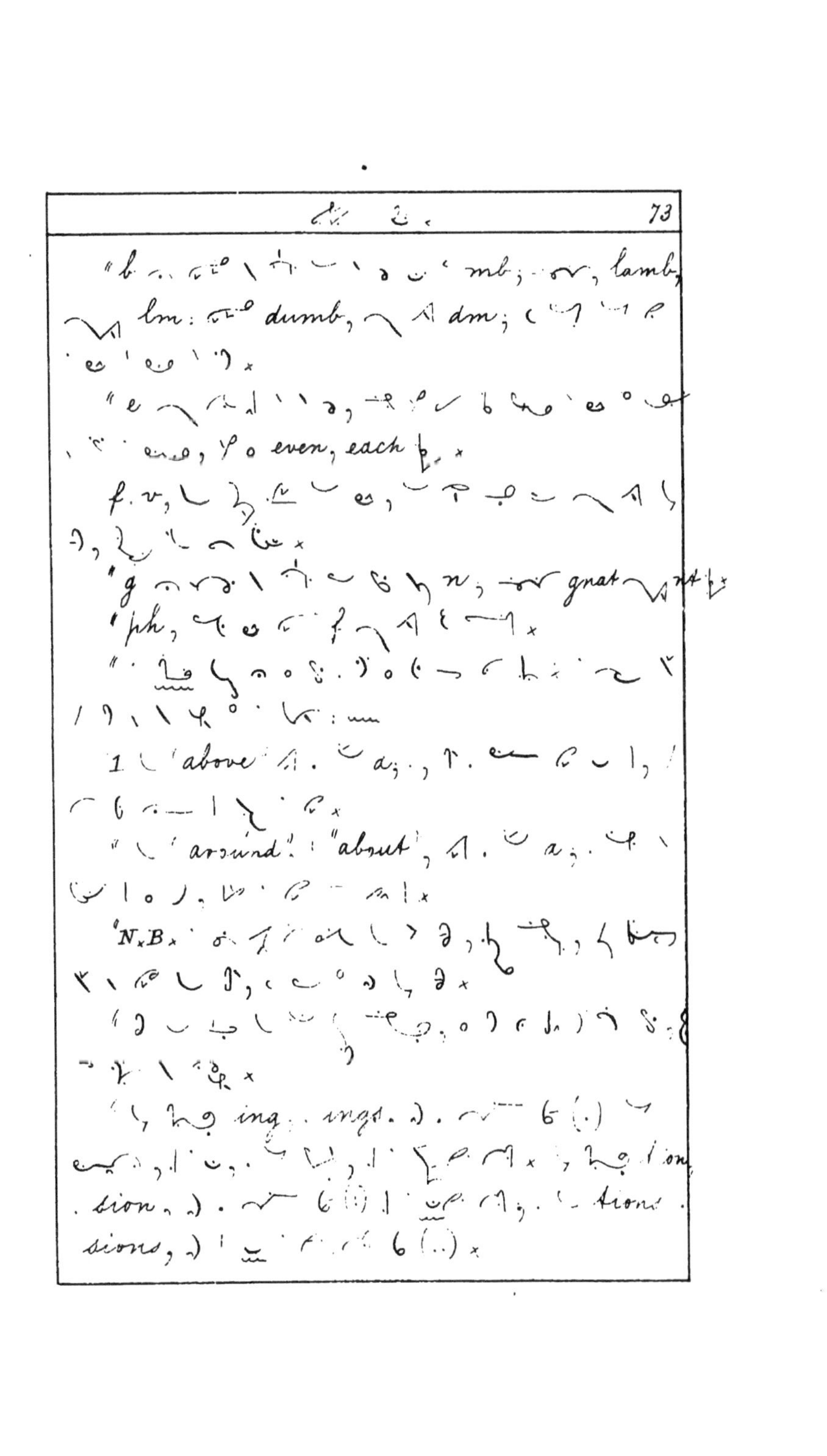

b … mb; … lamb, … bm: … dumb, … dm; …

e … even, each …

f. v, …

g … n; … gnat … nt …

ph, … f …

1 … above … a; …

… around … about, … a; …

N. B. …

… ing … ings …

… ion, … sion … tions … sions …

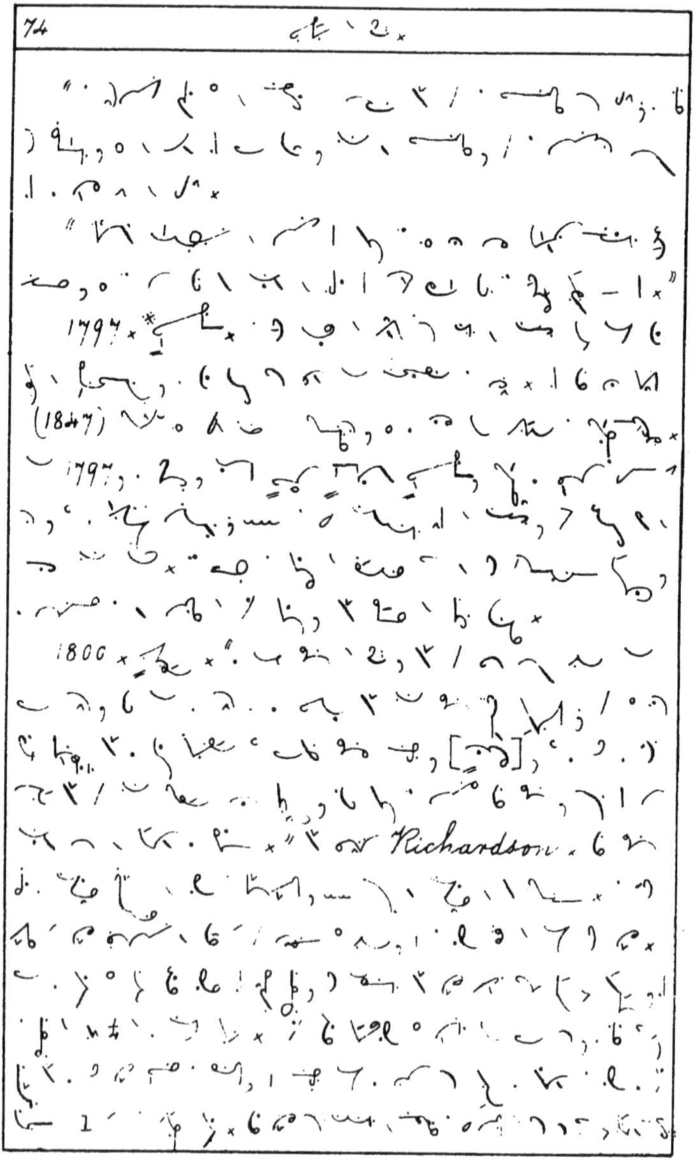
1797
(1847)
1797
1800
Richardson

Fig. 1.

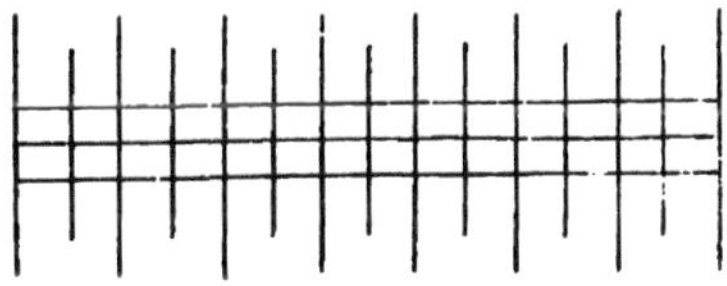

Fig. 2.

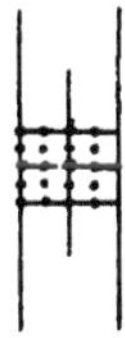

Fig. 3.

A	B	L	S
E	D	M	T
I	F	N	W
O	G	P	X
U	K	R	Y

[shorthand] 2. [shorthand] 3.

[shorthand] a, [shorthand] a; [shorthand]

[shorthand] b, [shorthand] b, [shorthand]

[shorthand] h, ch, sh, th, [shorthand]

ou, qu, str, v.

[shorthand] at,

[shorthand] a [shorthand] A, [shorthand] and [shorthand]

[shorthand] e, [shorthand] nd; [shorthand] inference [shorthand]

[shorthand] i, [shorthand] nfrns. [shorthand]

[shorthand]

"know, nigh," "knows;"

"in the, in him, in her, in it,"

"near, nearer, nearness, nearly"

"nevertheless". "notwithstanding."

63

123

525, 276, 646

393, 768, 301

1603

Harwin, … 17(

19 … 12

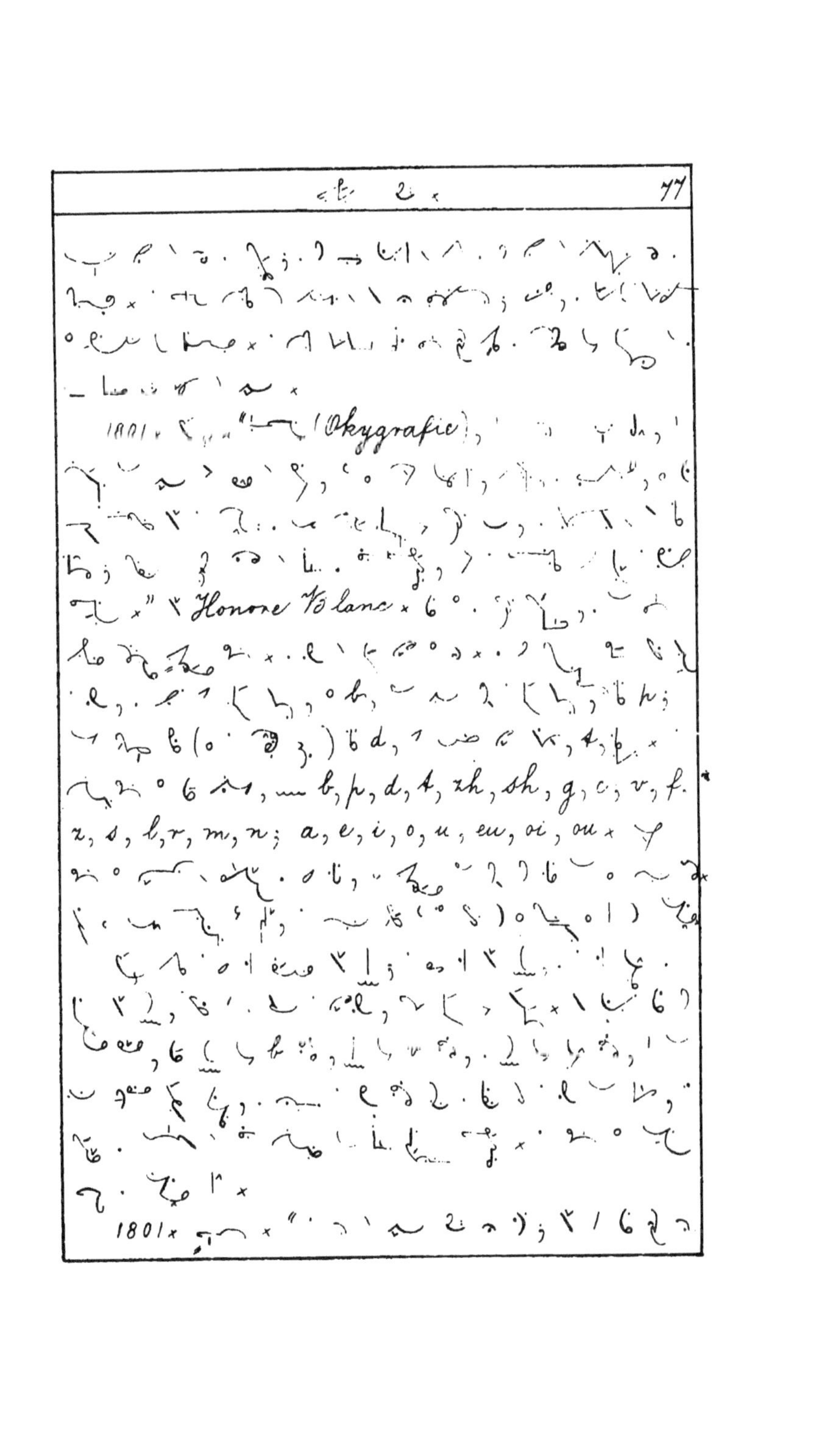

[illegible]

1801. [illegible] (Okygrafic), [illegible]

[illegible] Honore Blanc. [illegible]

[illegible] b, p, d, t, zh, sh, g, c, v, f. z, s, l, r, m, n; a, e, i, o, u, eu, oi, ou. [illegible]

[illegible]

1801. [illegible]

Crome,

'by' 'be',

'can' 'come'

'do, did' d, f, 'of, off' 'if',

g 'go,' 'God,' 'give':

h 'he, how,' l 'all' 'ill';

m 'am me' 'my'

n 'in', 'on', 'one',

p 'up' 'upon';

'our, or', 'are,' r

'as, is, us, so, see,' s;

t 'at, it, to, thee, that,'

w 'we, who, was,' 'what;'

y 'ye, yea, you, yet,' 'yes;'

B, B, b, b, □,

|, £, *,

+, W, M,

[illegible]

1802. [illegible]

[illegible] Roe. [illegible] 1821, [illegible]

[illegible] u, au, ŏ, ah, a, e, ay, ĭ, ee, ō, ōō, ŏŏ, [illegible] ü (lute, vue). [illegible] ī, oi, aye, ow. [illegible] y, w. [illegible] b, v, d, th, g, k, ([illegible] lough) — lok, [illegible]), z, zh, r, ly, ([illegible] "lieu, million, seraglio"); m, n, ny ([illegible] "new, annual,") ng. [illegible] b, d, g, [illegible] m, n, ny, ng, [illegible] v, th, k, sh, [illegible] r, l, ly, m, n, ny, ng [illegible] h.

[illegible] h, f, t, k, s, sh, th."

[illegible]

1802.* [illegible]

[illegible]

1803. [illegible] Prosser. [illegible] a, b, c, [illegible] a, e, i, o, u. [illegible]

1806. [illegible] Nicholson, [illegible] l. r, m. s. [illegible]

1810. [illegible]

Clive

1811 "Curso de Taquigrafia Española,"

a, e, i, o, u,

1812

1829

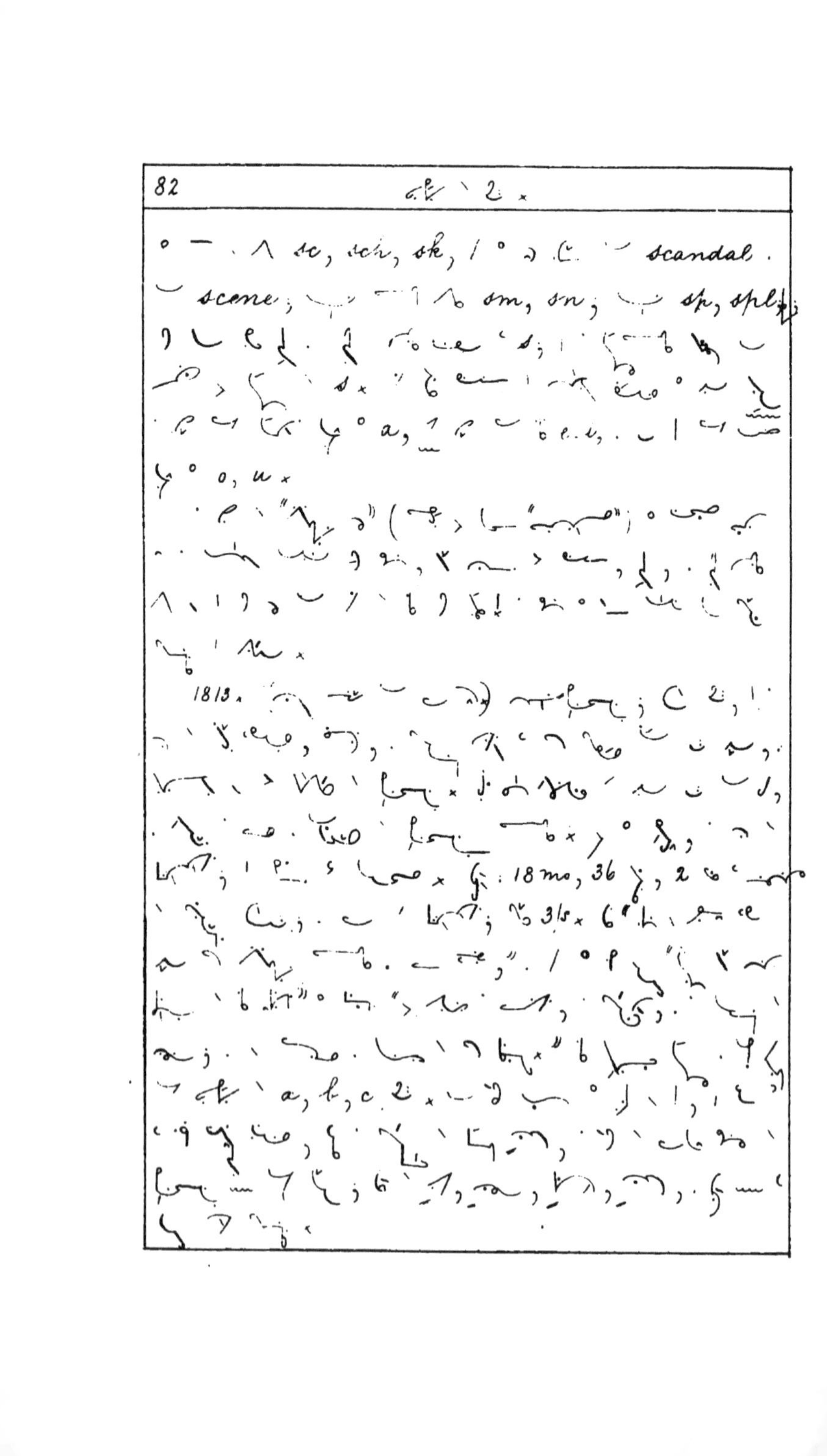

sc, sch, sk, … scandal … scene; … sm, sn; … sp, spl; …

… s; … s. …

… a, … l, …

… o, u.

…

1813. …

… 18 mo, 36 … 3/s. …

… a, b, c. …

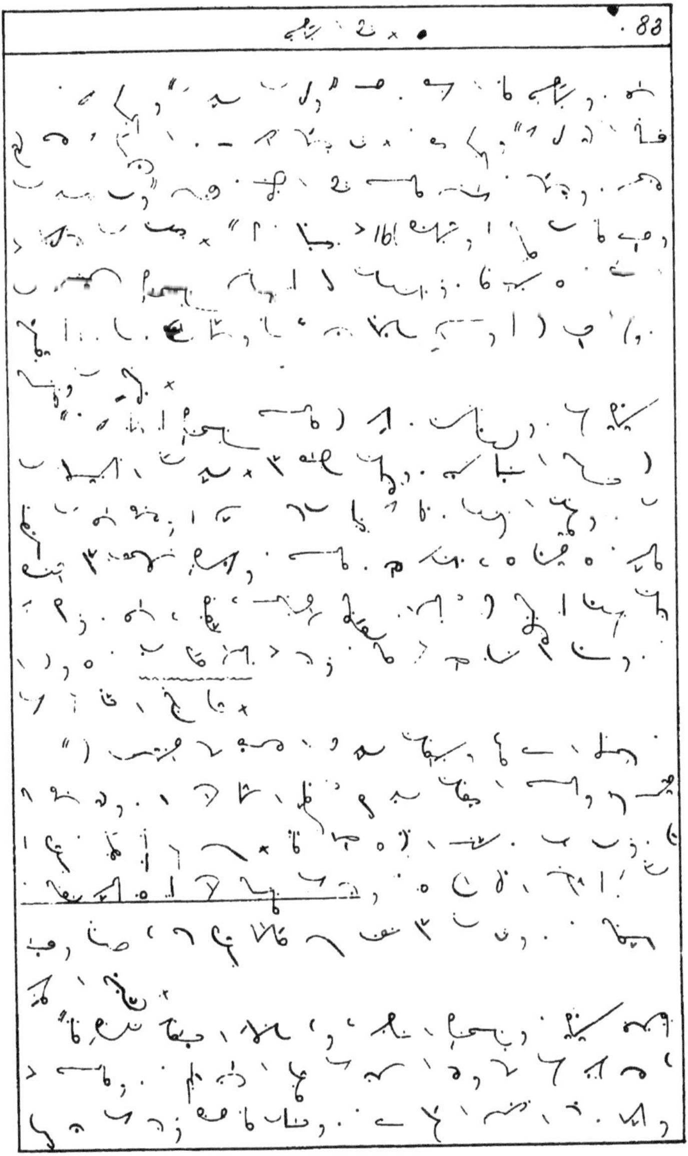

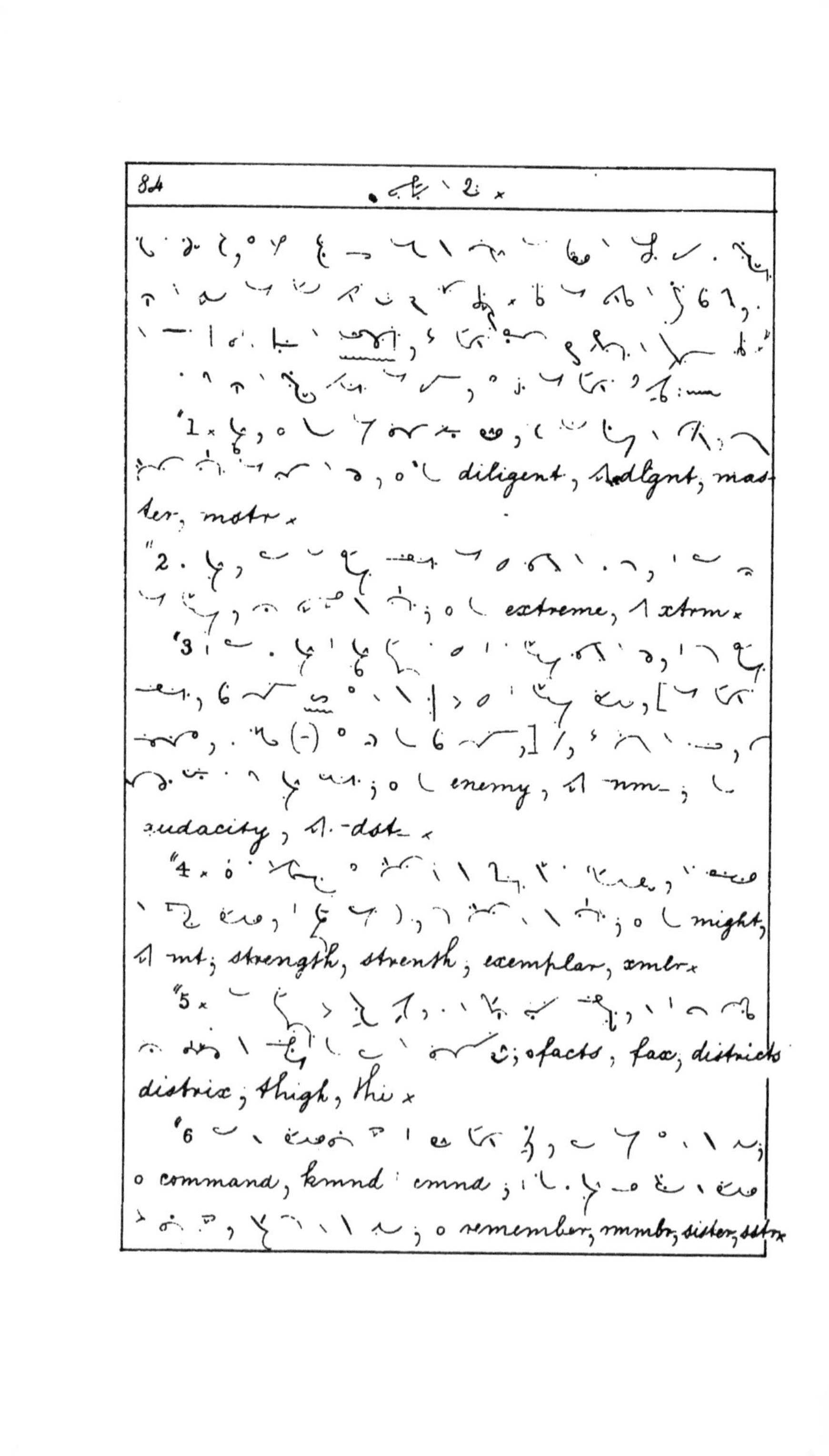

[illegible]

1\. [illegible] diligent, [illegible]dlgnt, master, mstr.

2\. [illegible] extreme, [illegible] xtrm.

3\. [illegible] enemy, [illegible] nm; [illegible] audacity, [illegible]-dst.

4\. [illegible] might, [illegible] mt; strength, strenth; exemplar, xmlr.

5\. [illegible] facts, fax; districts, districx; thigh, thi.

6\. [illegible] command, kmnd, cmnd; [illegible] remember, rmmbr; sister, sstr.

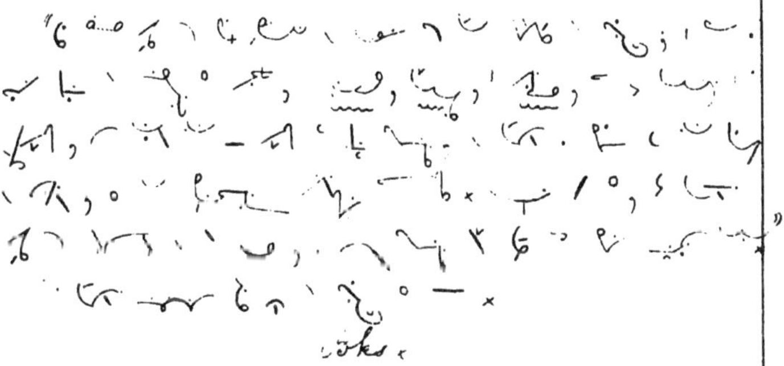

"Ft rlst -gs. Bks hv bn t. sls -f t ws & t dlt -f t nqsv -n e kntr- whr svlstn ws nn & w -t thm wht- blnk wd lf -pr; -l t nlg. w- kn -gr f -ktl xprns -s xtrml- lmtd bt bks ids -s t- t -qntns -f tms lng pst -f nsns nw n- mr -f snss nw-td kltvtd & brt t- prfkson bt lrnd & ngns -f e klm & -g.

"T dskvr- -f ltrs -s -f sch mprtns tht mn- hv -skrbd -t t- -dvn -ngn. W- -n vn ndvr t- trs -t t- -ts srs. Bt lrnng w -t nfnt lbr kd nvr hv bkm g hd -t nt bn dfsd thr- t mdm -f t prs. Tht nbl nvnsn t rt -f Prnting plss t mdrns -n -mst nvb ston cmprd w t nnts & n bt grs ntnsn -r crmnl ndf cn nw plt -gnrns -r hrcld k. T -vns -f nfrmsn -r nw pln & drk t fntns -f sns -r nlkd & t lvng wtrs not -s t- tst. T sprngs f t mss -r -n- lngr fbls & nthr rlgn nr mrls -r rpd -p -n t vl -f mstr -r cnsld f ngrng mnds.

"Hw thnkf thn -t w- t- b- fr t tr prolgd t- wh w- wr brn & hw grt -t yth t- cltvt tst fr ltrtr wh wl fl -p t blnks -f lf w -ms -m -kp- t ists f njm & la t- tht mprvm f t sl wh w- hw svn t- sps wl nkrs t hpns f tnt."

'Mors Fthrs Gft, vl 1 pg 1.'

Books.

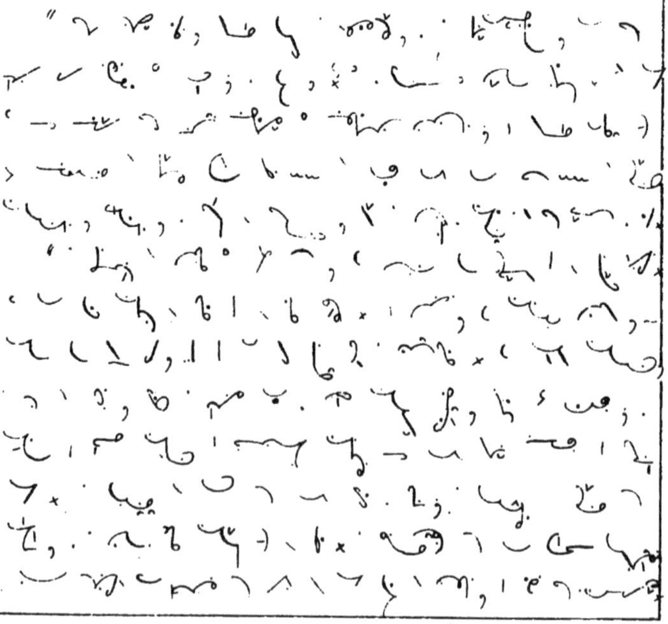

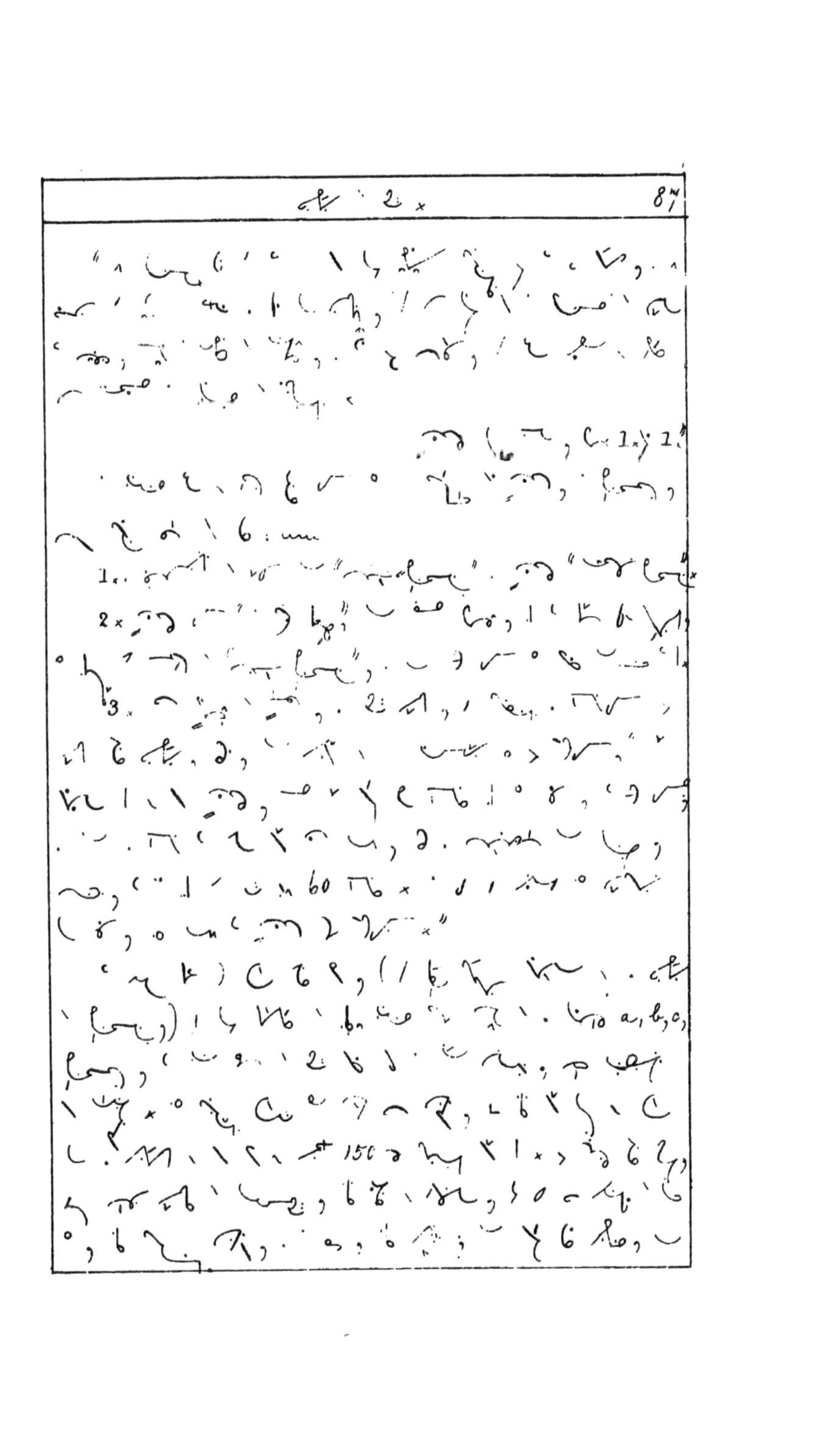

[illegible]

[illegible] 1. [illegible] 1.

[illegible]

1. [illegible]

2. [illegible]

3. [illegible] 2 [illegible] 60 [illegible]

[illegible] 10 a, b, c, [illegible] 2 [illegible] 150 [illegible] 6 [illegible]

1813. Lawson, (subpoena)

1814. 1824, s, x, z, j, ch, sh. b, p,

1815,

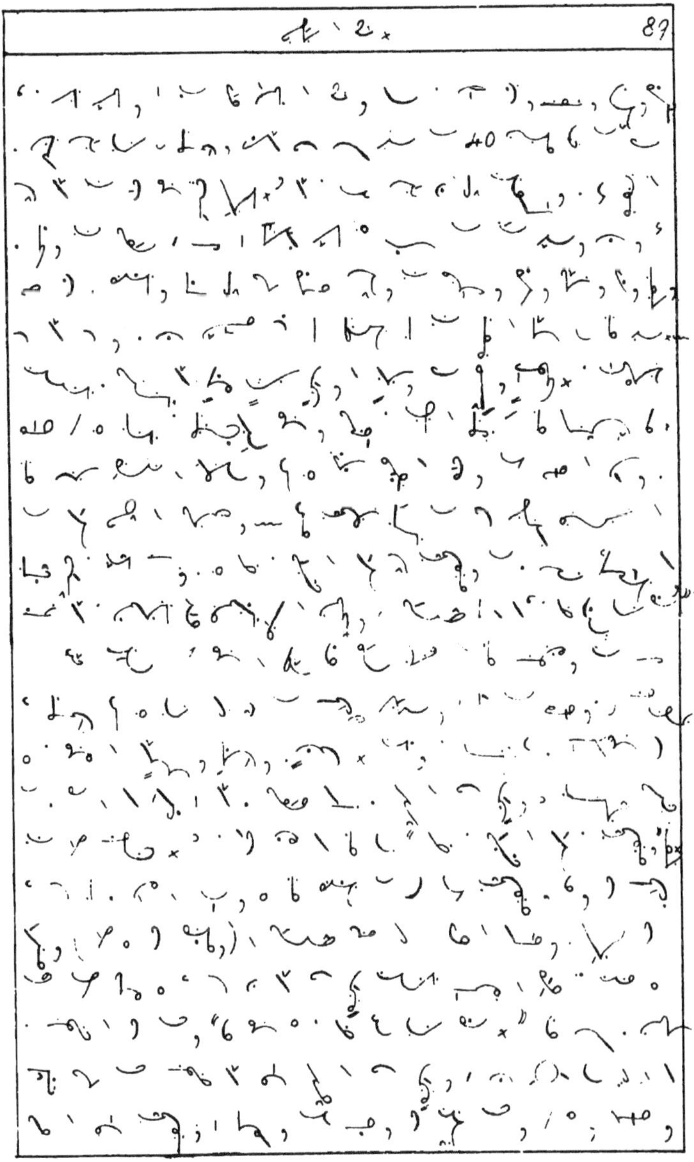

g. j, k, x. ch

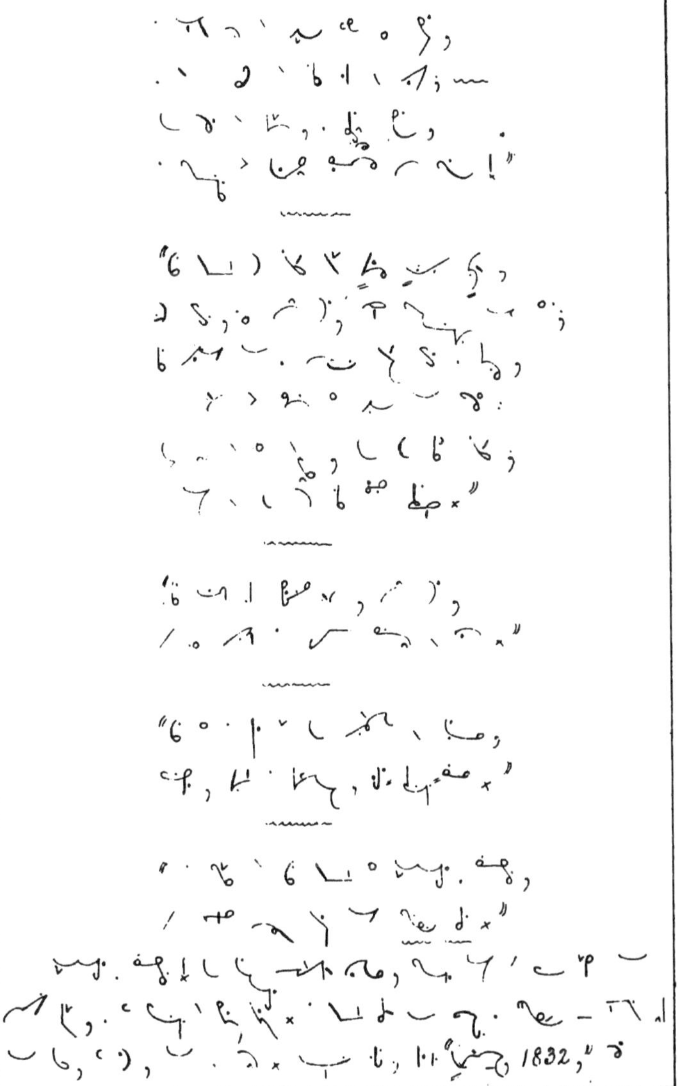

"object, discover, frequent, govern, habit, kind, lawful, imitate, necessary, public, quick, respect, scarce, time, wicked, expect, yield."

"observe, deliver, forgive, general, happy, know, labour, imagine, neglect, perfect, question, reflect, serious, temper, worthy, extraordinary, yourself."

"ct an, and; he, thee; my, may; no, so; you, your."

"f, for, from; g give, gave; (m) can, come; every, every; f of, often; our, own; that, there, therefore; up, upon; (n, n) only, over;"

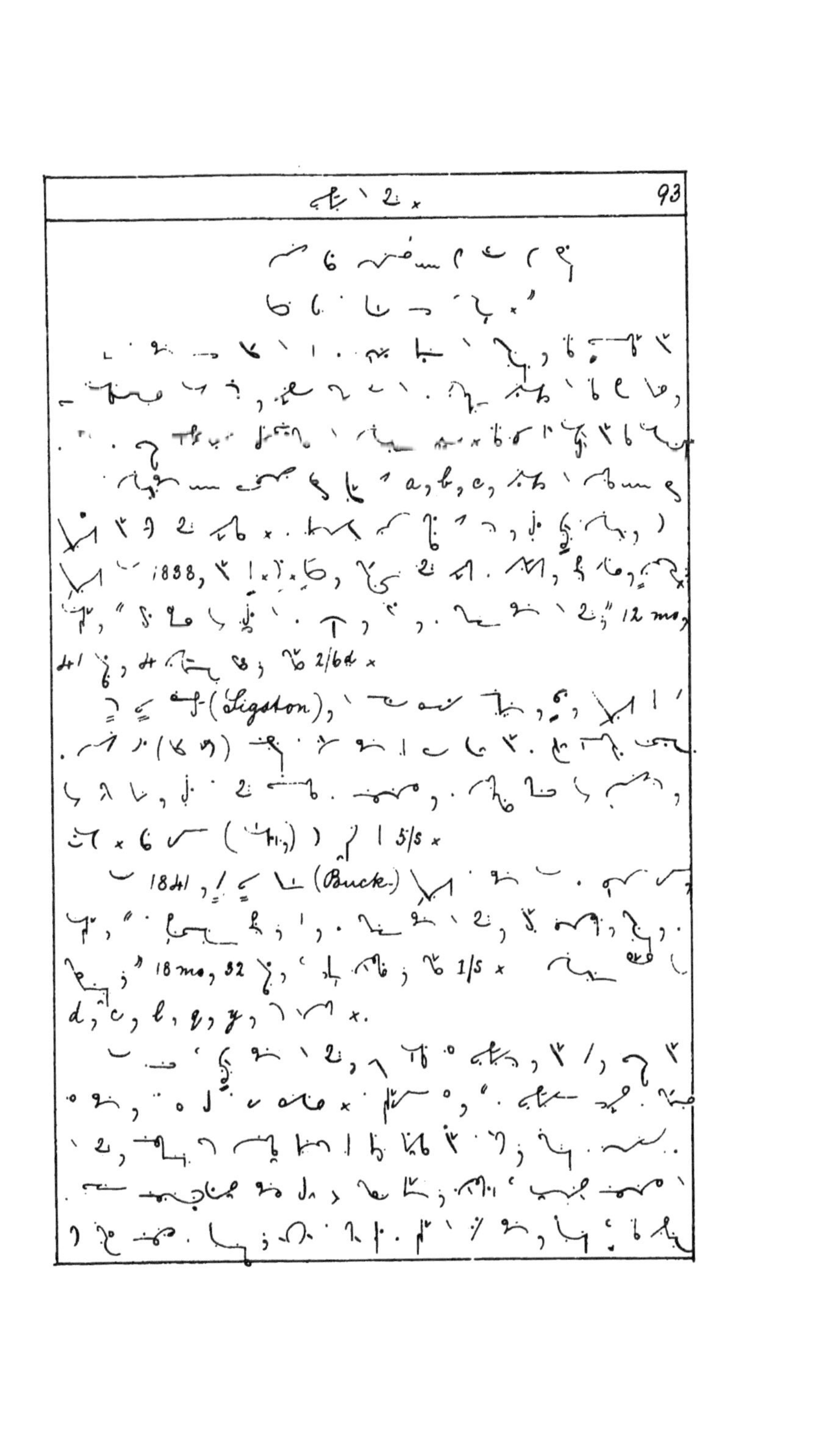

a, b, c,

1838, 12 mo,

41 2/6d

(Ligston),

5/5

1841, (Buck)

18 mo, 32 1/5

d, c, l, q, y,

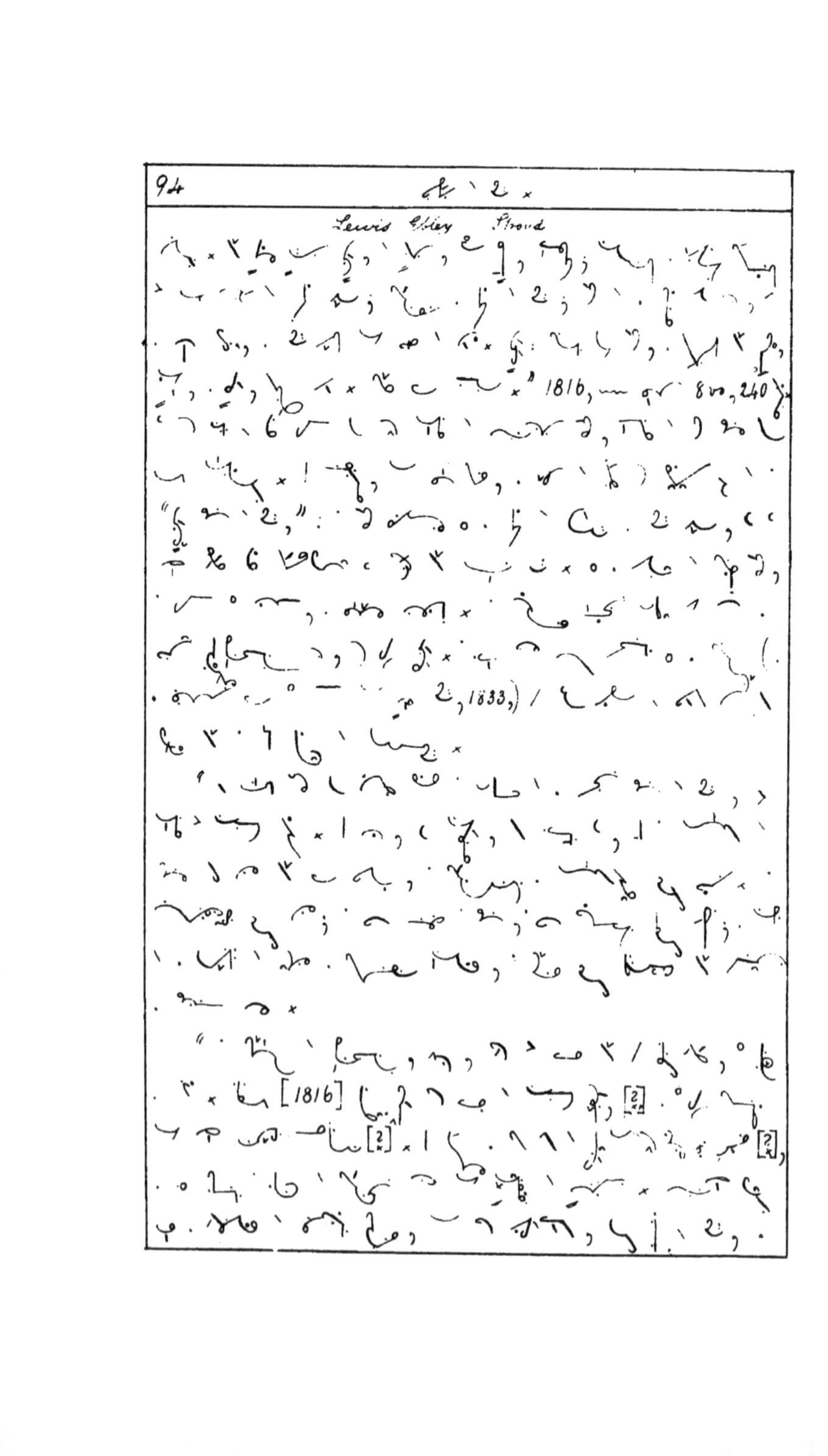

Lewis Ebley Stroud

1816, 8vo, 240

1833,

[1816] [2] [2] [2]

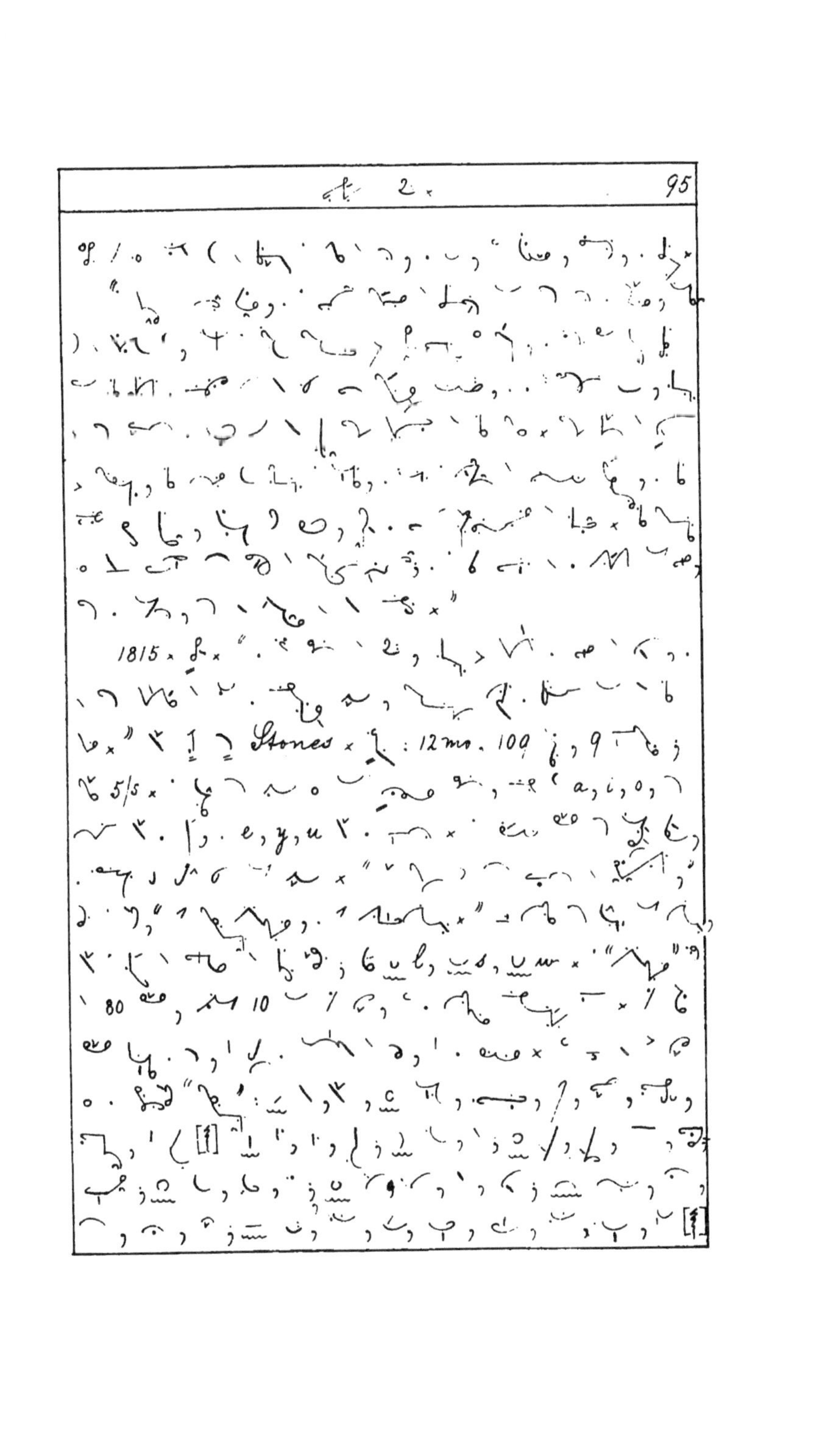

1815

Stones : 12mo. 100 9

5/s a, i, o,

e, y, u

6 u l, s, u w

80 10

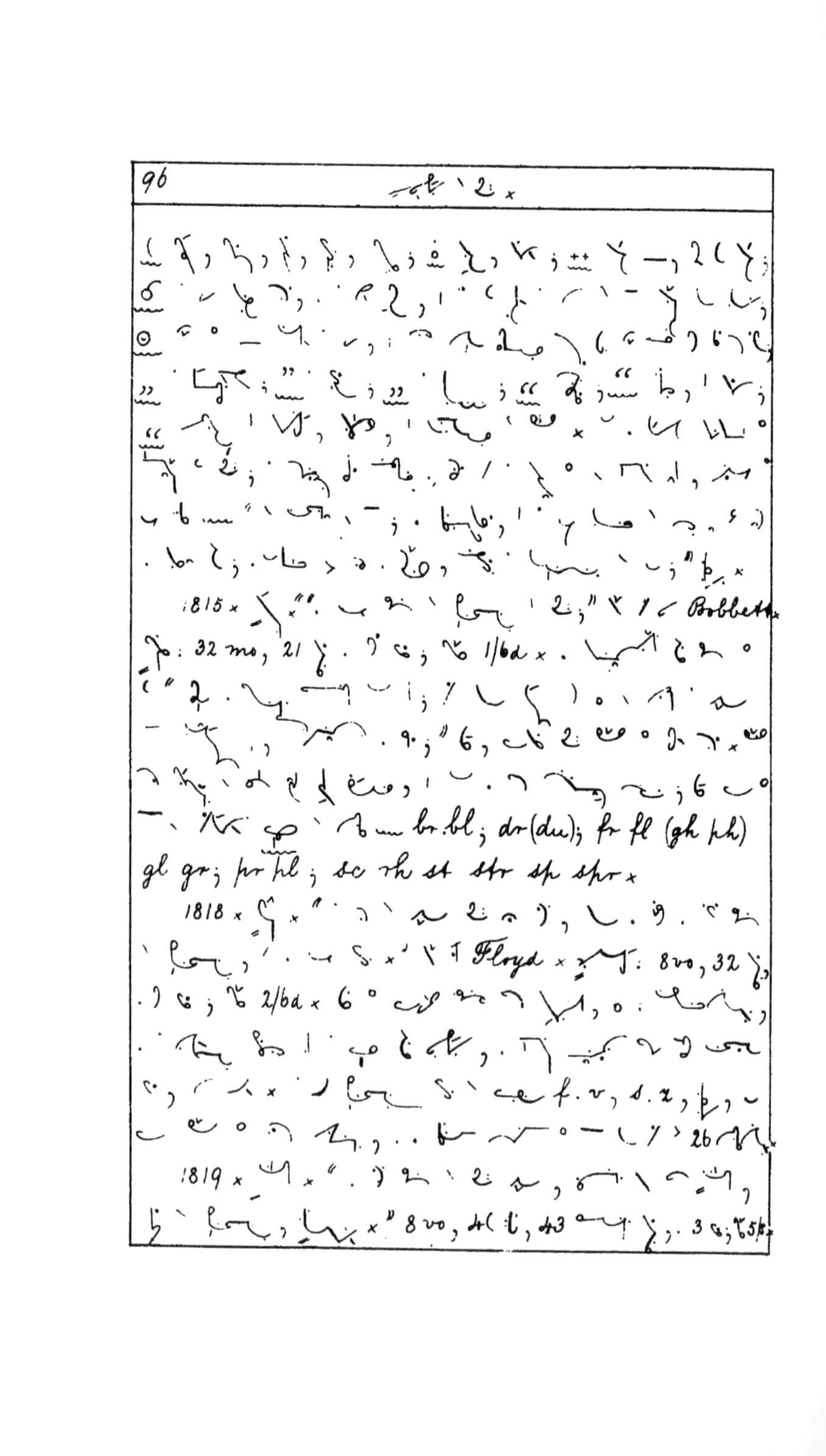

[shorthand]

1815 × [shorthand] Bobbett × [shorthand]: 32 mo, 21 [shorthand] 1/6d × [shorthand] br. bl; dr (dw); fr fl (gh ph) gl gr; pr pl; sc sh st str sp spr ×

1818 × [shorthand] Floyd × [shorthand]: 8vo, 32 [shorthand] 2/6d × [shorthand] f. v, s. z, [shorthand] 26 [shorthand]

1819 × [shorthand] 8 vo, 4 [shorthand], 43 [shorthand] 3 [shorthand] 5 [shorthand]

1819

Farr 8vo, 74 3 6/5 6

a, e, i,

o, u, y,

fig,

1823

Jackson 12mo, 32

3 5/6d 21

6 k q

4 c d m x

b v, w p s, z h g j f n y

l * r

(*)

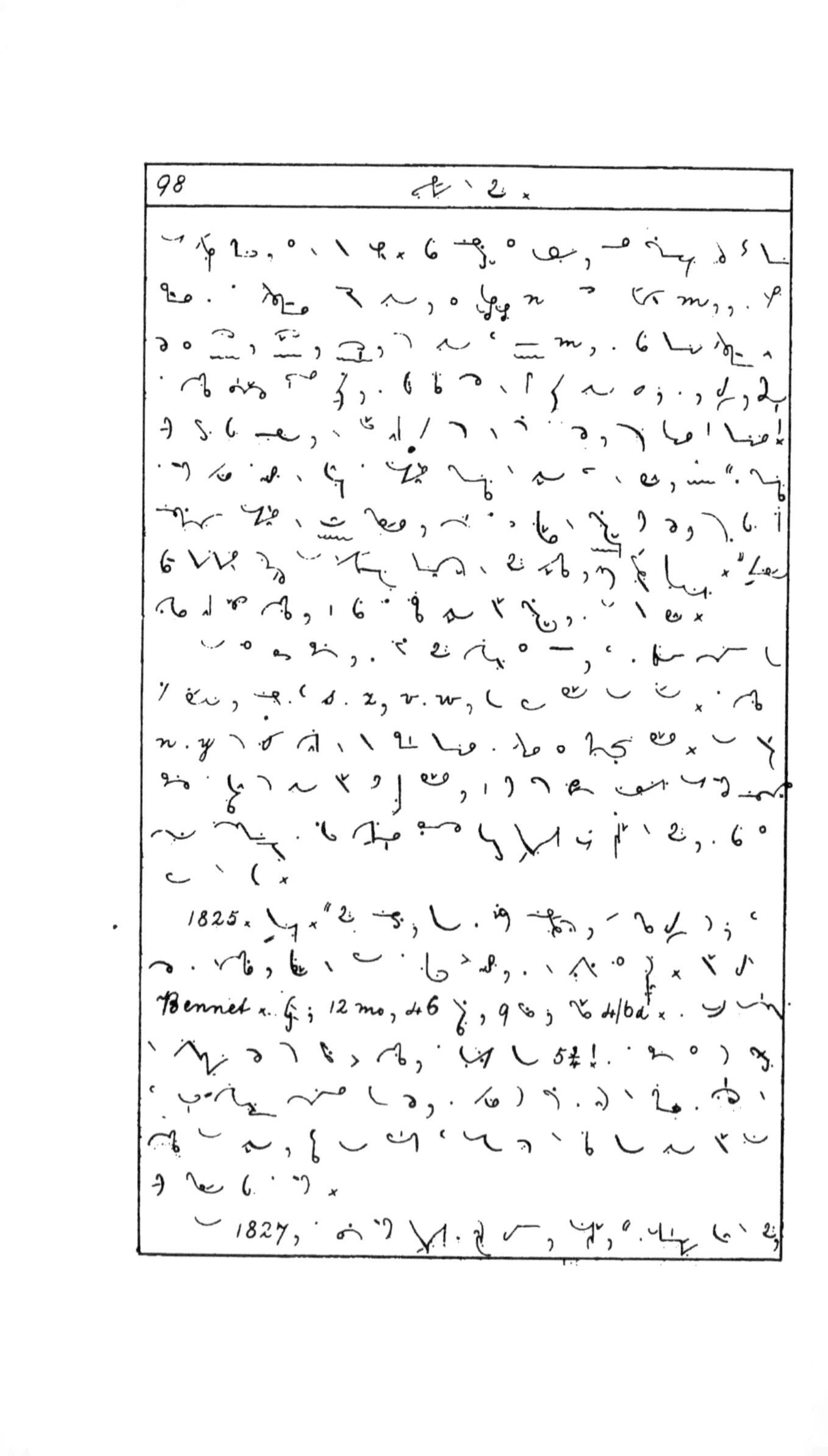

1825.

Bennet. 12 mo, 4/6 , 9 ; 4/6d.

5¼!

1827,

[illegible] 12mo, 36 [illegible] 2/8 [illegible]

1824 [illegible] 8vo, 17 [illegible] 4 [illegible] 1/8 [illegible] b, ij, vw, y [illegible]

[illegible]

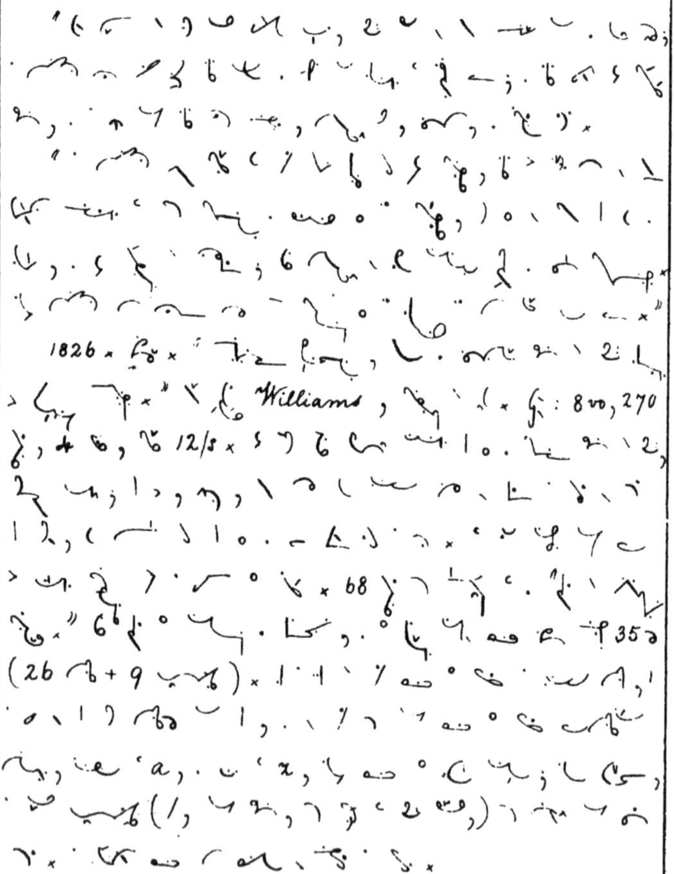

Ac (&)

academical	a	accidence	d
accelerate	b	acoustics	x
acceptance	c	acquaintance	1

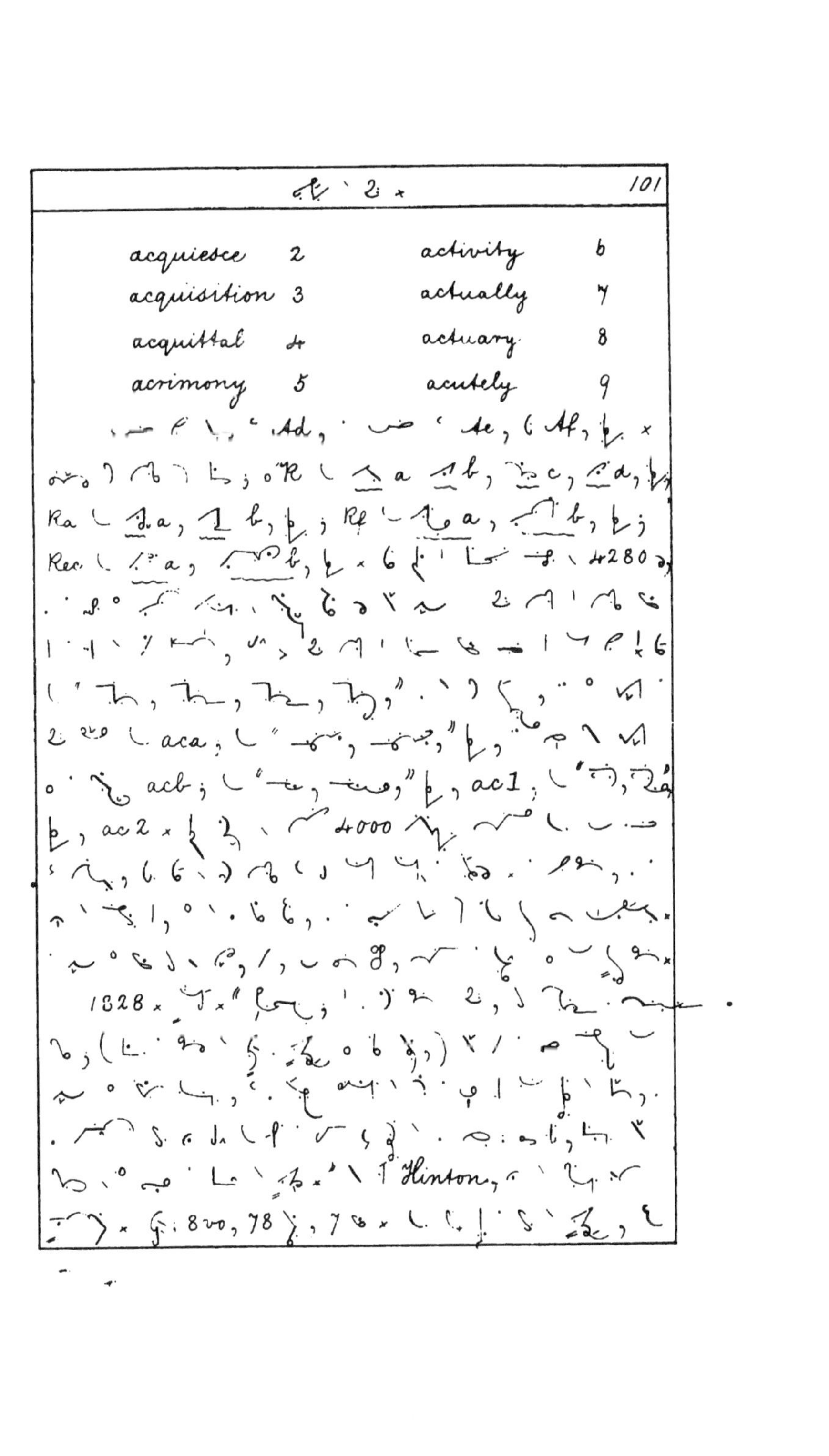

acquiesce	2	activity	6
acquisition	3	actually	7
acquittal	4	actuary	8
acrimony	5	acutely	9

1828 … Latham … 8 vo, 17 … 2 … 2/6d … pr. pl. …

1828 … 18 mo, 6 … 1 … 1/s … Kitchingman … J. S. …

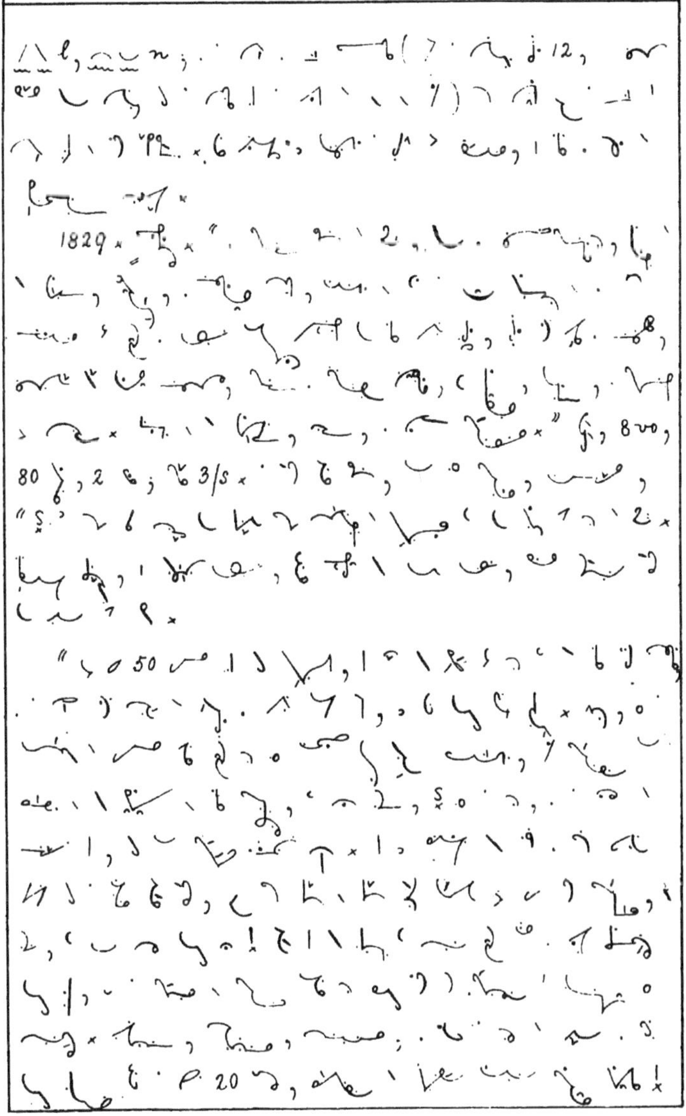

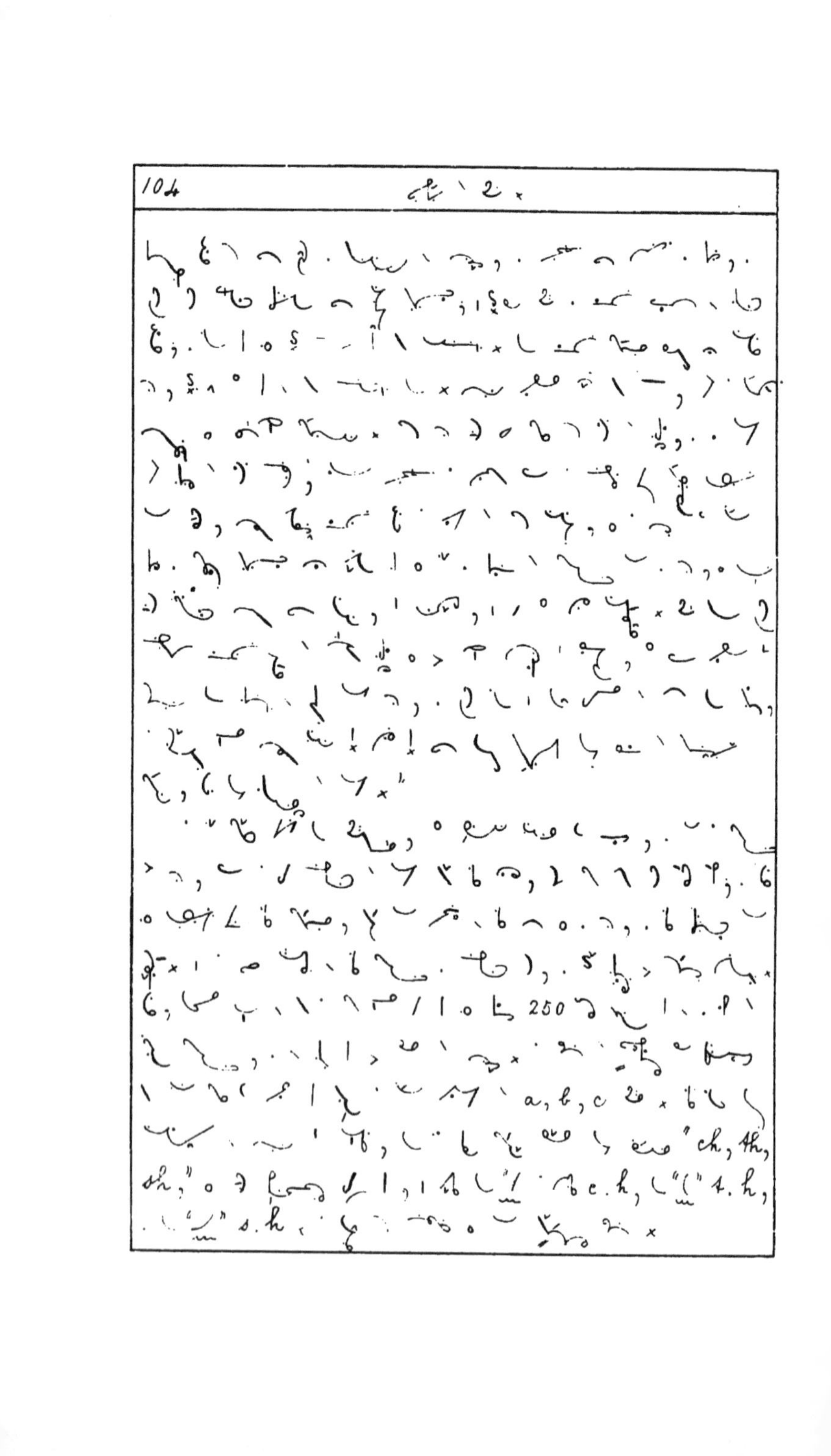

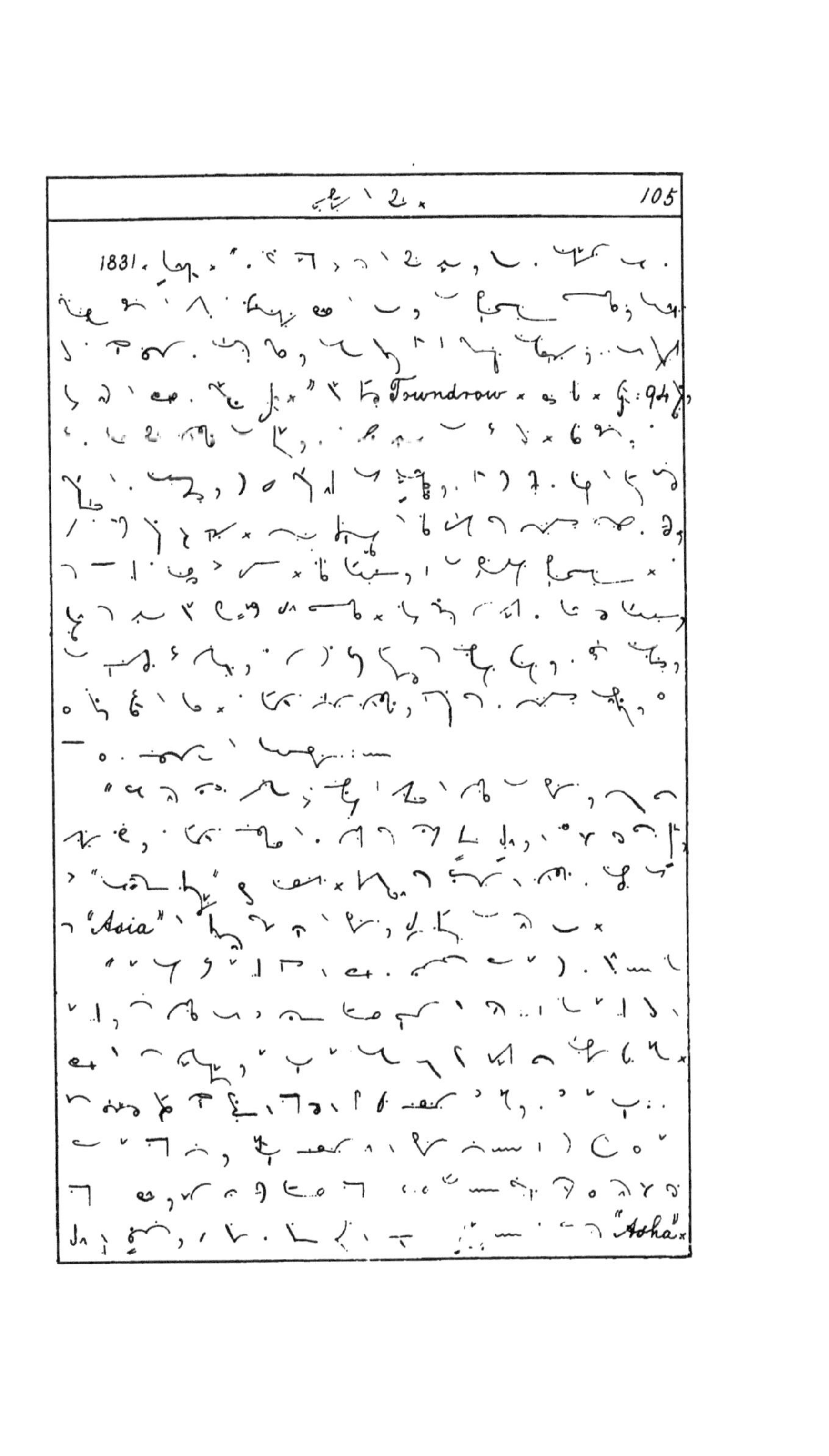

1831. … Towndrow … 94 …

… "Asia" …

… "Asha".

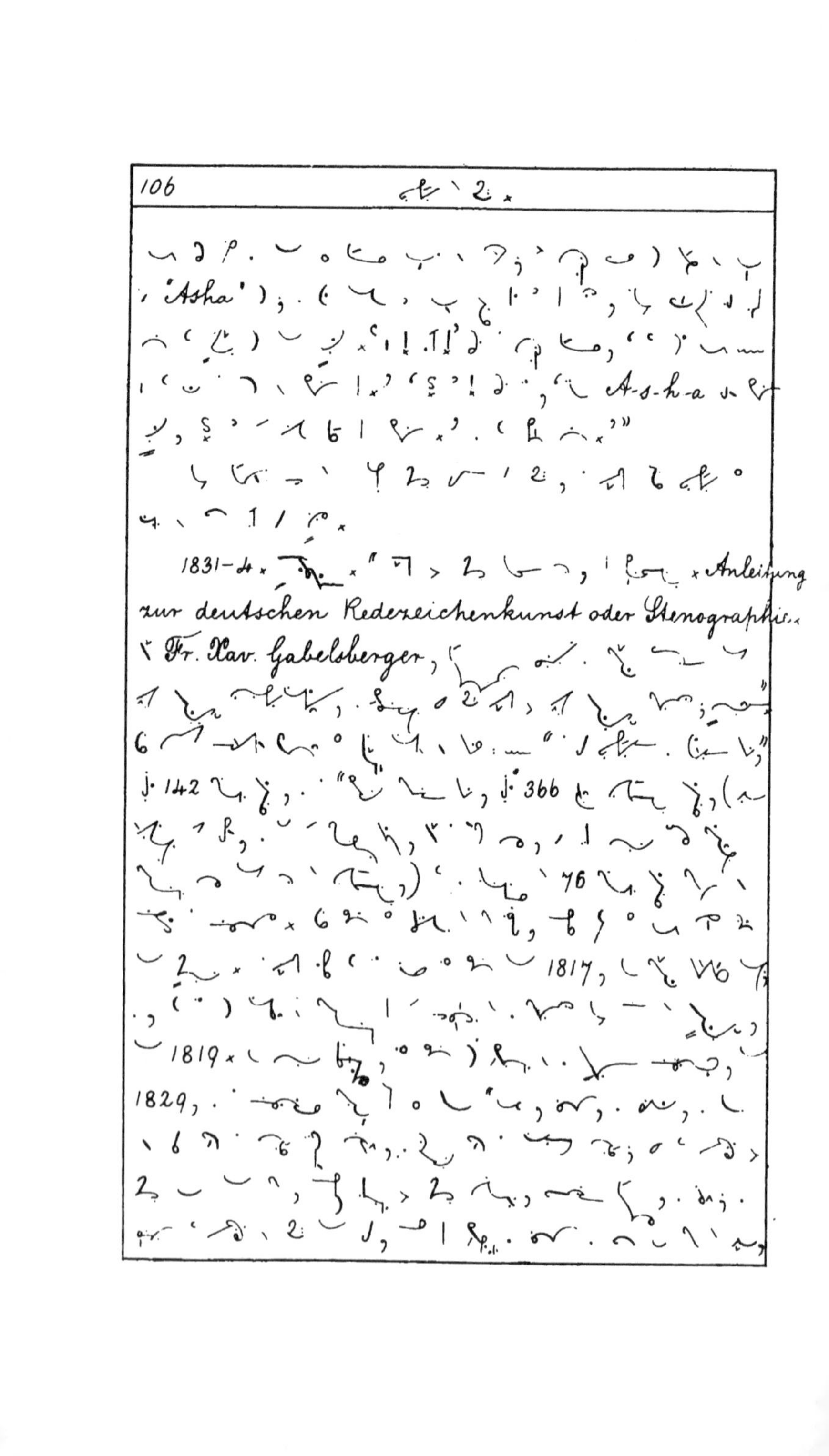

'Asha'

A-s-h-a

1831-4 … Anleitung zur deutschen Redezeichenkunst oder Stenographie … Fr. Xav. Gabelsberger

142 … 366

76

1817

1819

1829

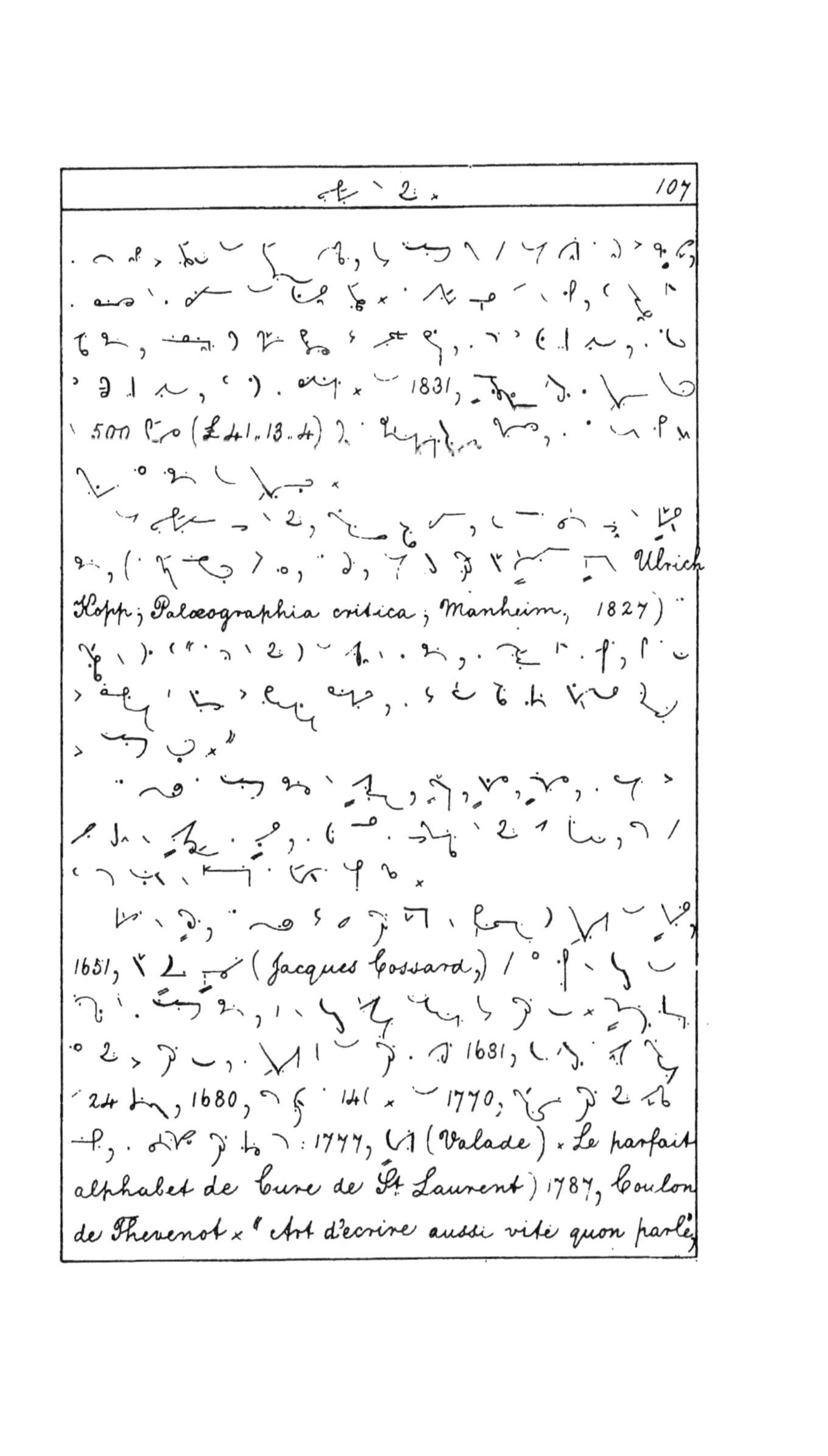

1831,

500 (£41.13.4)

Ulrich Kopp; Palæographia critica; Manheim, 1827)

1651, (Jacques Cossard,)

1631,

24, 1680, 141 1770,

1777, (Valade). Le parfait alphabet de Cure de St Laurent) 1787, Coulon de Thevenot. "Art d'ecrire aussi vite quon parle,

, 1787, (,)
400
1792,
(Mahie,) 1810
(Grosselin), 1822
(Clement) 1801, (Blanc), IX-1801,
(Montigny), (Vital)
(Conen de Prépéan), 1823, (Fosse)
1829, Cours théorique et pratique de Sténographie, (Dutertre) (Painparé)
1831,
(Jomard,) " " " ," 1832,
(Fayet; Nouvelle Écriture et Sténographie,) 1832,

1823, 500 (£40. 12. 3,) (Silfverstolpe, Hjerta) 1828,

(Ridderskapet) 1825 (?)

(Morhof), 1666, 1679, (Leipzig) 1681 1743, 1796, (Mosengeil)

1796 (Erleichterte Deutsche Stenographie,) (Danzer), 1800, " R " 1808,

(2) 1819, (Julius Leichtlein; 1819),

(Berthold) (Heim)

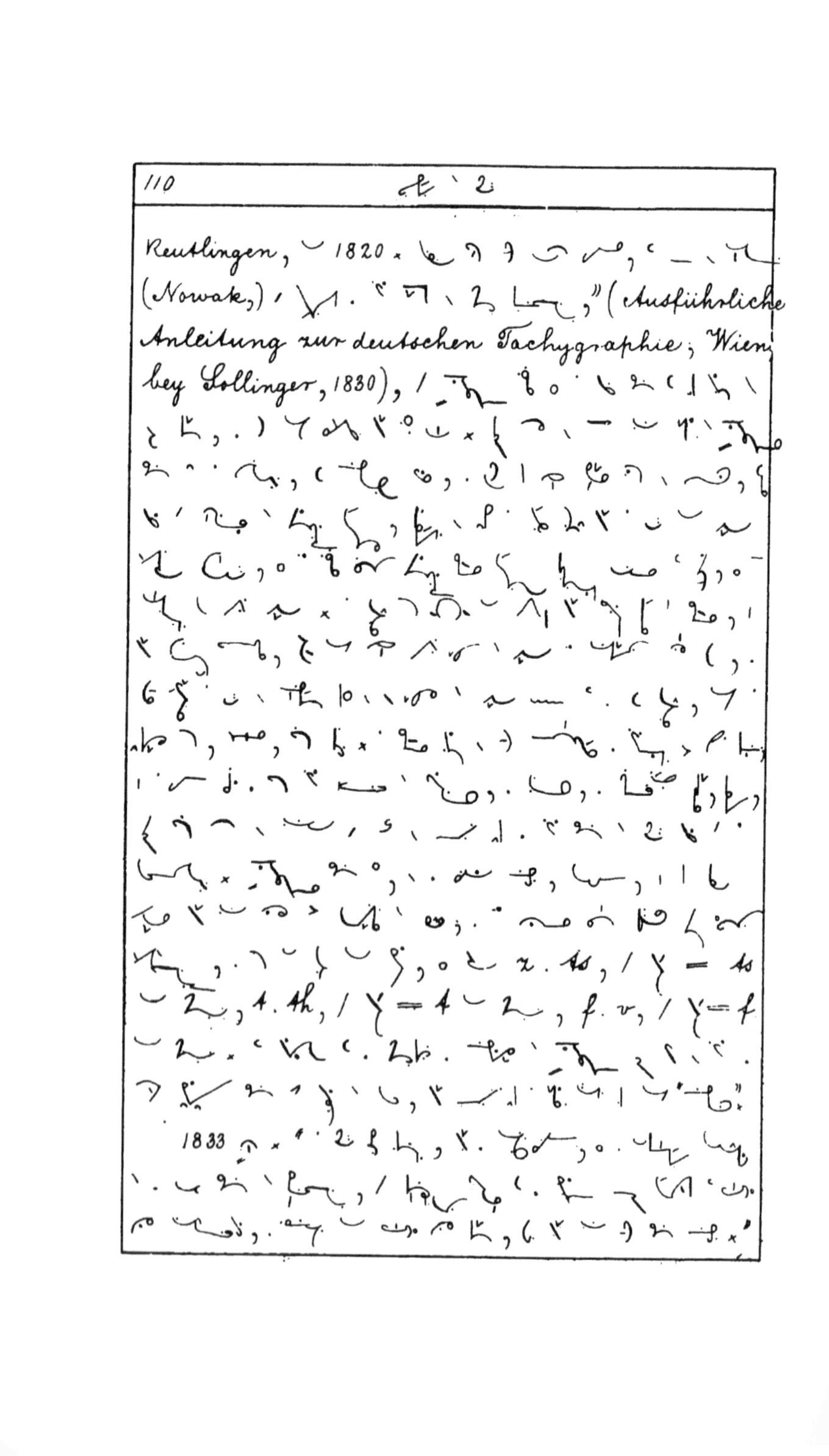

Reutlingen, 1820 … (Nowak,) … "(Ausführliche Anleitung zur deutschen Tachygraphie, Wien, bey Sollinger, 1830), …

… z. ts, / … = ts … t. th, / … = t … f. v, / … = f …

1833 …

Moat 8vo, 120, 24, 8s

24

22½

3/10

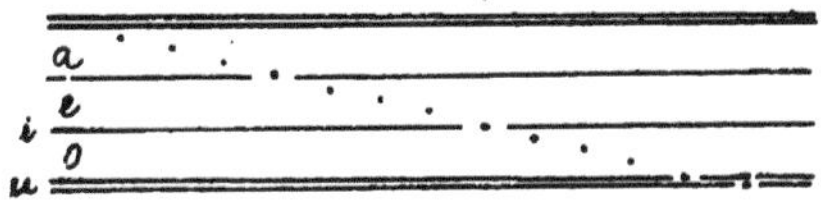

that, at, a,

e, ever, every, everything, the,

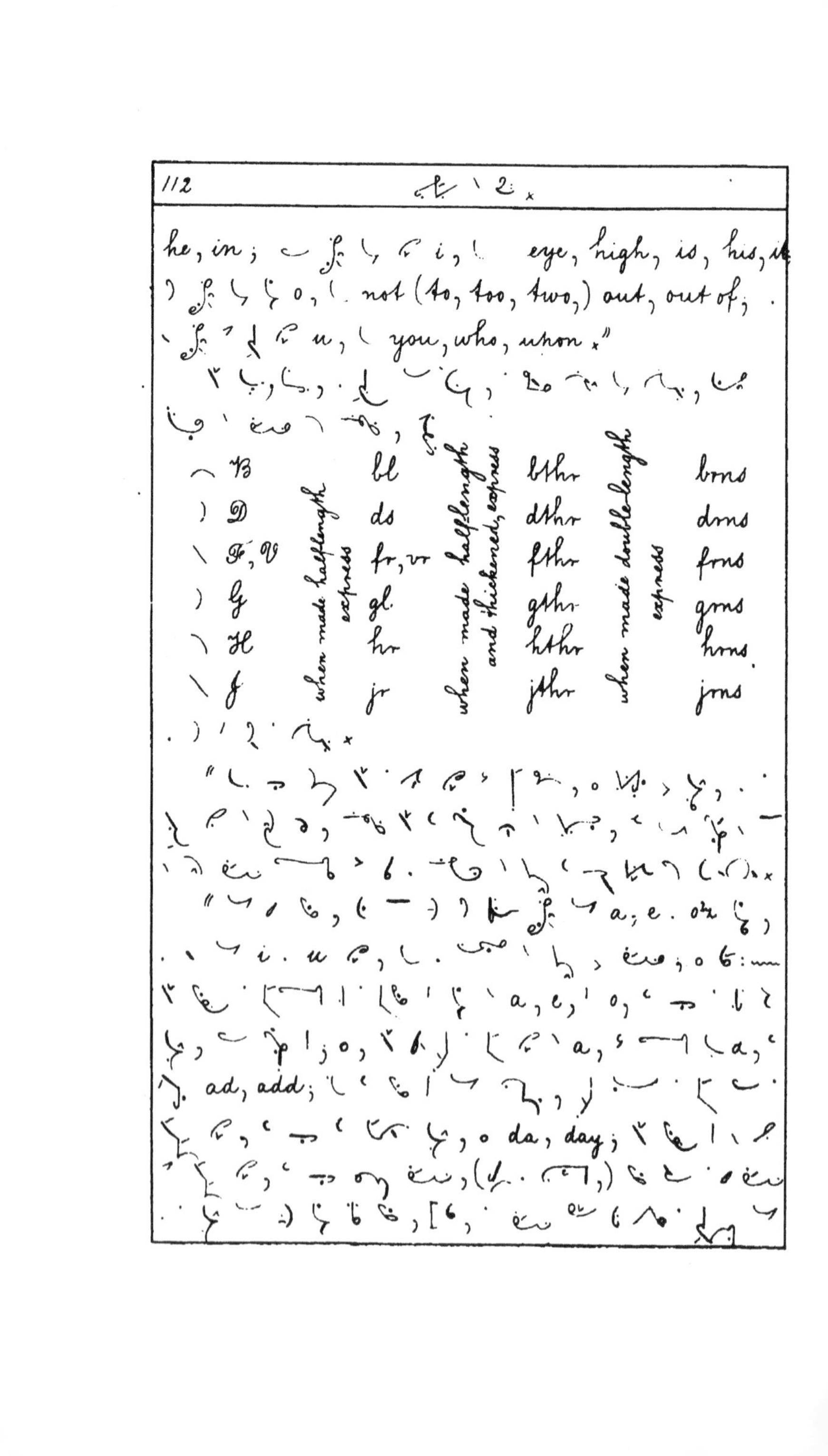

he, in; i, eye, high, is, his, it

o, not (to, too, two,) out, out of;

u, you, who, upon."

B	when made halflength express	bl	when made halflength and thickened, express	bthr	when made double-length express	brns
D		ds		dthr		drns
F, V		fr, vr		fthr		frns
G		gl		gthr		grns
H		hr		hthr		hrns
J		jr		jthr		jrns

a, e. o

i. u

a, e, o,

o, a, a,

ad, add;

o da, day;

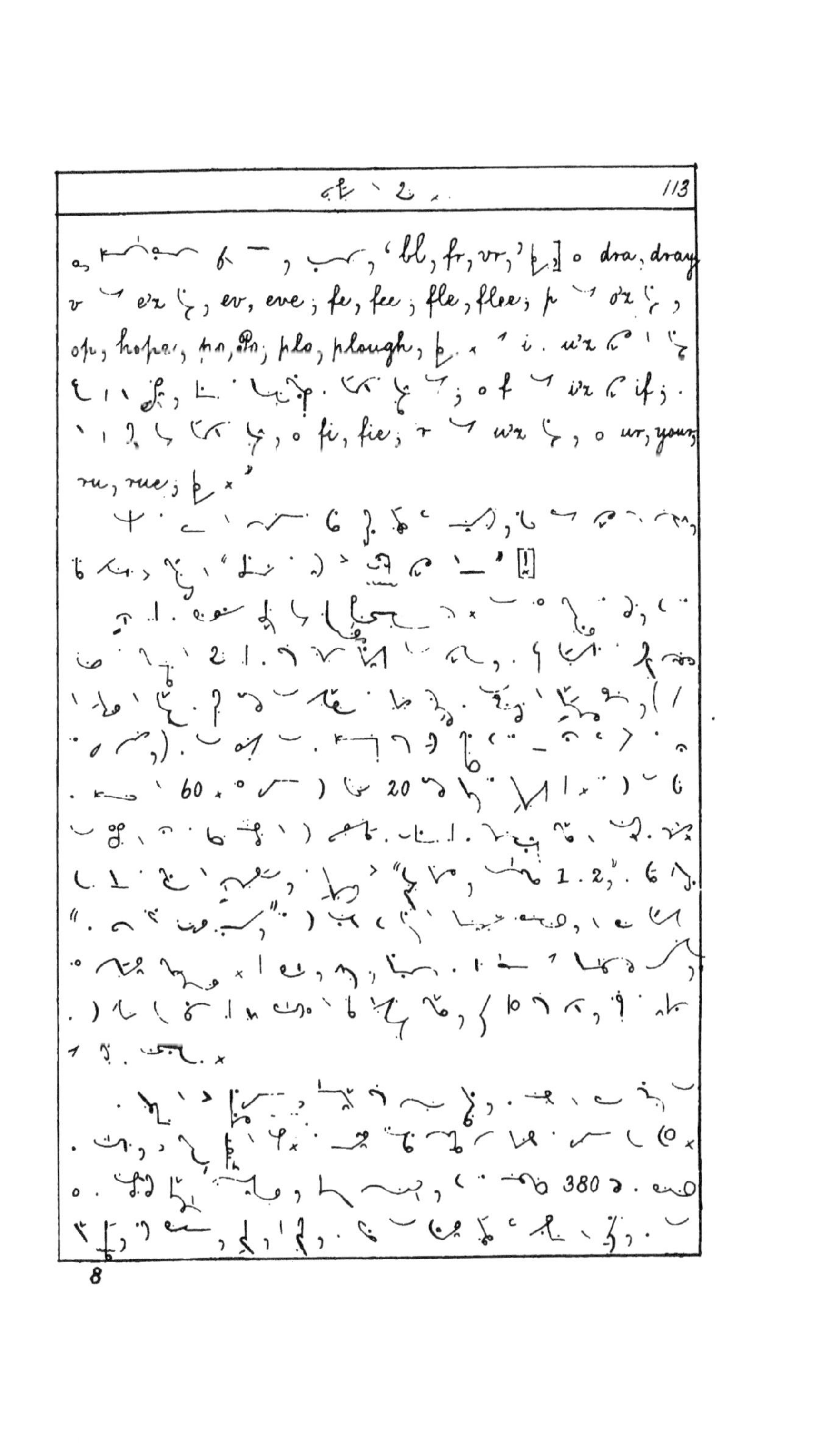

'bl, fr, vr,' dra, dray

ev, eve; fe, fee; fle, flee;

op, hope, plo, plough,

of if;

fi, fie; ur, your,

ru, rue;

60 20

"1.2,"

380

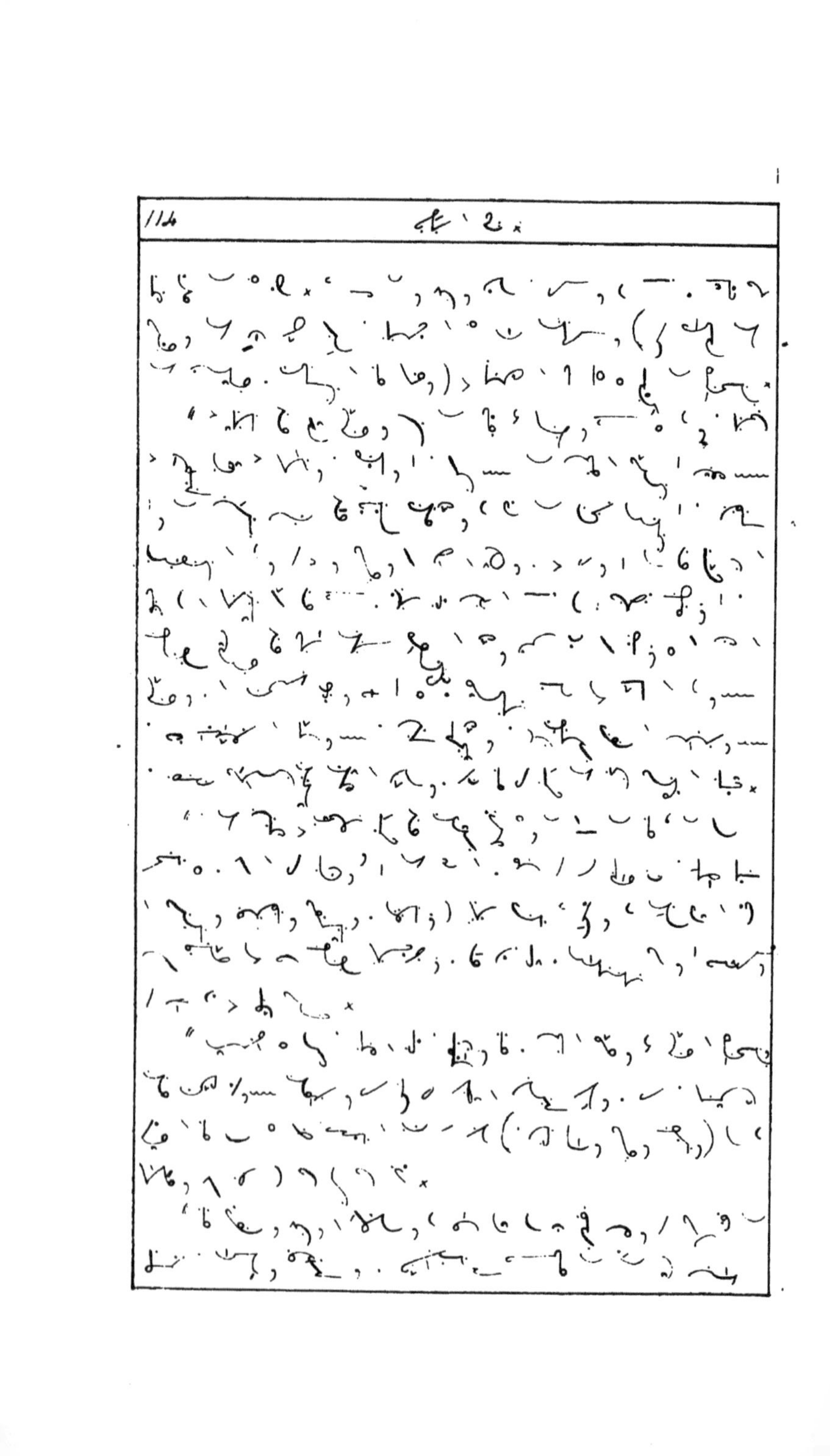

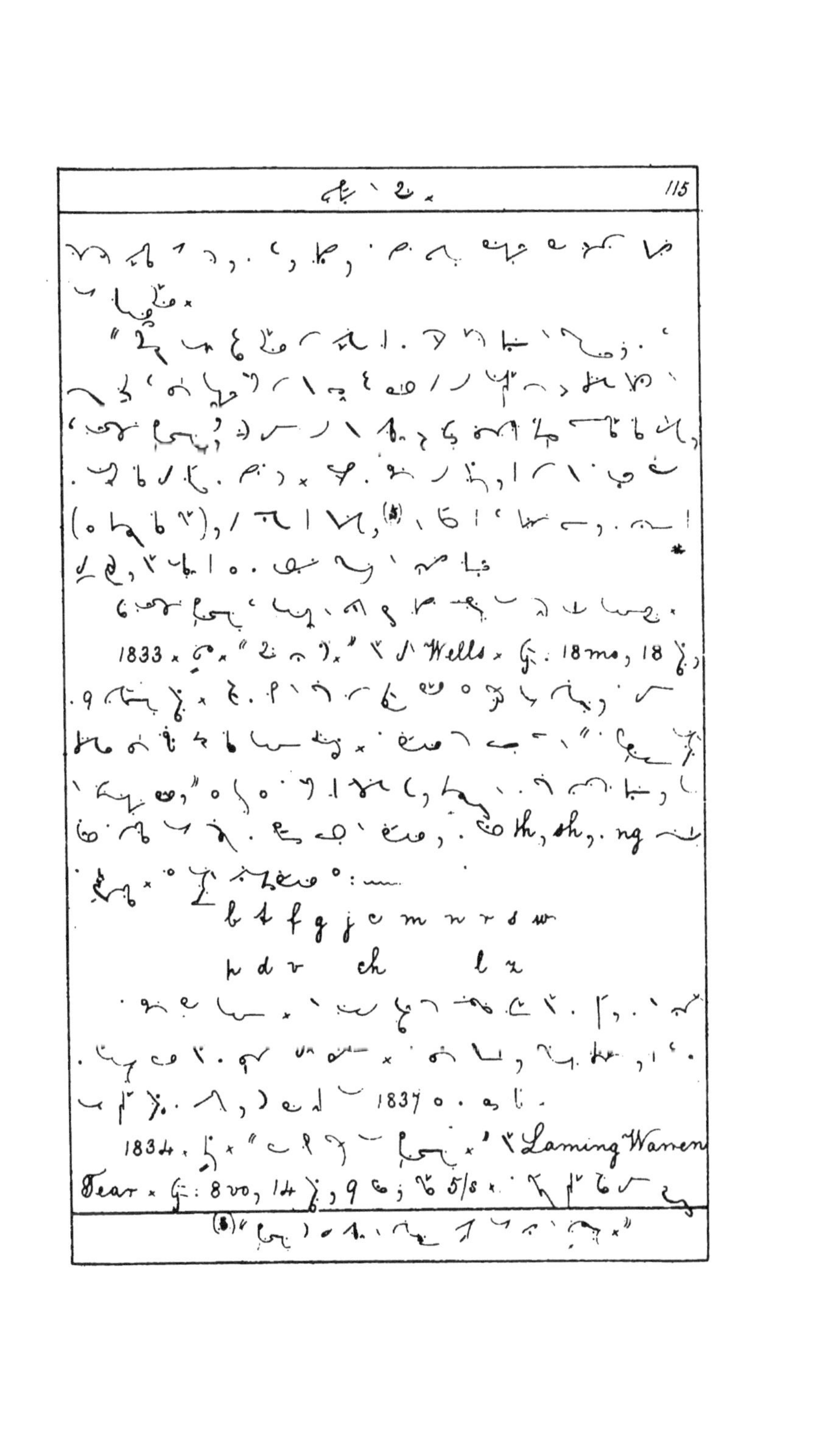

1833. " " Wells. 18mo, 18

th, sh, ng

b t f g j c m n r s w

p d v ch l z

1837

1834. " Laming Warren

Tear. 8vo, 14 ; 9 ; 5/s.

(5)

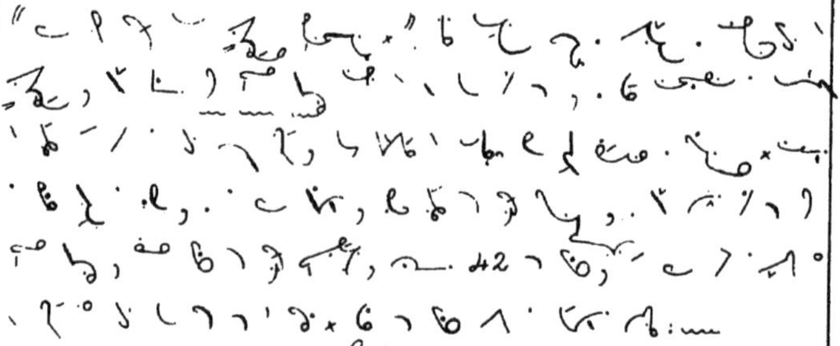

Scheme 1.

ab abs	th	sh shr	ch chr	dr ds	h
a	e	i	o	u	y
b	d	f,v	g	c	l
m	n	p	(qu)	r	s
t	w	(x)	gr,gl	fr,vr	pr
mr,ms	ps	pl	cr	fl,vl	sub,super,satis
tr,trans	br	st str	imp,ins	com,con,contra	sp,spr

Scheme 2.

ac	am,an	ar	dm,dn	dp,dsp	cl
ad,advan	ef,ev	inter,intro	over,out	un,under	as,at
bl	df,dv	inf,v	sc	rc	lr,ls
mag,multi	nr,ns	op	ir,or	rf,rv	sr,ss
en,in em,im	wr	rl	rp	fm,fn	pm,pn
mm,mn	comp	al	sm,sn	rs,rt	mn,nn
tm,tn	wm,wn	ap	bn	rm,rn	recom,recon

(1) ... (2)

ity ... (1) ...

(2) ...

42 ...

not ...

1 ...

2 ... en, em; ...

we ...

155 ...

"a, after, from, my, an, to, and, him, the, of, say, you, me, therefore, which, who, though."

...

[illegible]

[illegible] 1835. [illegible] Cadman [illegible] 8 vo, 22 [illegible], 6 6. [illegible]

[illegible]

(6) [illegible] 3.0 [illegible] 1847, [illegible] 181 [illegible] 296 [illegible] 253 [illegible]

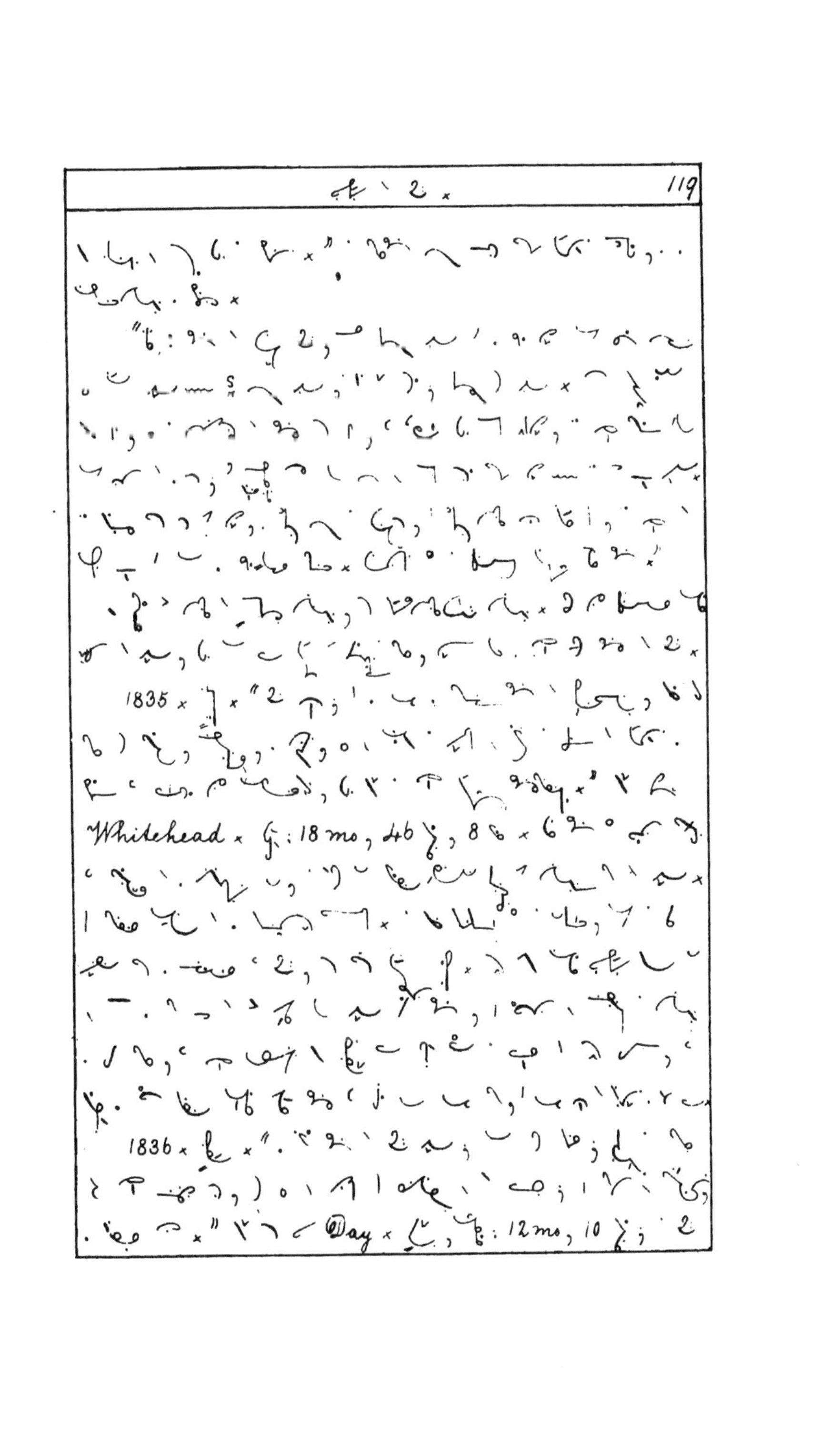

1835

Whitehead : 18 mo, 46, 8

1836

Day : 12 mo, 10

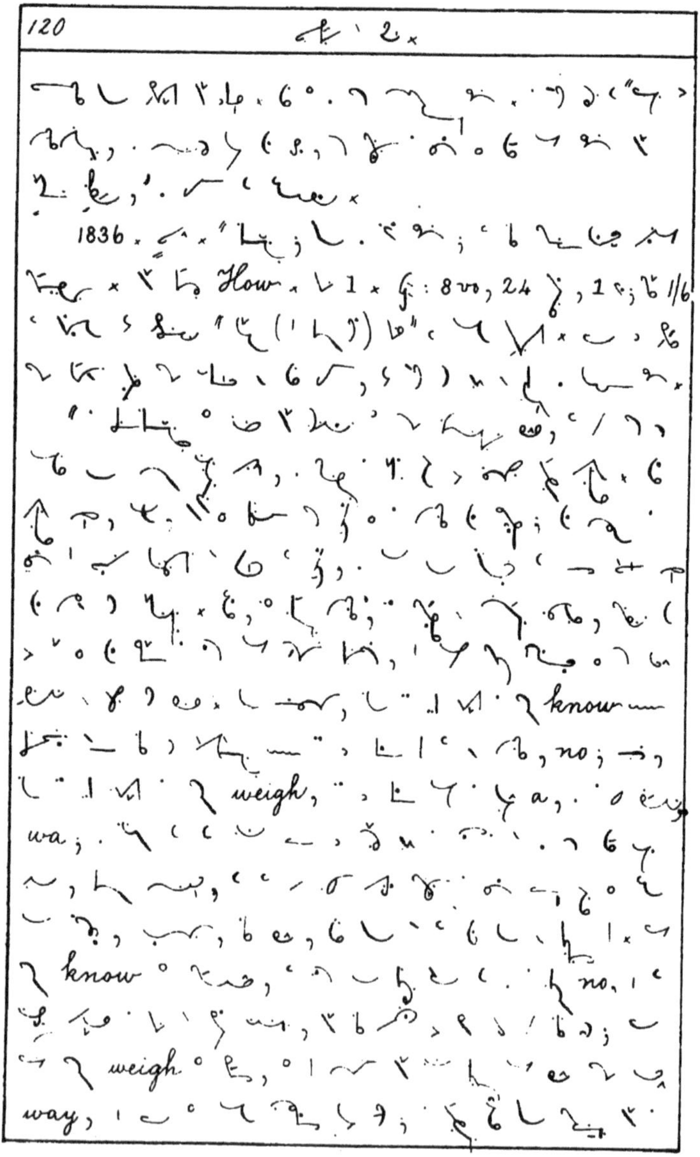
1836
How
1
8vo, 24
1/6
know
no
weigh
a
wa
know
no
weigh
way

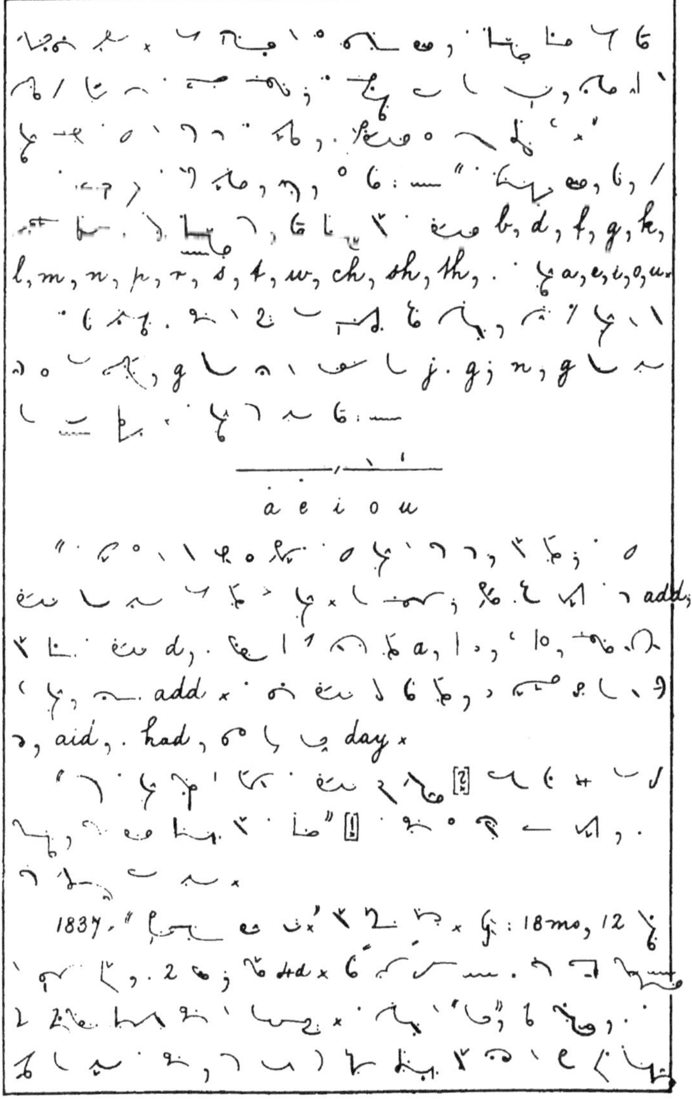
b, d, f, g, k,
l, m, n, p, r, s, t, w, ch, sh, th,
a, e, i, o, u.
j. g; n, g
a e i o u
add;
d,
a,
add
aid,
had,
day
1837
18mo, 12
2
4d

1837 . 1840

"both, burr, but,"

2 1840, 6 4to; 1d;

8 6½ 3000

3 1840, 8vo, 23

14 100

2/,

18d

4(1841; 4to, 1d.

5(1842, 32mo, 64 2/

8vo,

[illegible] 1/ [illegible] 32mo, 24 [illegible] 3d.

6([illegible] 1844; [illegible] 4to, [illegible] 6d. [illegible]

[illegible] pn, pshn [illegible] cur cut [illegible]

[illegible]

7([illegible] 1845; [illegible] 8vo, 64 [illegible] 1/ [illegible]

[illegible] 2/.

8([illegible] 1847; [illegible] 8vo, 64 [illegible] 8 [illegible] 1/6.

9([illegible] 1852; [illegible] 8vo, 64 [illegible] 8 [illegible] 1/6.

1837? [illegible]

[illegible]

" [illegible]

" [illegible] 25 [illegible]

[illegible]

25

a, e, i(y), o, u;

20

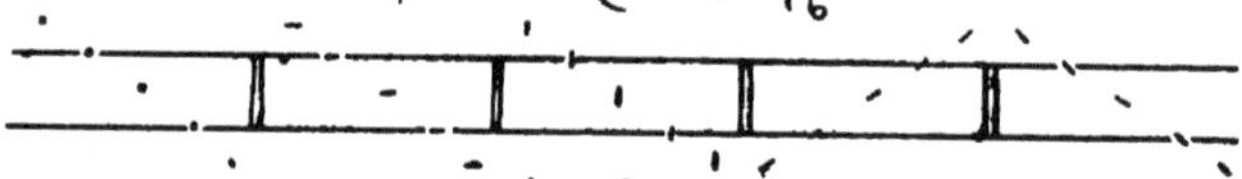

a e i y o u b c d f g h j k l m n p q r s t v w x z

Follow good advice

1837 Galloway

18mo, 12

m n

t s f

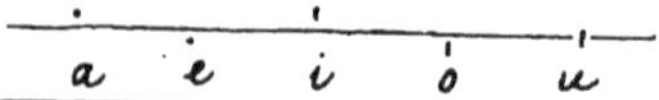

a e i o u

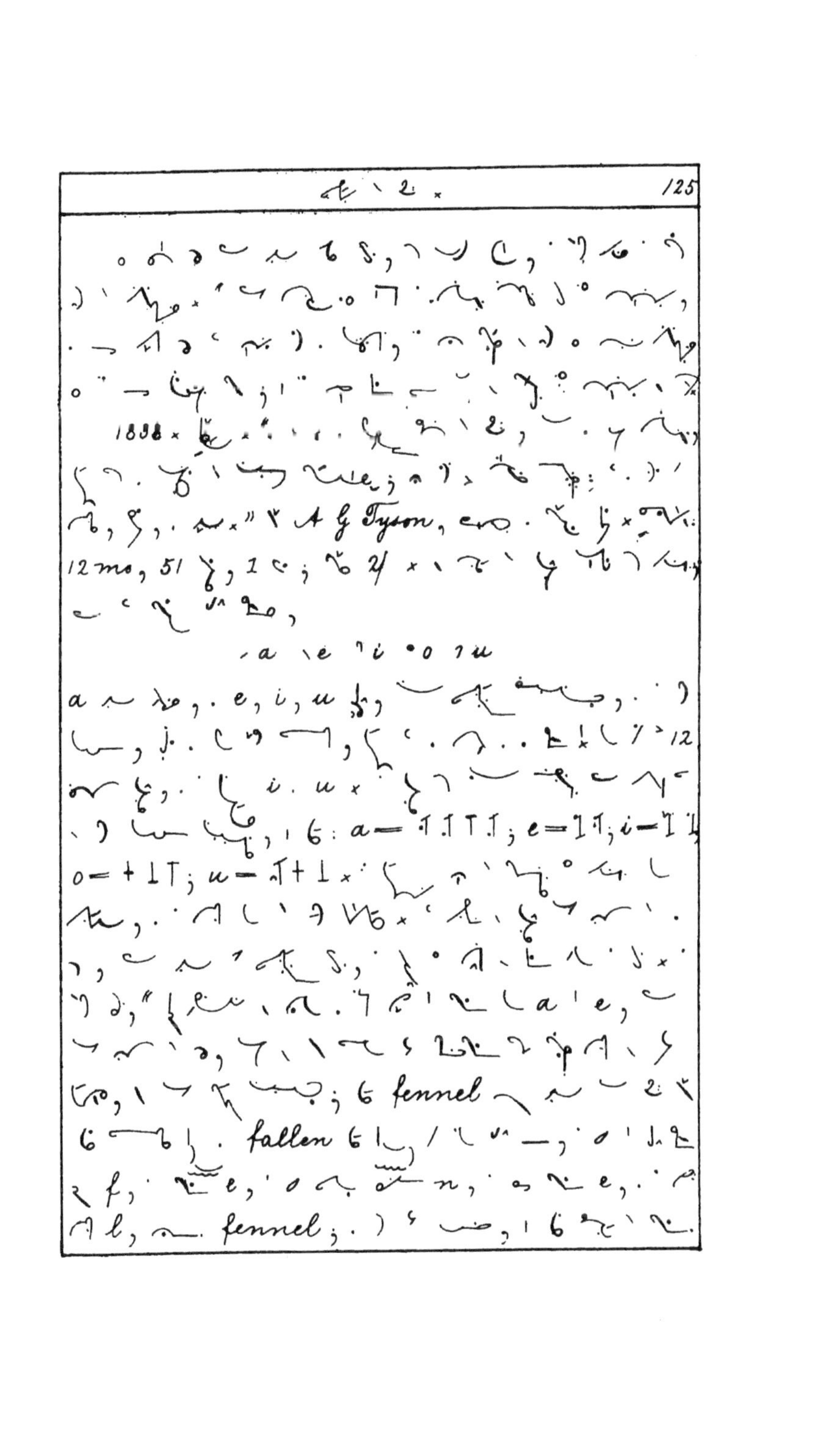

1838

A G Tyson

12 mo, 51

a e i o u

a, e, i, u

12

i, u

6: a = ; e = ; i =

o = ; u =

a e

6 fennel

6 fallen 6

f, e, n, e

l, fennel; 6

[illegible] b p, d t, f v, g j, h, c, l, m, n, r, s z, zh, sh, ng, th [illegible] w, y [illegible]

1838 [illegible] Leonard [illegible] 12mo, 50 [illegible] 10 [illegible] 3/ [illegible]

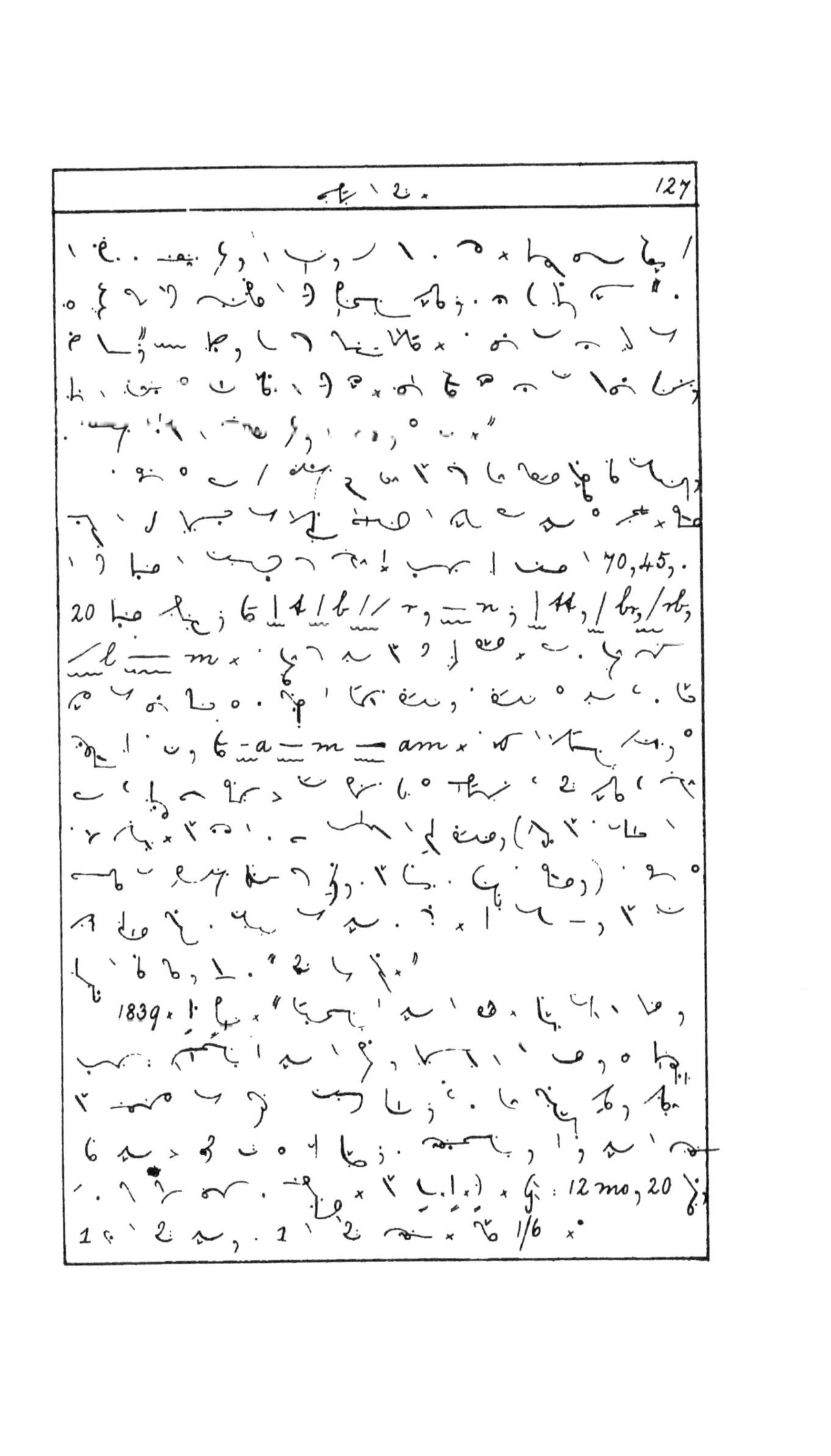

[illegible] 70, 45, [illegible]

20 [illegible] t [illegible] b [illegible] r, [illegible] n; [illegible] tt, [illegible] br, [illegible] rb,

[illegible] l [illegible] m [illegible]

[illegible] a [illegible] m [illegible] am [illegible]

1839 [illegible]

[illegible] 12 mo, 20 [illegible]

1 [illegible] 2 [illegible] 1 [illegible] 2 [illegible] 1/6 [illegible]

1842)

8vo, 208 ; 9 ; 10

V. D. De Stains

a, b, c

3

1

1, 2,

3,

II

1.

2

10 3

6

III. 2 1

2, 6 . 6 2 2

3

6

1 … 2 … 3 … 4 … 1/6 … 5 …

… ē i, … u, … ō, ŭ, ā, ĕ, ŏ, ō, ōō, ă, au; … c g, t d, p b, sh zh, s z, th (…) f v, ng, n, m, h, r, l … b … m, …

… 1839, …

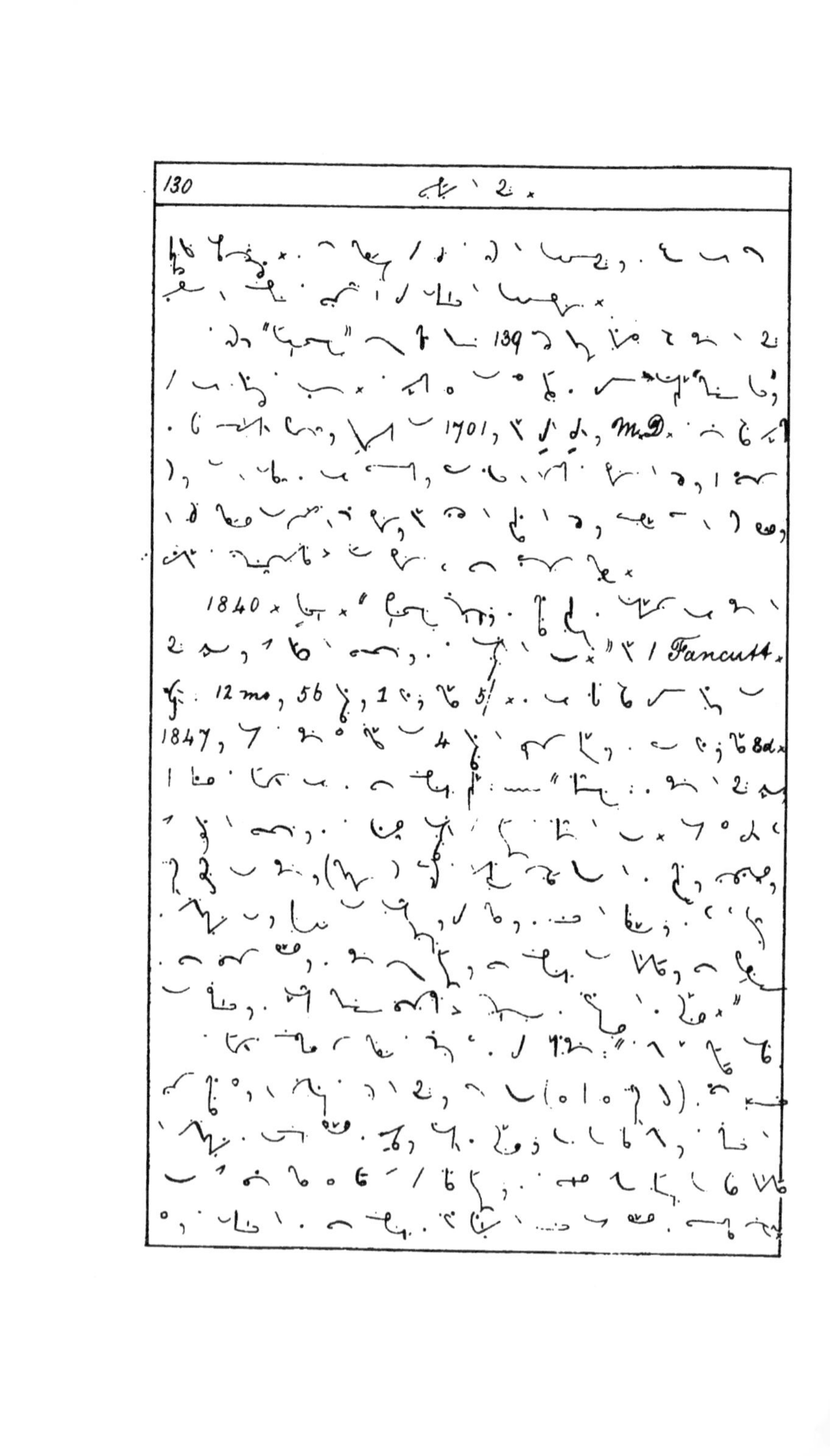

139

1701, M.D.

1840

Fancutt.

12 mo, 56

1847, 4, 8d.

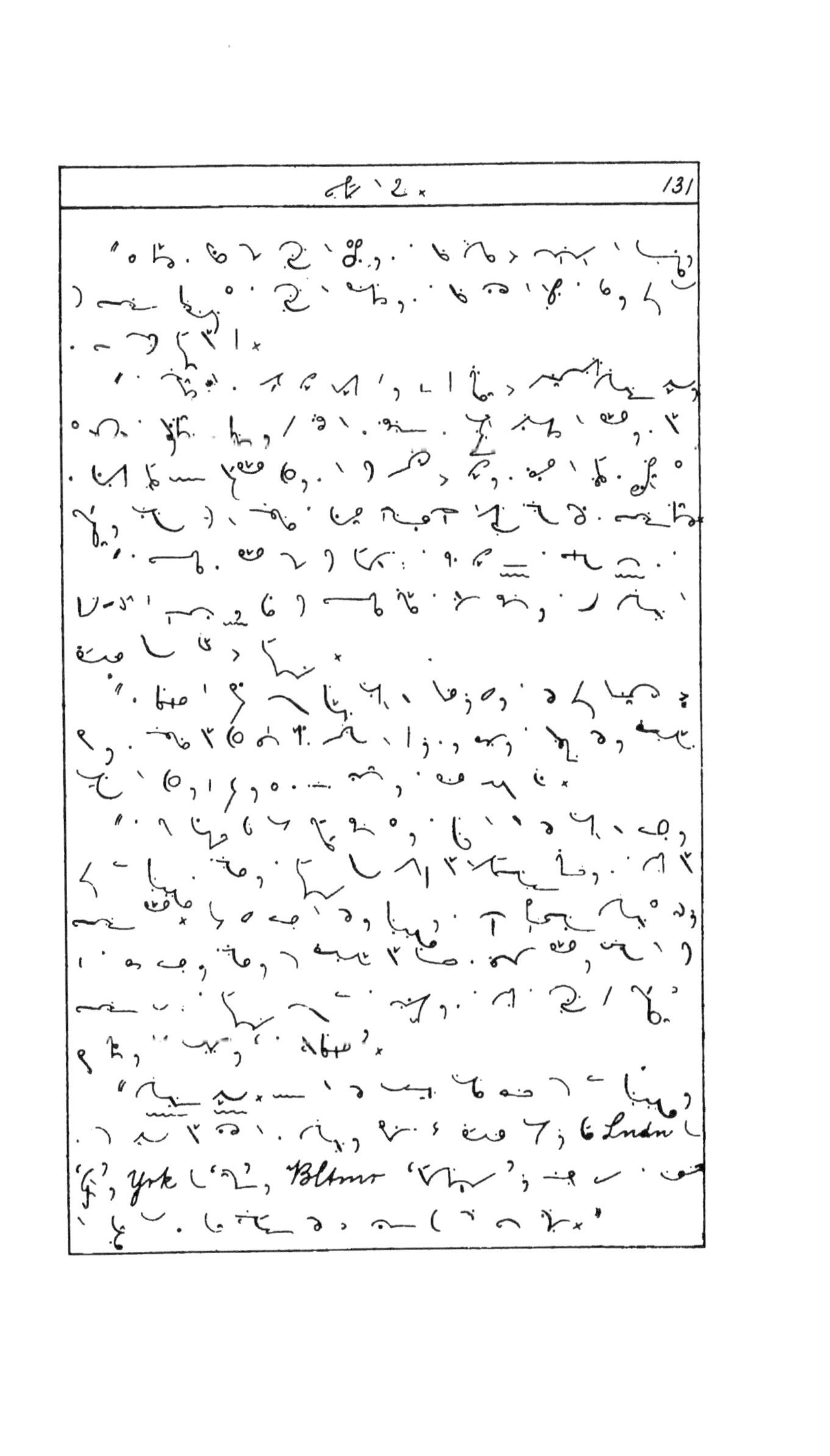

Lndn

York

Bltmr

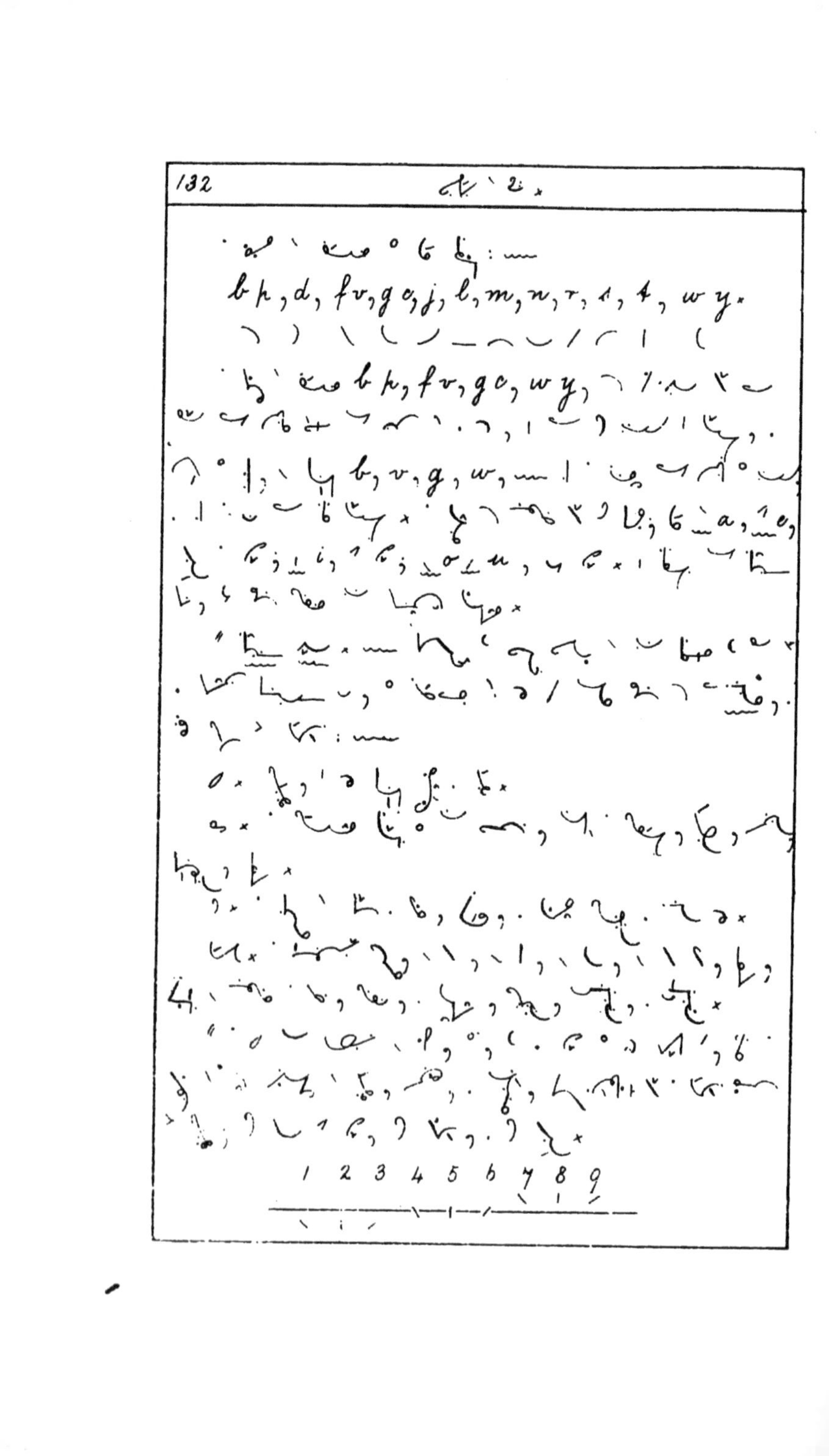

b p, d, f v, g c, j, l, m, n, r, s, t, w y.

b p, f v, g c, w y,

b, v, g, w,

a, e,

i,

o u,

1 2 3 4 5 6 7 8 9

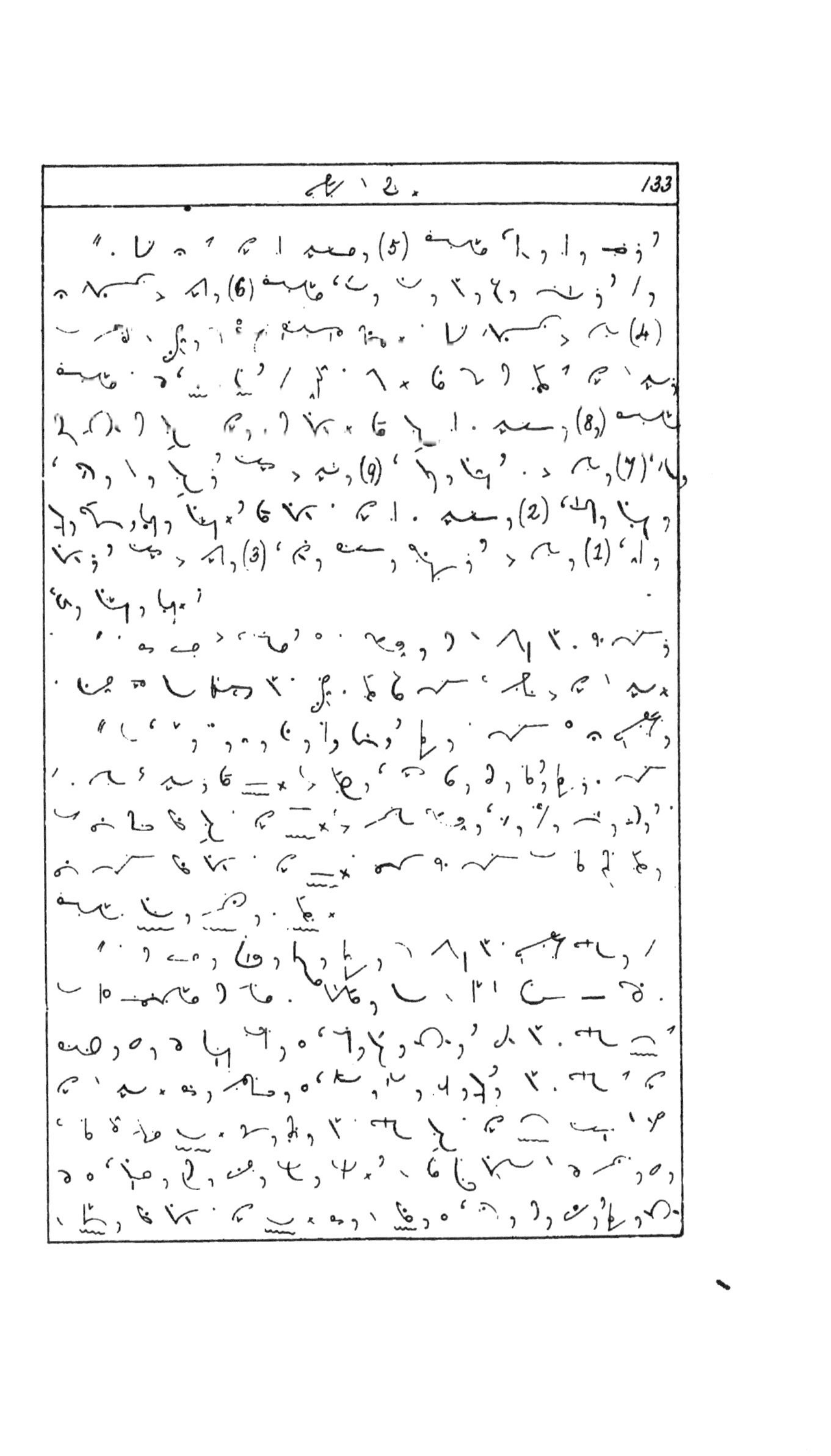

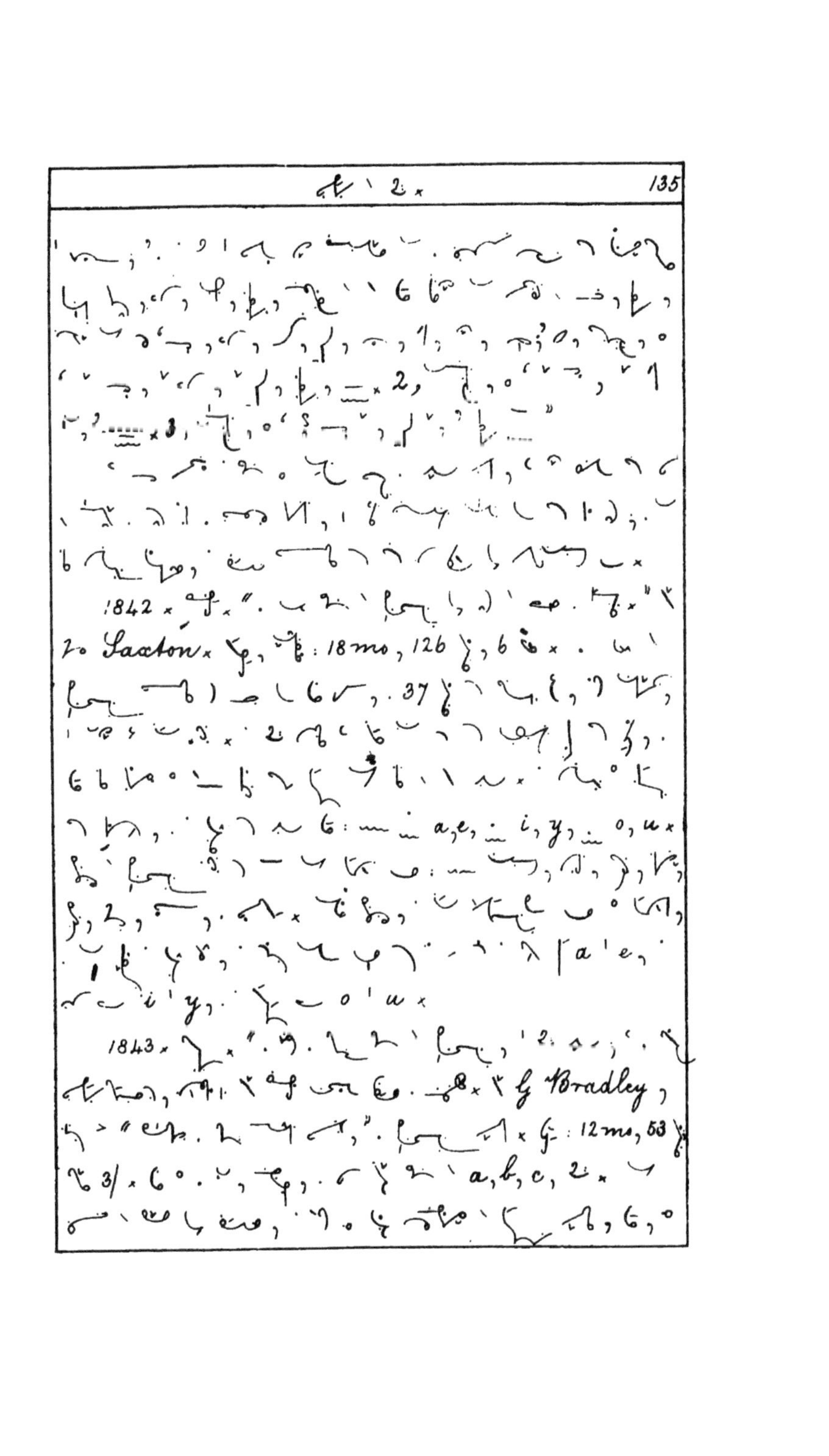

1842 … Saxton … 18mo, 126 … 6 … 37 … 2 … a, e, … i, y, … o, u … a … e, … i … y, … o … u

1843 … 2 … Bradley, … 12mo, 53 … 3/ … 6 … a, b, c, 2 … 6, 6, [illegible] m, [illegible] n, [illegible] r, [illegible] l [illegible] b, d, [illegible] l, [illegible] f, v, [illegible] w [illegible] g, h, (k, q, x,) y, [illegible]

1844. [illegible] 8vo, 40 [illegible] (7) [illegible] 10 [illegible]

(7) [illegible] 1803, [illegible] 1805, [illegible] Ewington, M. M., [illegible]

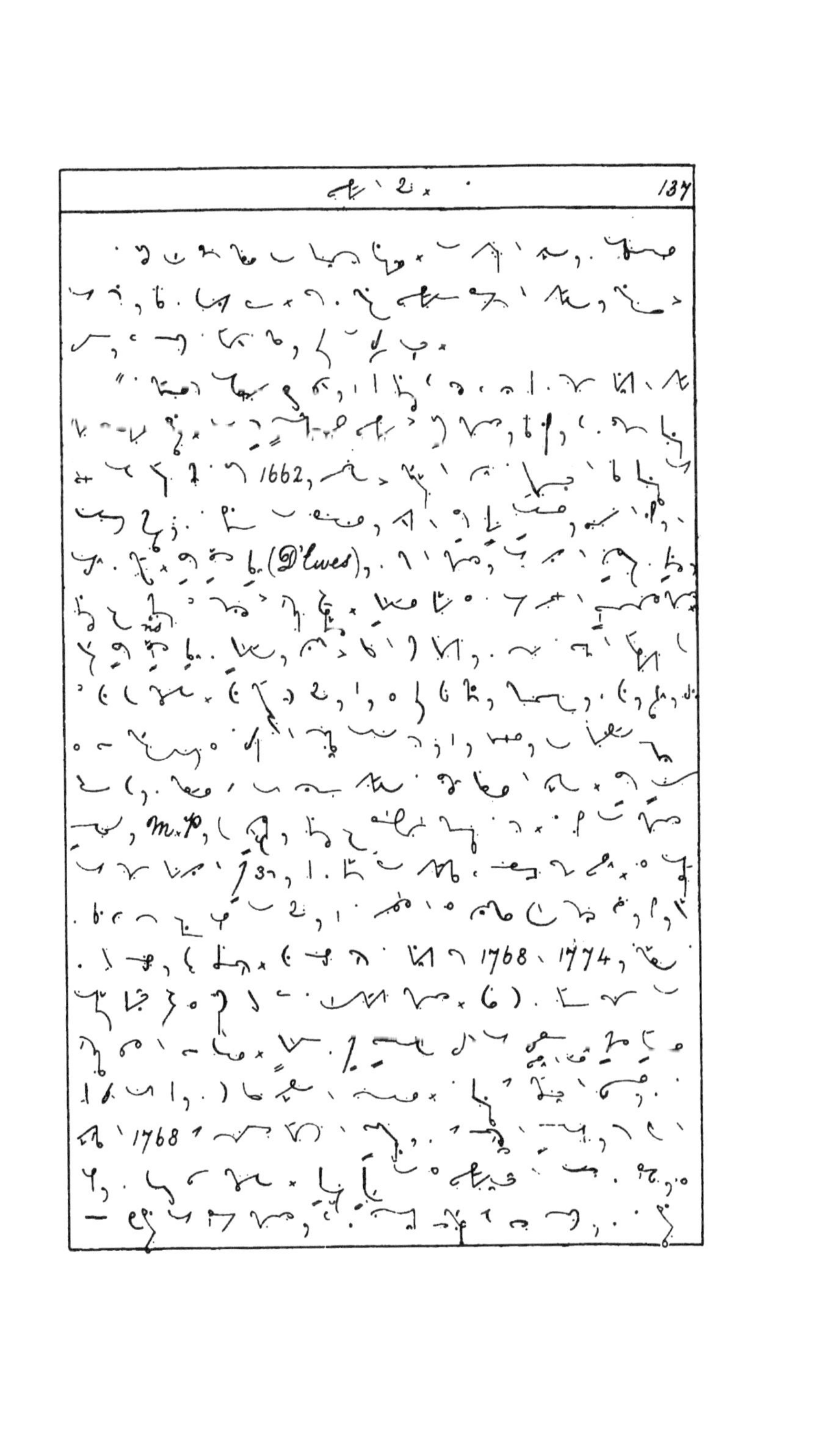

1662

(D'Ewes)

M.P.

1768 1774

1768

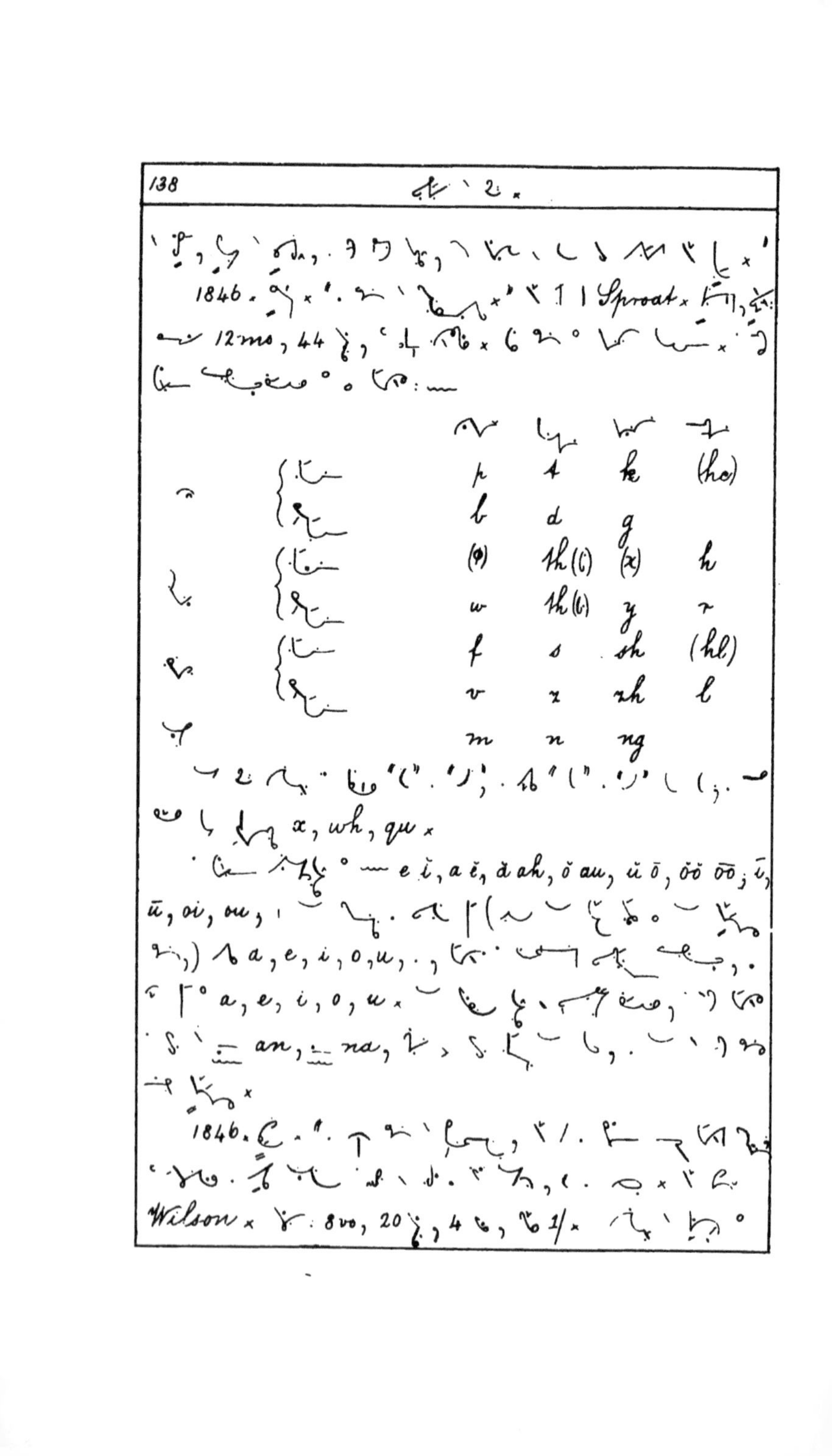

1846. Sproat.

12mo, 44

p	t	k	(kc)
b	d	g	
(φ)	th (c)	(x)	h
w	th (b)	y	r
f	s	sh	(hl)
v	z	zh	l
m	n	ng	

x, wh, qu.

e ĭ, a ĕ, ă ah, ŏ au, ŭ ō, ŏŏ ōō; ī, ū, oi, ou,

a, e, i, o, u,

a, e, i, o, u.

an, na,

1846.

Wilson. 8vo, 20, 4, 1/.

ă a, ĕ e, ĭ i, ŏ ō, ŭ ōō, u, au, oi, ou

1847 … Davidson, … 12 mo, 24 … 4 … 2/

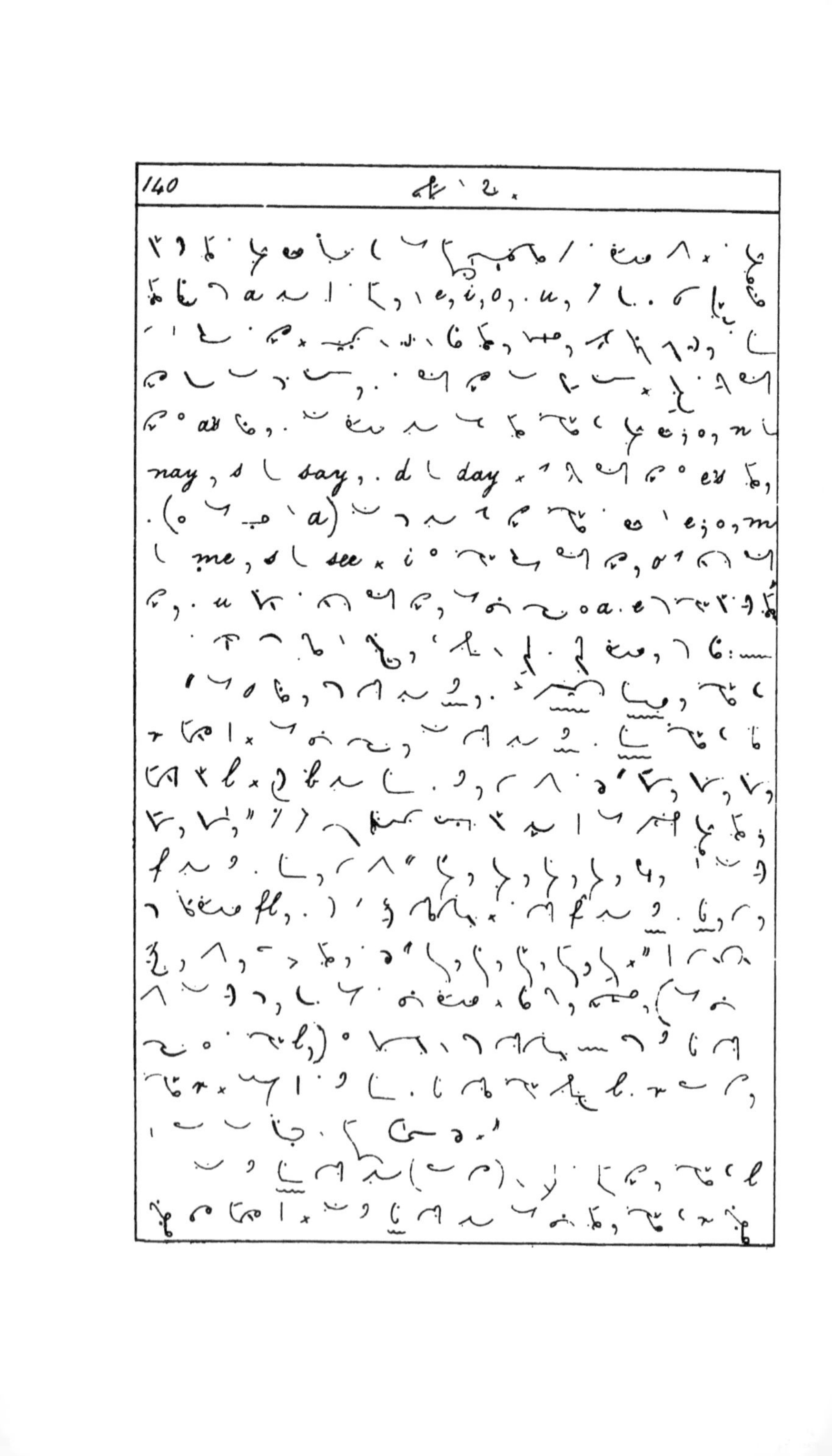

a ... e, i, o, u,

nay, s ... say, . d ... day ... e

(o ... a) ... e; o, m

me, s ... see ... i

u ... o a . e

l ... b

f

fl ... f

l,)

l.

l

spr

str ms

ns

st

a, b, c

253 260

"1848"

sh; th th

1847

Snaith 12 mo

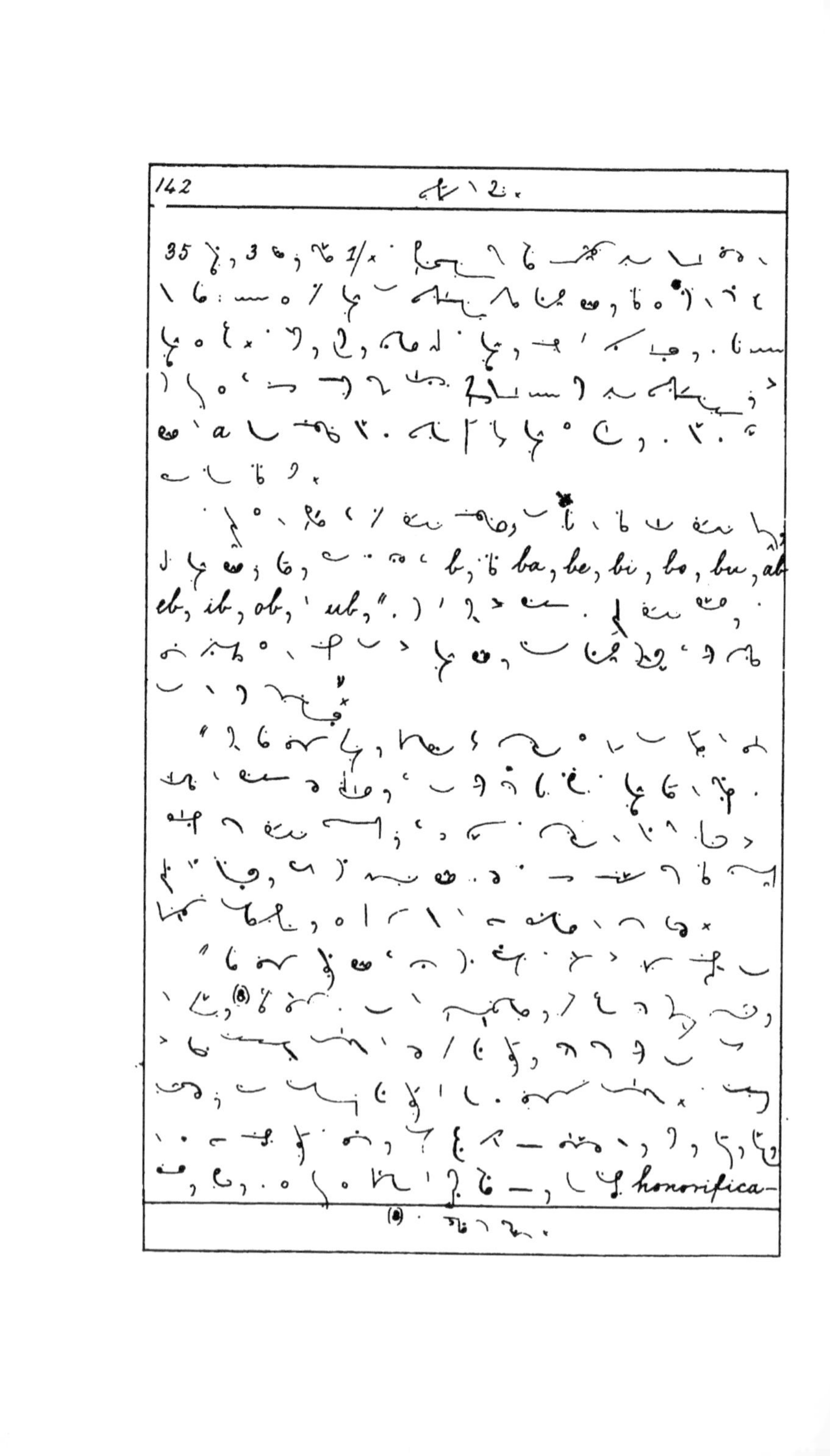

35 [illegible] 3 [illegible] 1/ [illegible]

[illegible] ba, be, bi, bo, bu, ab eb, ib, ob, ub, [illegible]

[illegible] honorifica-

[illegible]

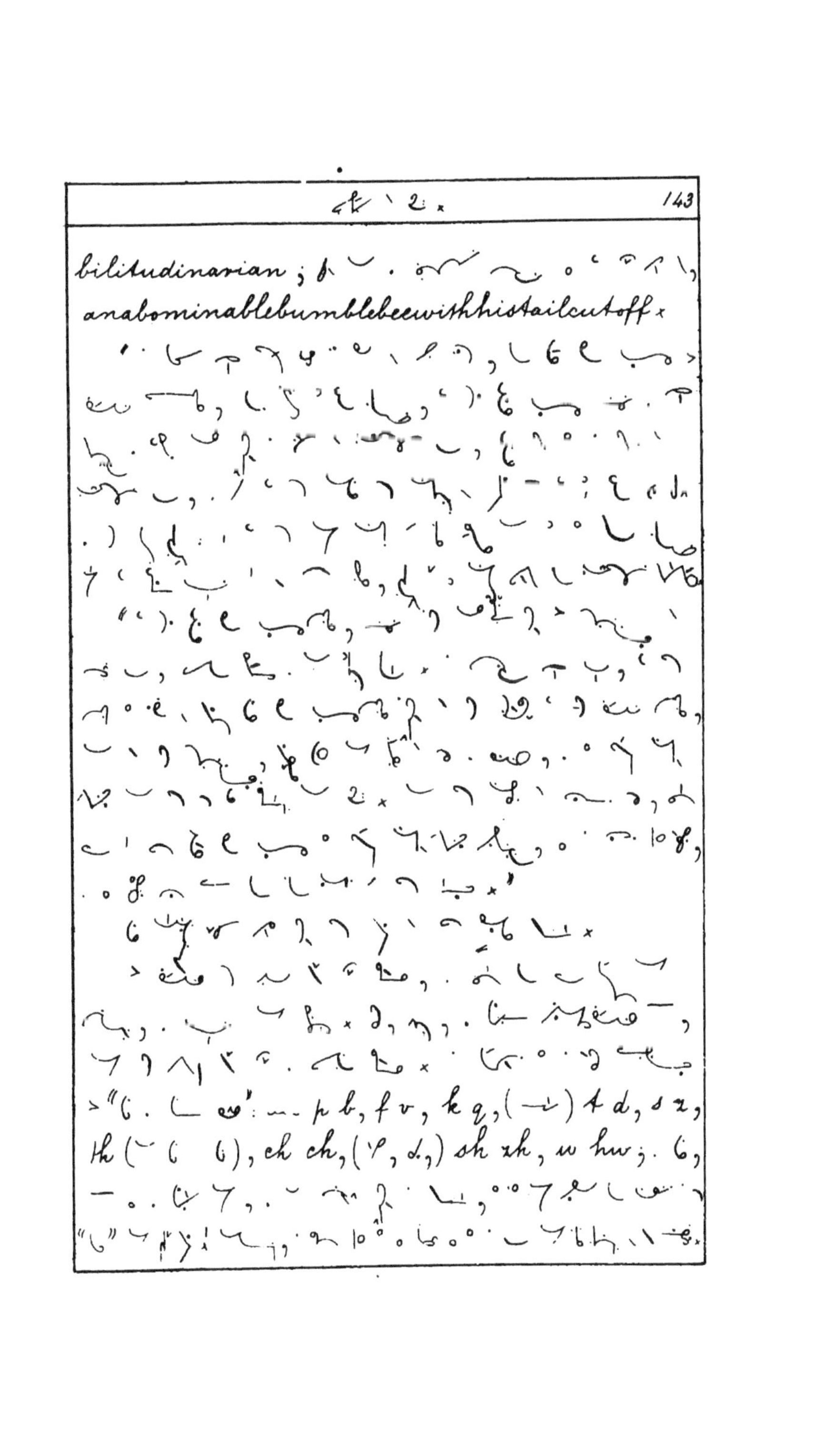

bilitudinarian;

anabominablebumblebeewithhistailcutoff

p b, f v, k g, ( ) t d, s z,

th ( ), ch ch, ( ) sh zh, w hw;

1847 … Selwyn.

… 12mo, 32 … 2 … 1/ …

… "ā ă, ē ĕ, ī ĭ, ō ŏ, ū ŭ; … "āū, ōō, ŏŏ." … "ō" … "ō" … "au."

… d, l, n, r, … d, … l, … n, … r, … f, …

… flow, … f, l, o, … fl, o.

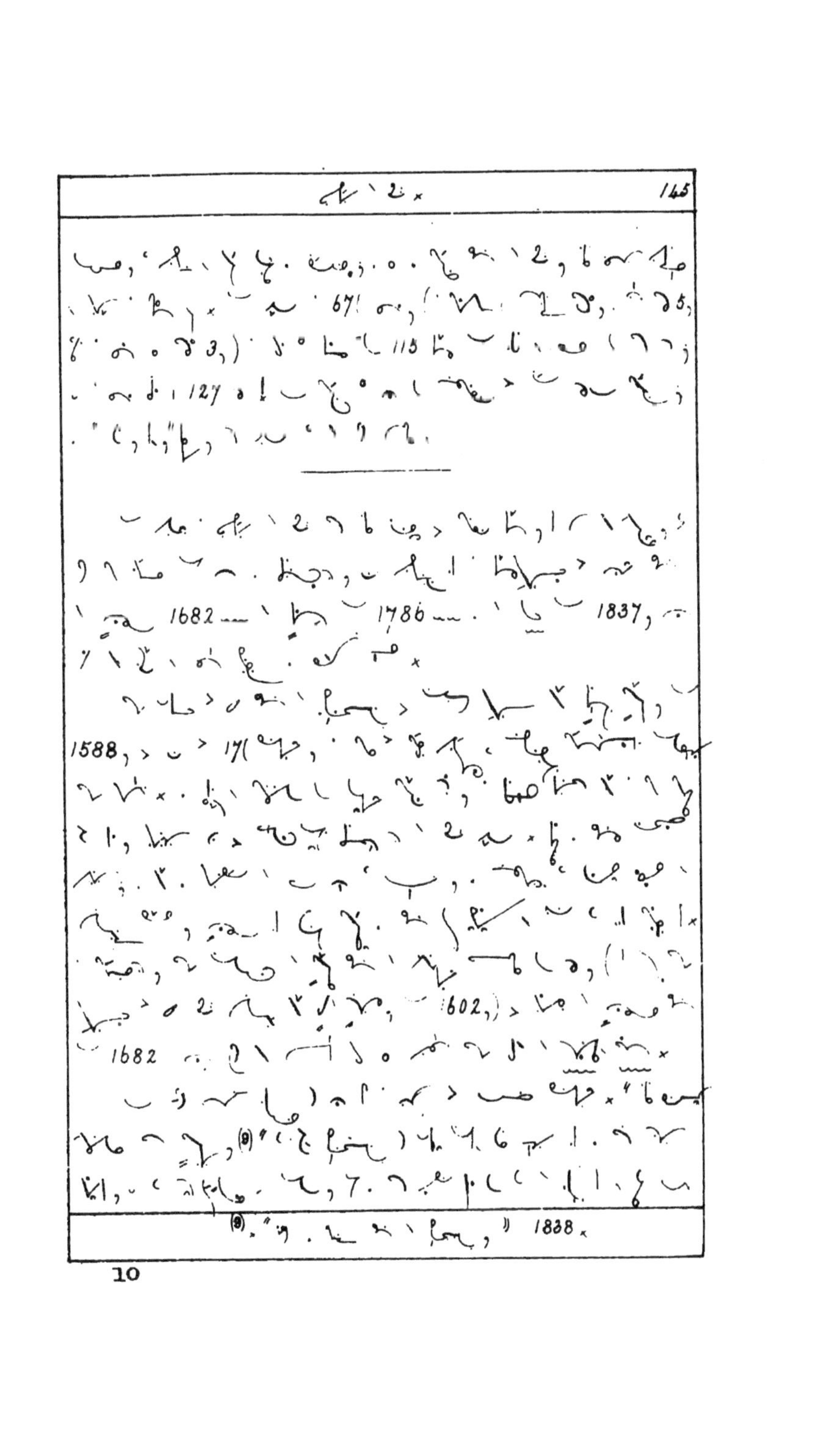

671 75 3 115 127

1682 1786 1837

1588 17

602 1682

(8) 1838

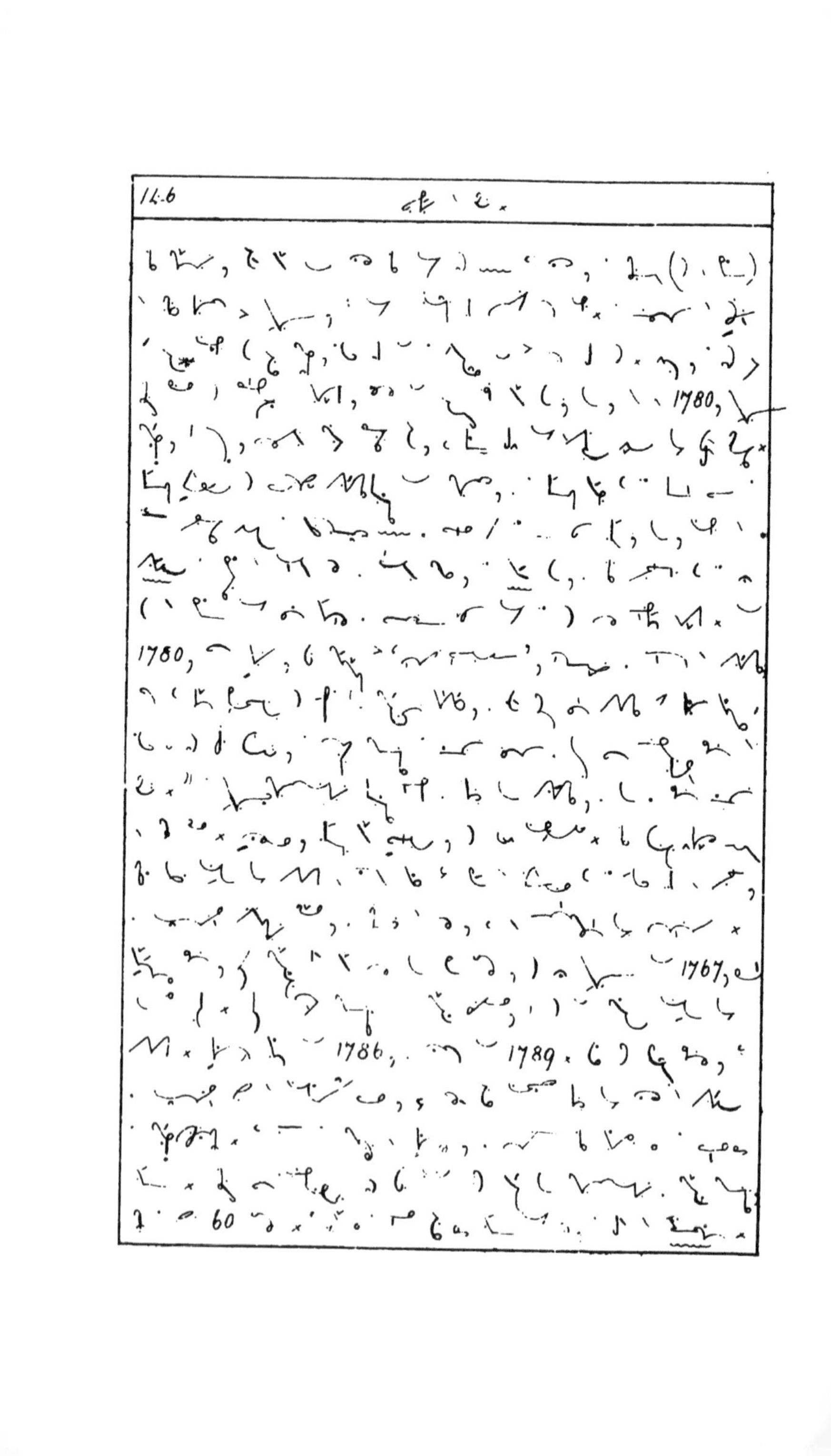

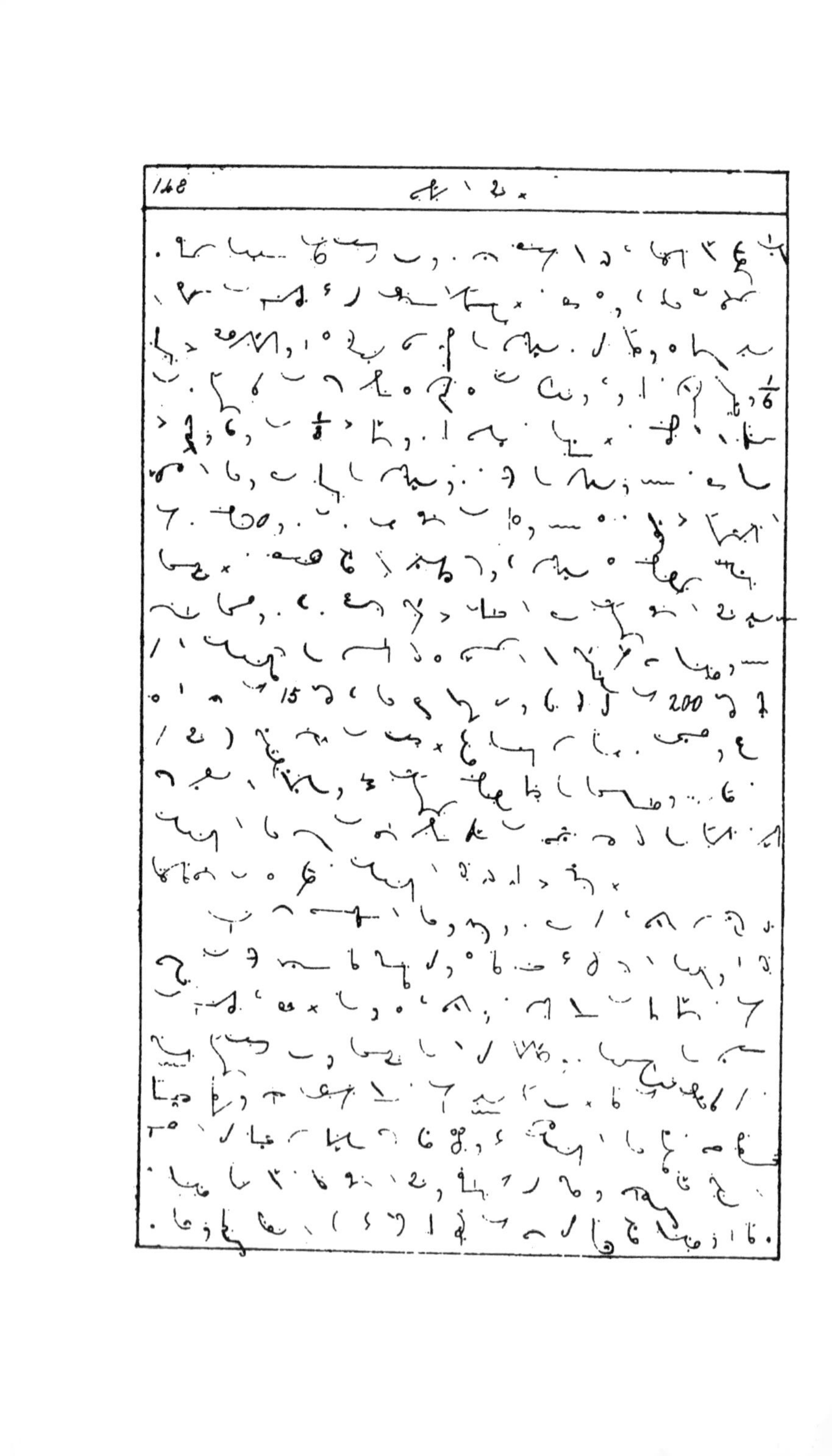

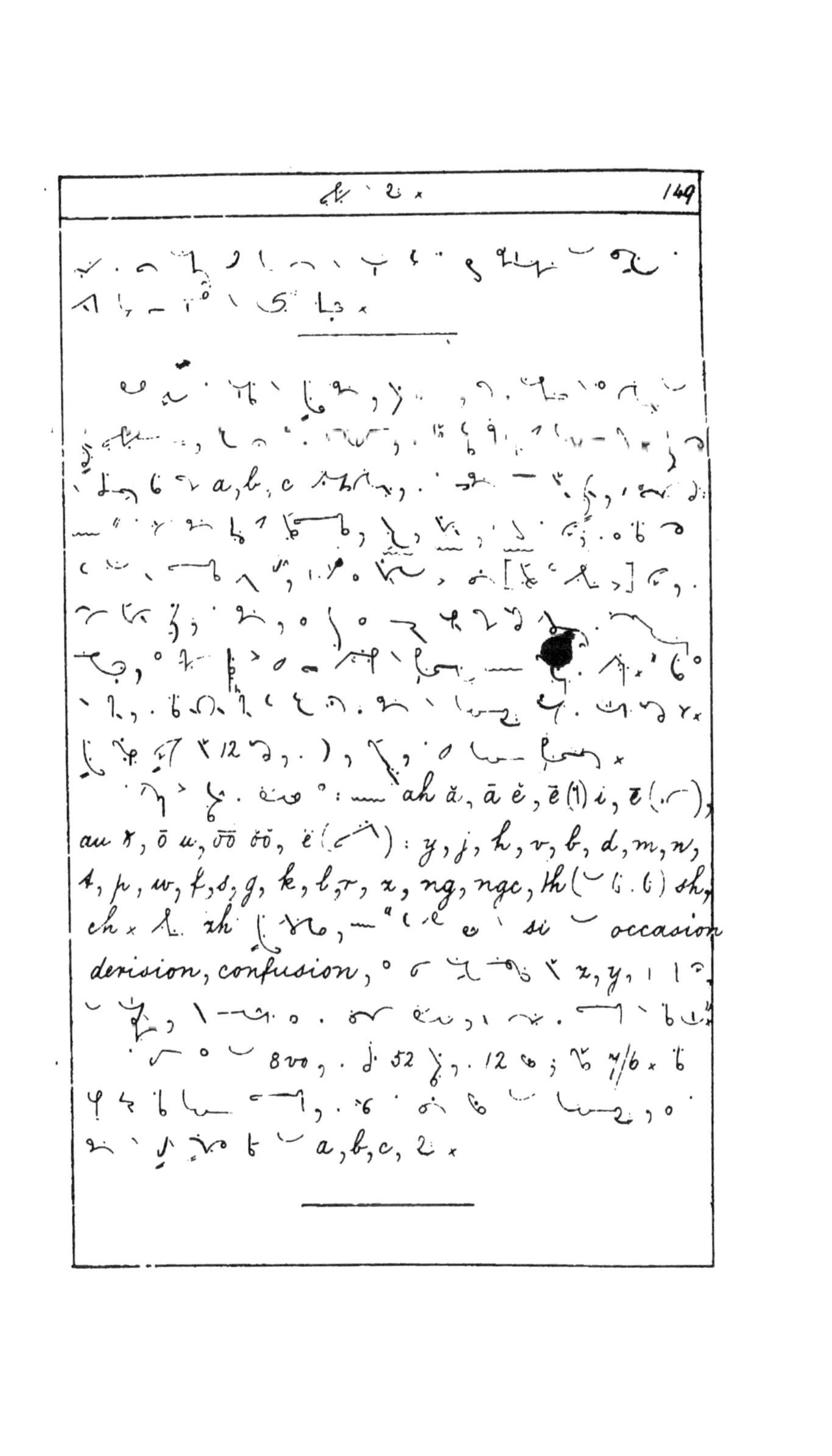

---

a, b, c

ah ă, ā ĕ, ē (?) i, ē ( ),
au ŏ, ō u, ōō ŏŏ, ė ( ): y, j, h, v, b, d, m, n,
s, p, w, f, s, g, k, l, r, z, ng, ngc, th ( ) sh,
ch. zh ( ) si occasion
derision, confusion, z, y,

8vo, 52, 12; 7/6.

a, b, c.

ALPHABETS AND SPECIMENS.

SHORTHAND NOTES IN TYRO'S SYSTEM.

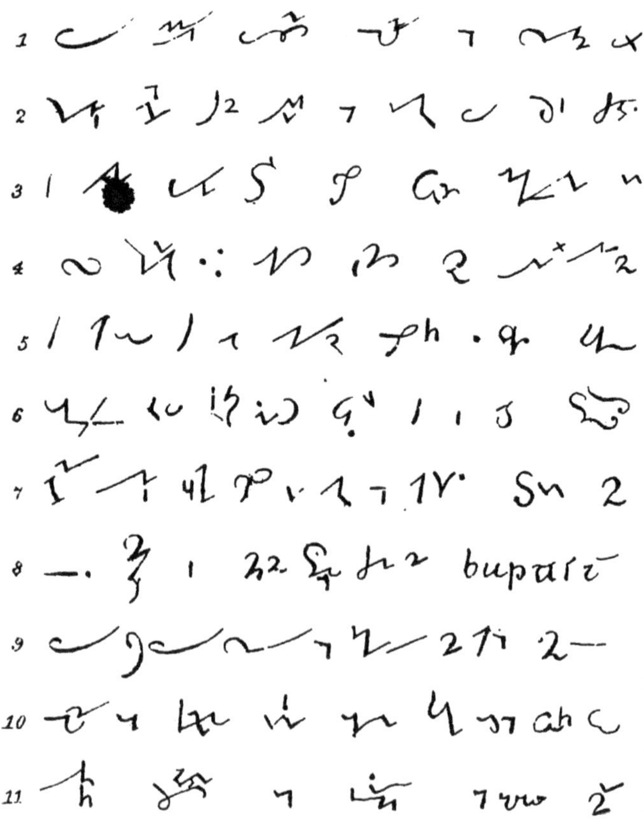

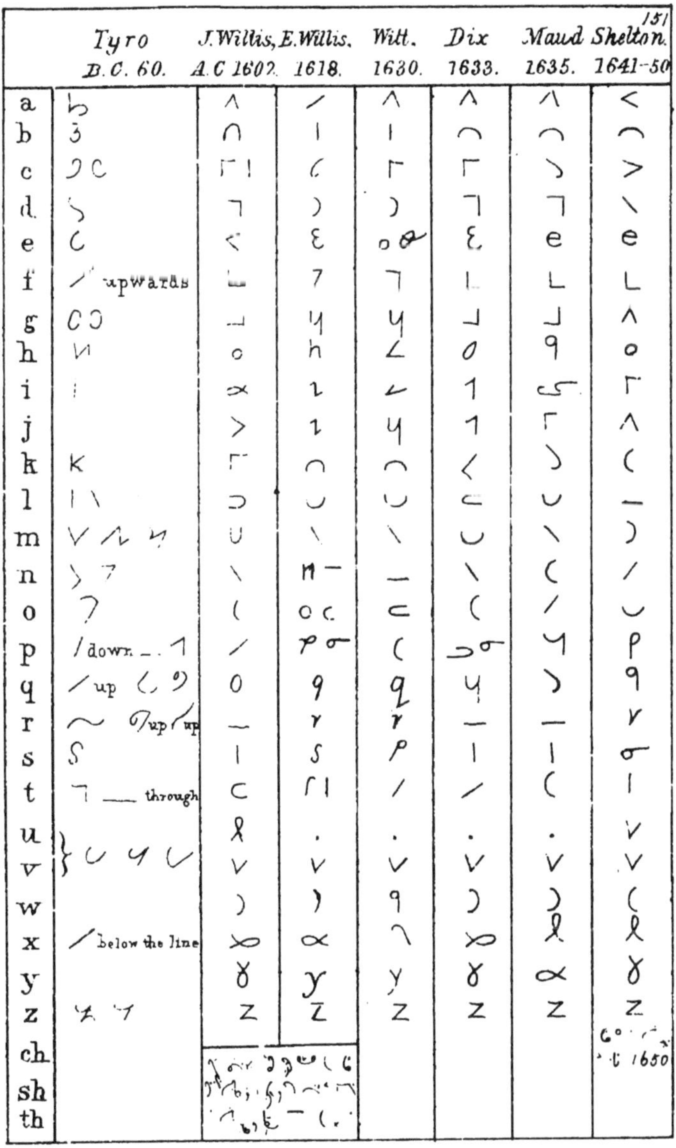
Tyro B.C. 60.
J. Willis, A.C 1602.
E. Willis. 1618.
Witt. 1630.
Dix 1633.
Maud 1635.
Shelton. 1641–50
a
b
c
d
e
f
g
h
i
j
k
l
m
n
o
p
q
r
s
t
u
v
w
x
y
z
ch
sh
th
upwards
down
up
up
up
through
below the line
1650

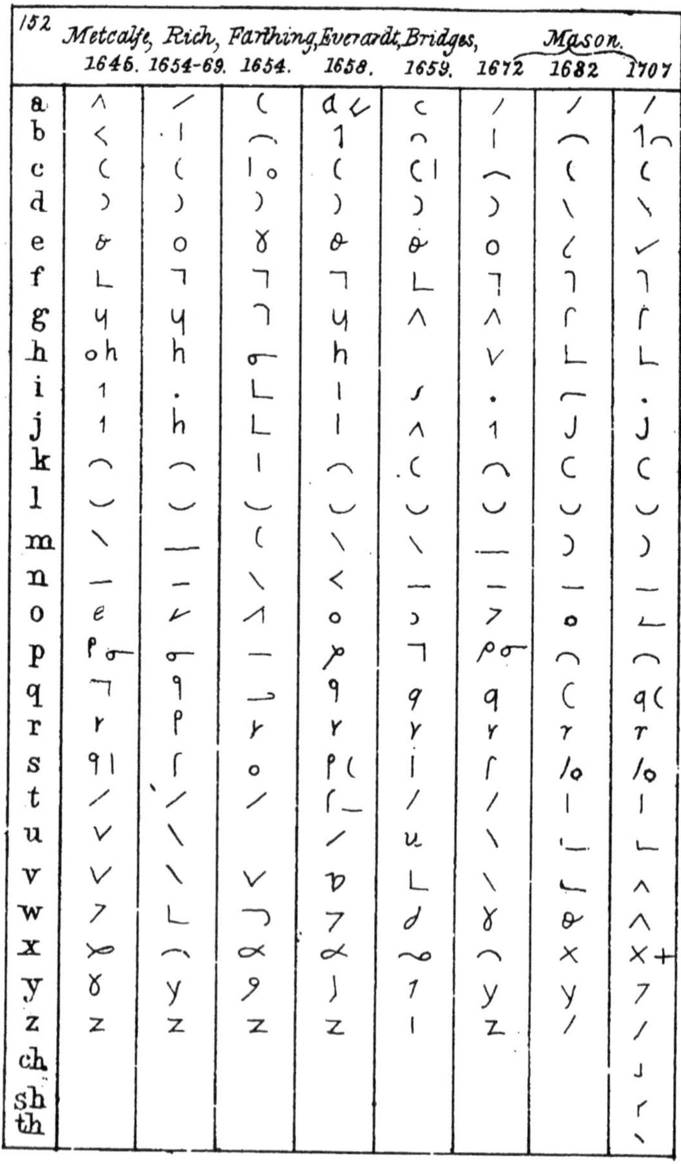
Metcalfe, 1646.
Rich, 1654-69.
Farthing, 1654.
Everardt, 1658.
Bridges, 1659.
1672
Mason. 1682
1707
a
b
c
d
e
f
g
h
i
j
k
l
m
n
o
p
q
r
s
t
u
v
w
x
y
z
ch
sh
th

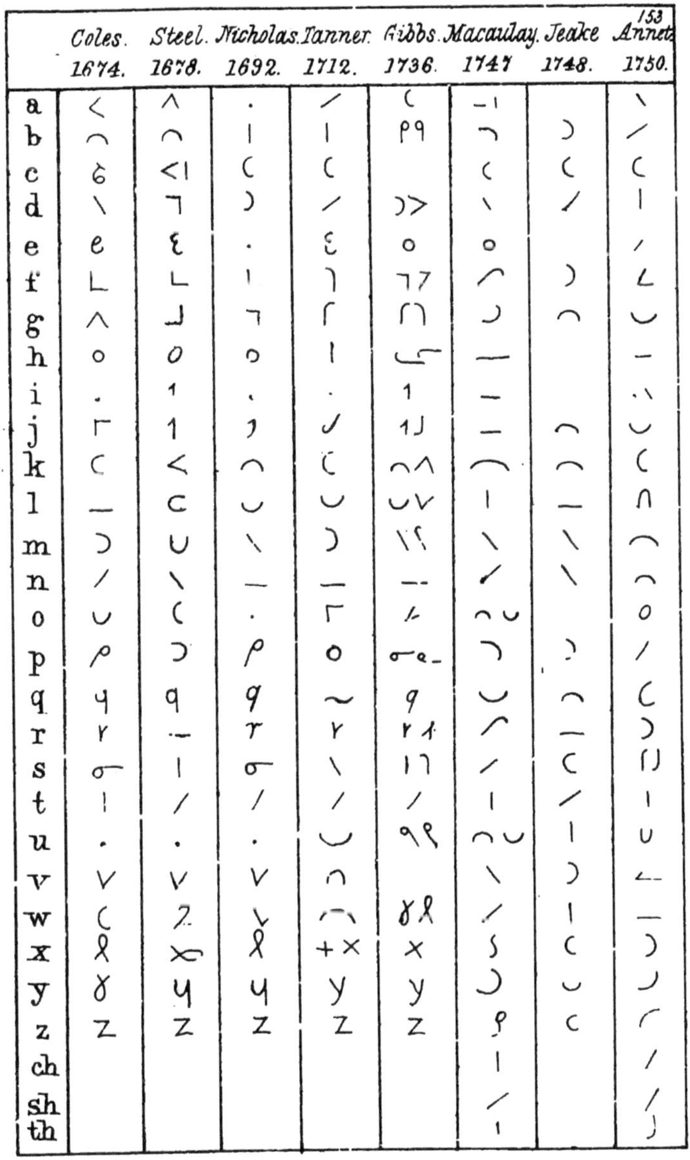
Coles. 1674.
Steel. 1678.
Nicholas. 1692.
Tanner. 1712.
Gibbs. 1736.
Macaulay. 1747
Jeake 1748.
Annet 1750.
a
b
c
d
e
f
g
h
i
j
k
l
m
n
o
p
q
r
s
t
u
v
w
x
y
z
ch
sh
th

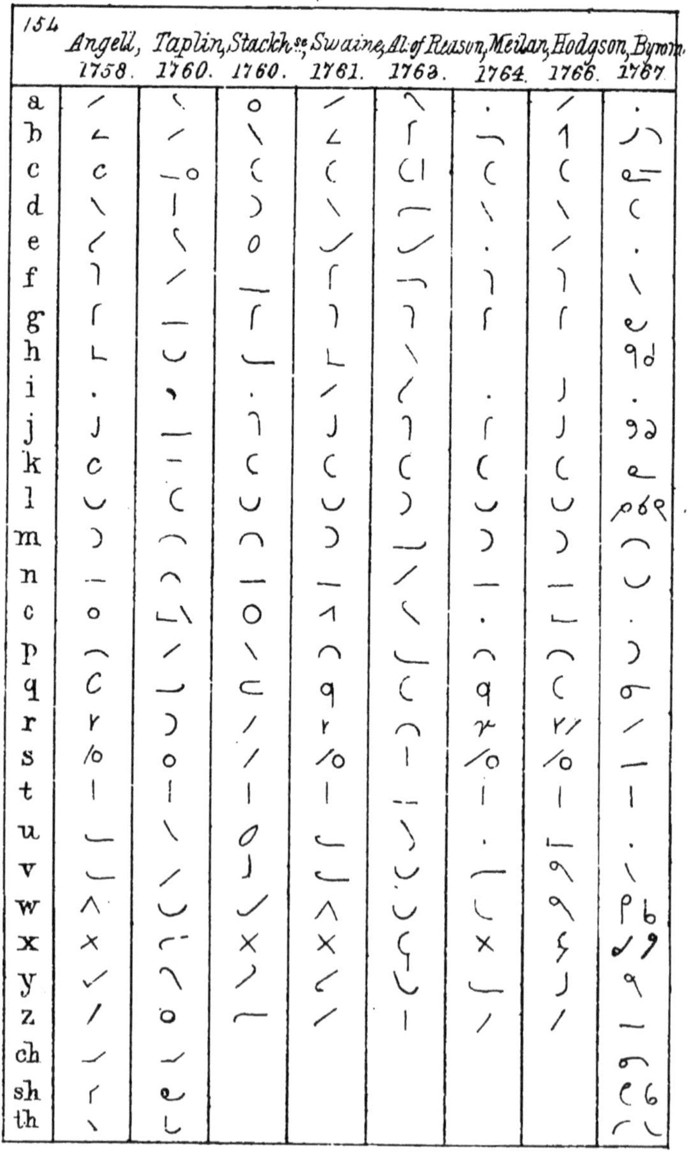
Angell, 1758.
Taplin, 1760.
Stackh.se, 1760.
Swaine, 1761.
Al. of Reason, 1763.
Meilan, 1764.
Hodgson, 1766.
Byrom. 1767.
a
b
c
d
e
f
g
h
i
j
k
l
m
n
o
p
q
r
s
t
u
v
w
x
y
z
ch
sh
th

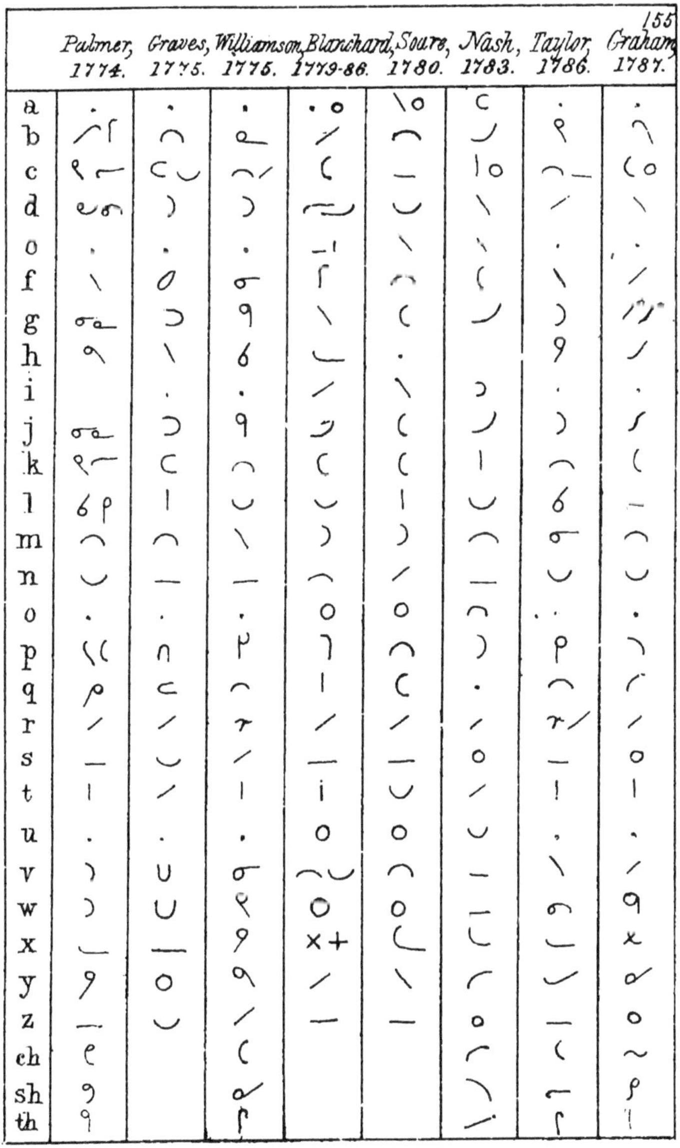
Palmer, 1774.
Graves, 1775.
Williamson, 1775.
Blanchard, 1779-86.
Soare, 1780.
Nash, 1783.
Taylor, 1786.
Graham, 1787.
a
b
c
d
e
f
g
h
i
j
k
l
m
n
o
p
q
r
s
t
u
v
w
x
y
z
ch
sh
th

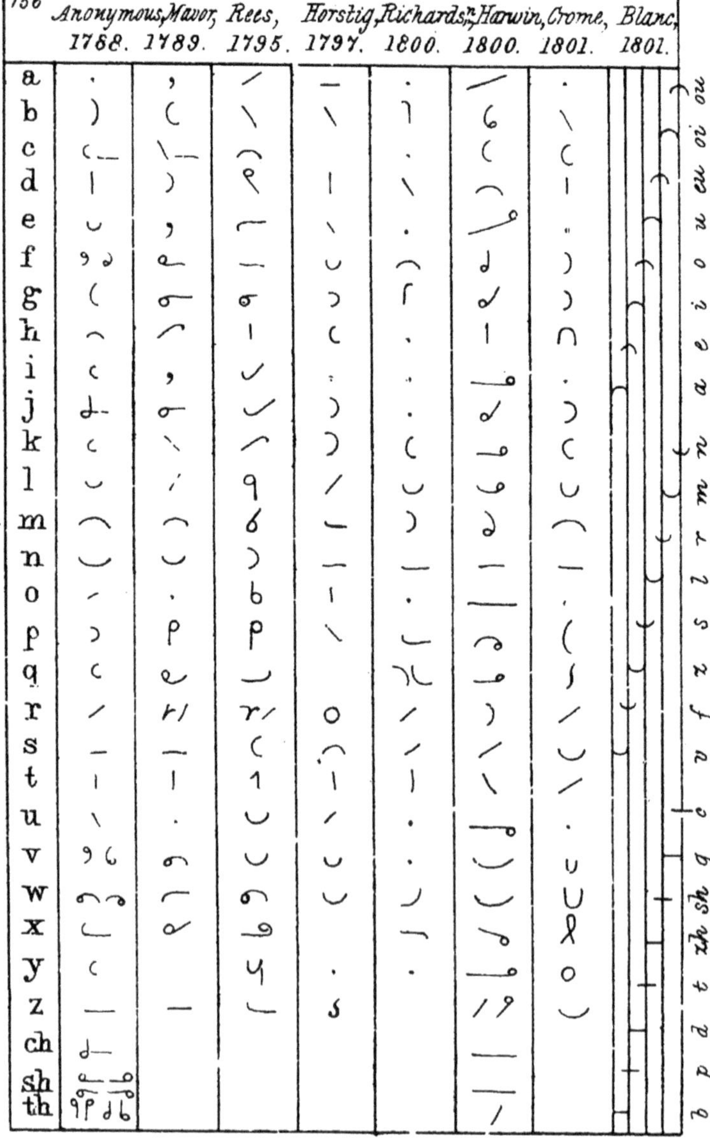
Anonymous, 1768.
Mavor, 1789.
Rees, 1795.
Horstig, 1797.
Richards, 1800.
Mr Harwin, 1800.
Crome, 1801.
Blanc, 1801.
a b c d e f g h i j k l m n o p q r s t u v w x y z ch sh th
b p d t zh sh g c v f z s l r m n a e i o u eu oi ou

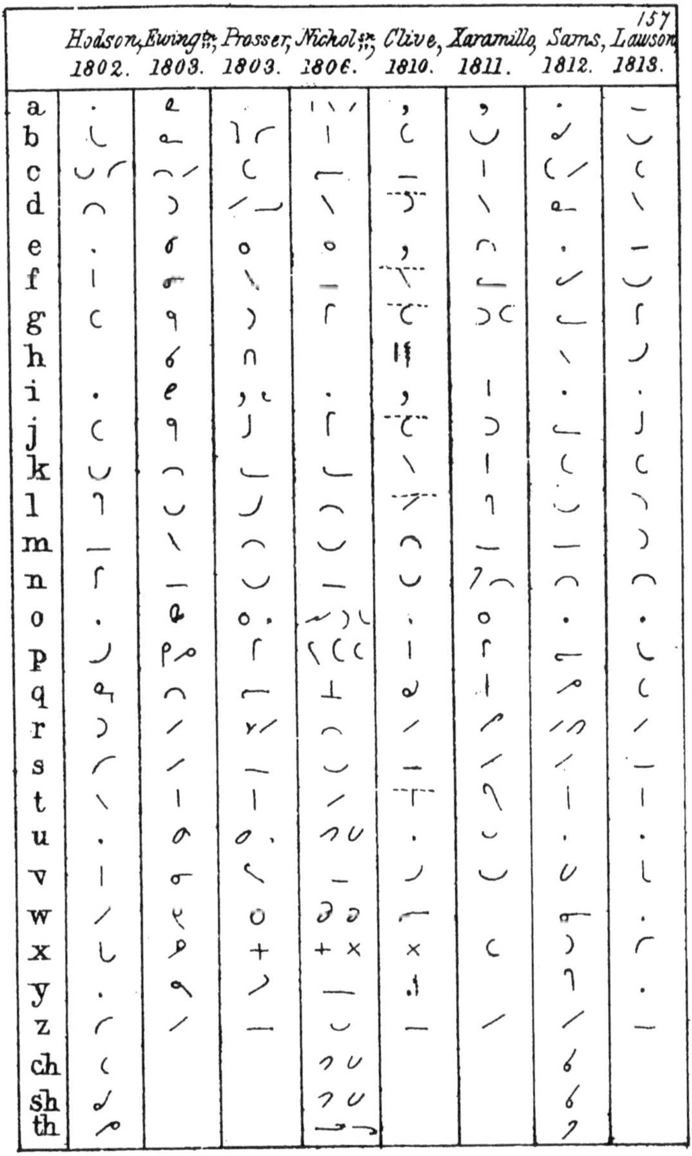
157
Hodson, 1802.
Ewing sr., 1803.
Prosser, 1803.
Nichol sr., 1806.
Clive, 1810.
Xaramillo, 1811.
Sams, 1812.
Lawson, 1813.
a
b
c
d
e
f
g
h
i
j
k
l
m
n
o
p
q
r
s
t
u
v
w
x
y
z
ch
sh
th

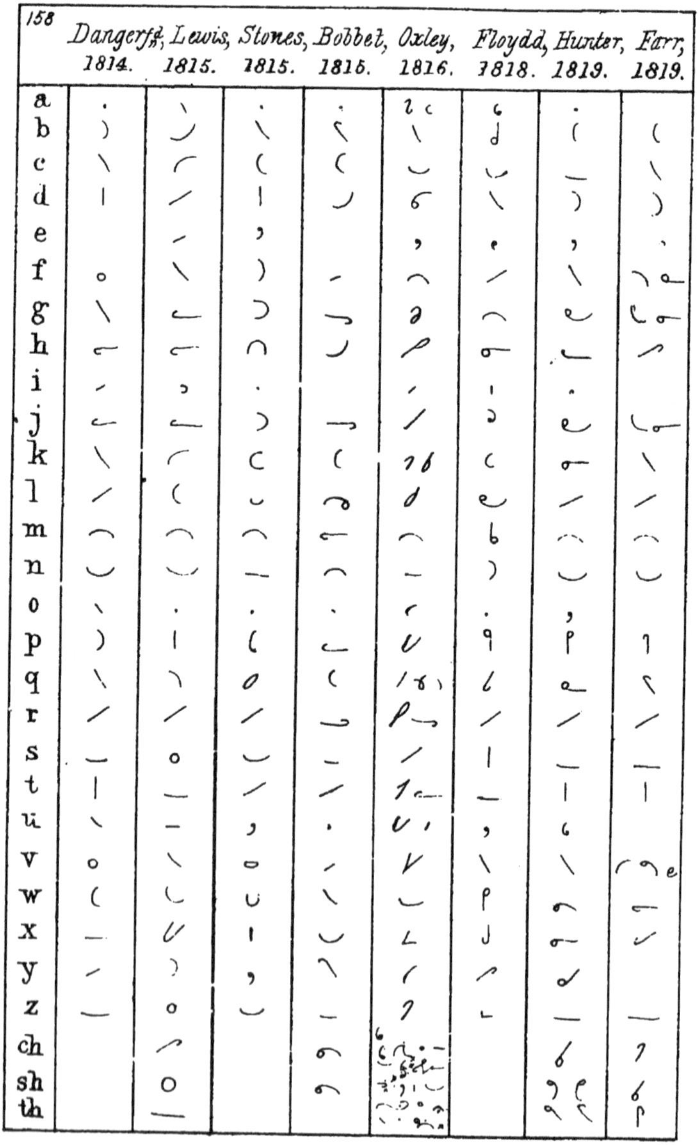
Dangerf^d, Lewis, Stones, Bobbet, Oxley, Floydd, Hunter, Farr,
1814. 1815. 1815. 1816. 1816. 1818. 1819. 1819.
a
b
c
d
e
f
g
h
i
j
k
l
m
n
o
p
q
r
s
t
u
v
w
x
y
z
ch
sh
th

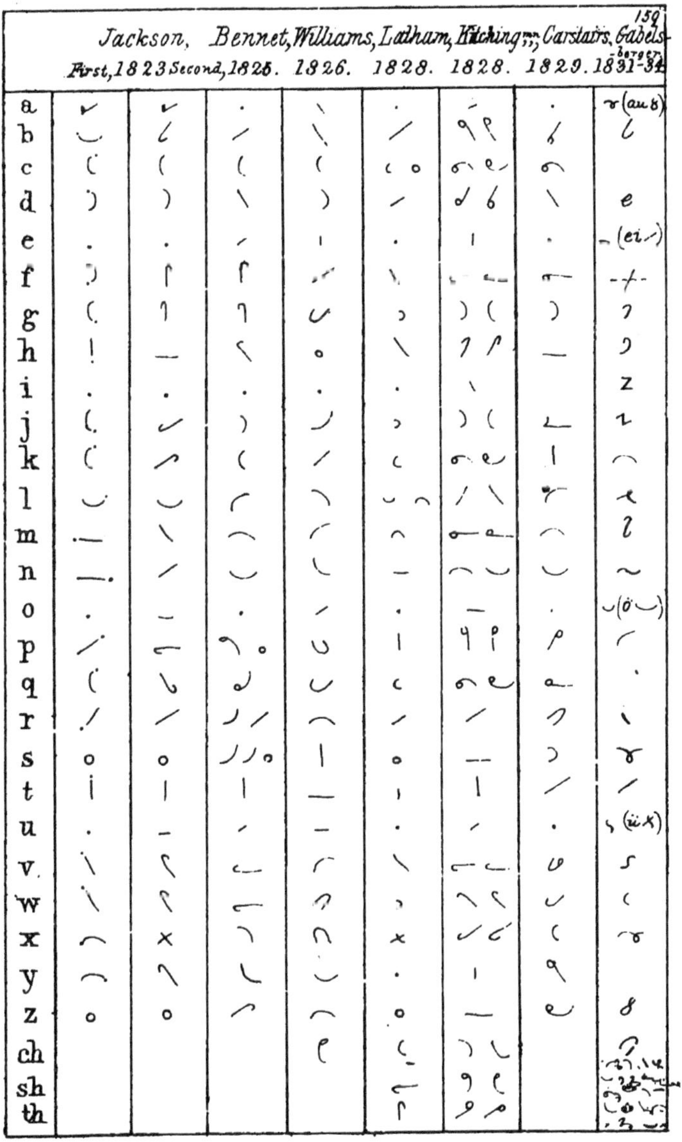
Jackson, First, 1823
Second, 1825.
Bennet, 1826.
Williams, 1828.
Latham, 1828.
Kitching, 1829.
Carstairs, 1831-34
Gabelsberger
a
b
c
d
e
f
g
h
i
j
k
l
m
n
o
p
q
r
s
t
u
v
w
x
y
z
ch
sh
th

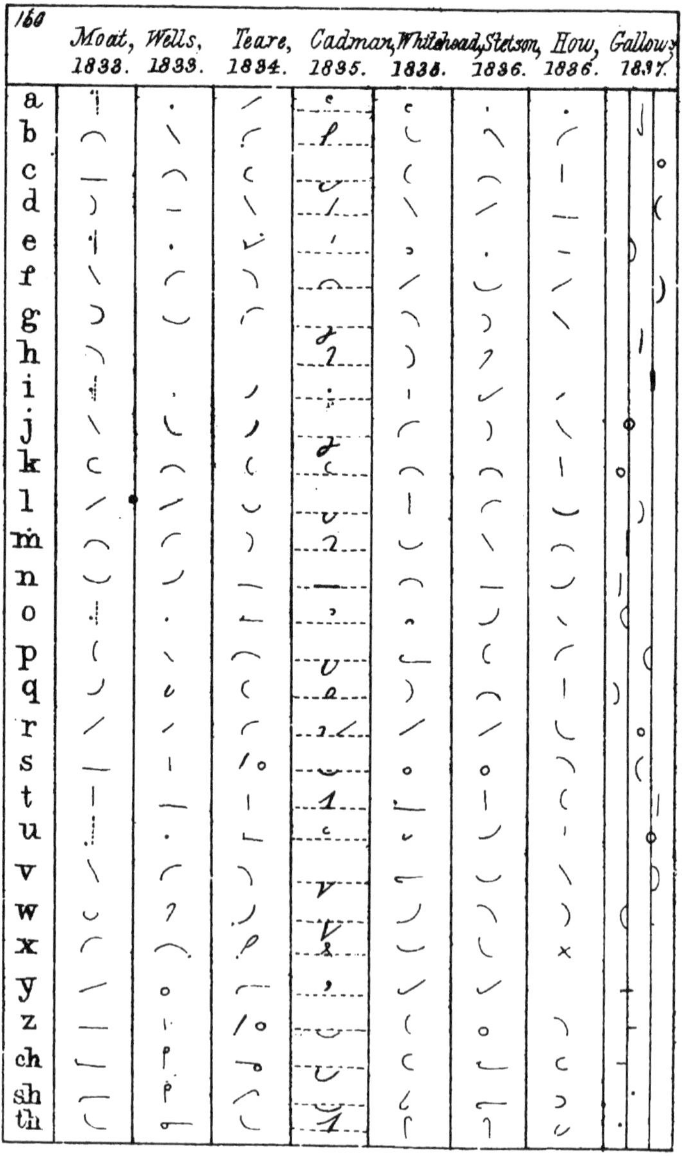
Moat, 1833.
Wells, 1833.
Teare, 1834.
Cadman, 1835.
Whitehead, 1835.
Stetson, 1836.
How, 1836.
Gallows, 1837.
a
b
c
d
e
f
g
h
i
j
k
l
m
n
o
p
q
r
s
t
u
v
w
x
y
z
ch
sh
th

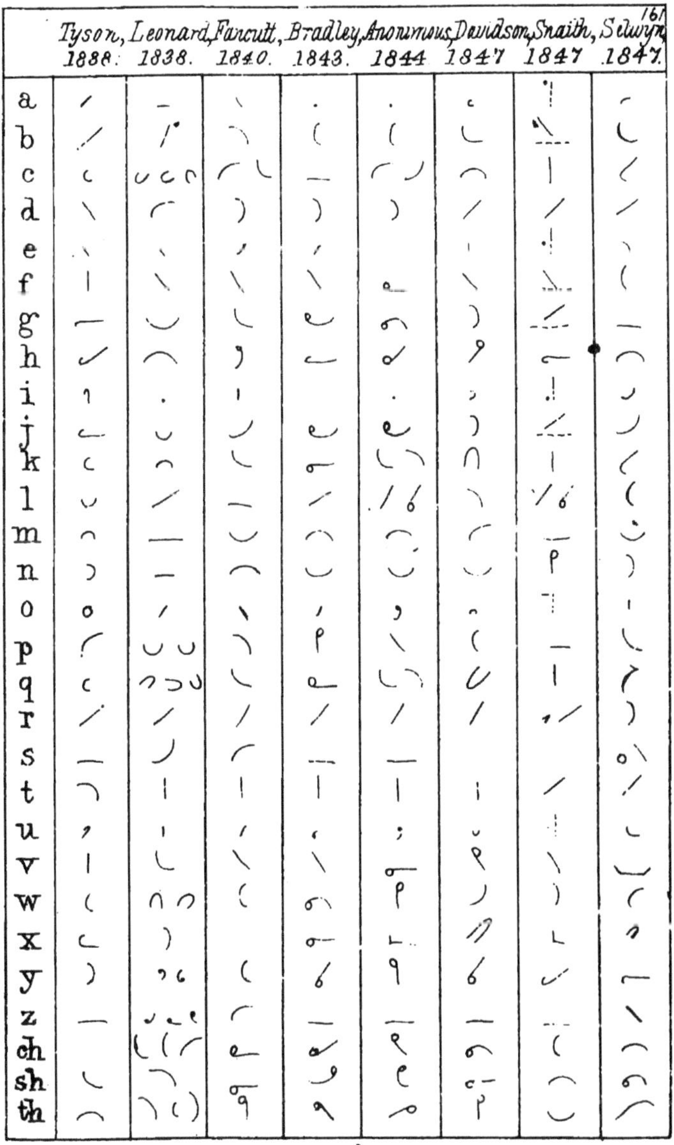
161
Tyson, 1888.
Leonard, 1838.
Fancutt, 1840.
Bradley, 1843.
Anonymous, 1844
Davidson, 1847
Snaith, 1847
Selwyn, 1847.
a
b
c
d
e
f
g
h
i
j
k
l
m
n
o
p
q
r
s
t
u
v
w
x
y
z
ch
sh
th

SPECIMENS OF A,B,C, SYSTEMS.

GURNEY'S MASON, 1753.

The Lord's Prayer.

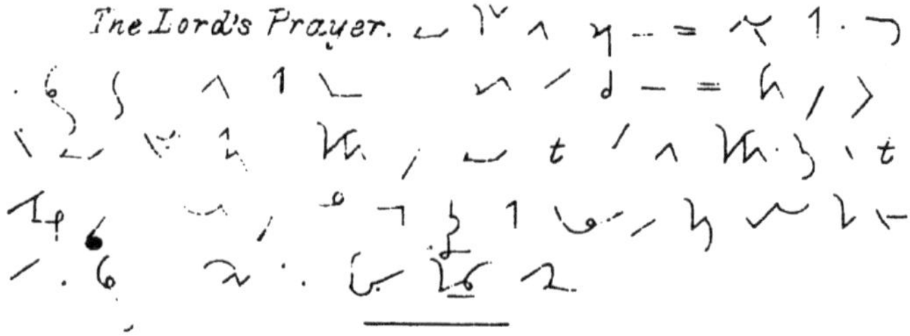

BYROM, 1767.

The Lord's Prayer.

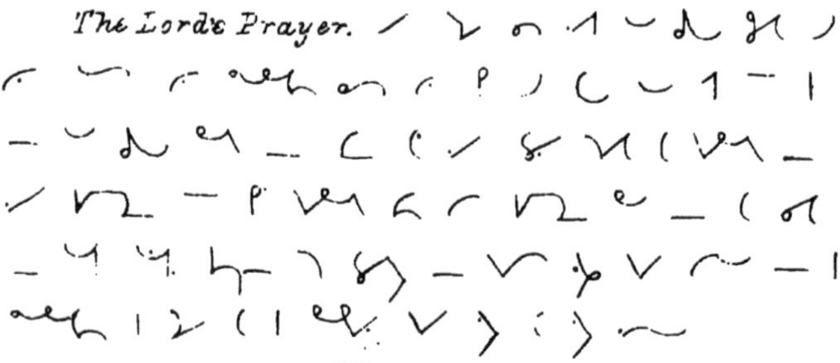

TAYLOR, 1786.

Psalm 15, 1-3

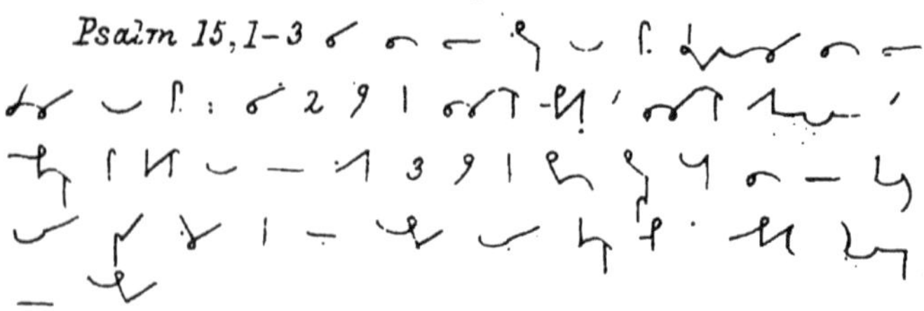

MAVOR, 1789.

Job 29, 11--13.

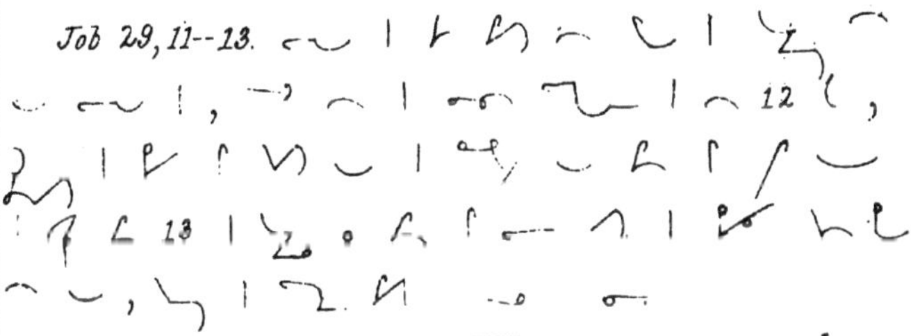

LEWIS, 1815.

Proverbs 9, 8-10.

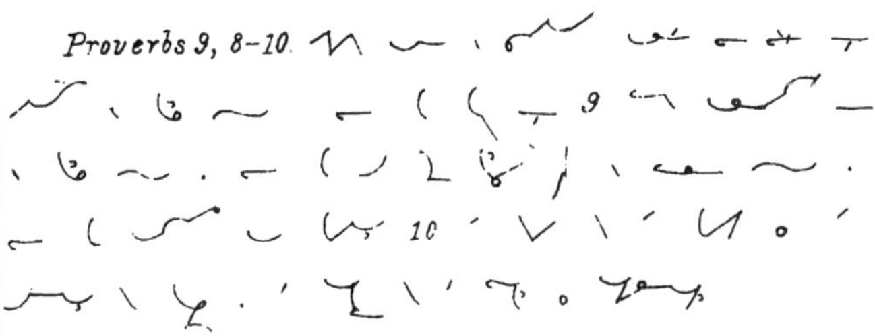

FLOYDD, 1818.

Psalm 93, 1.

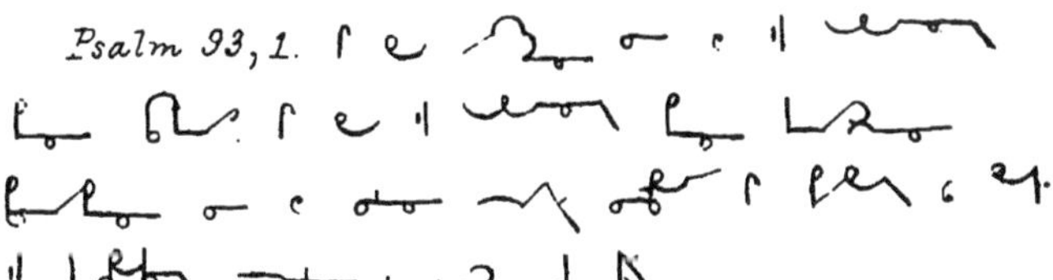

Phonography.

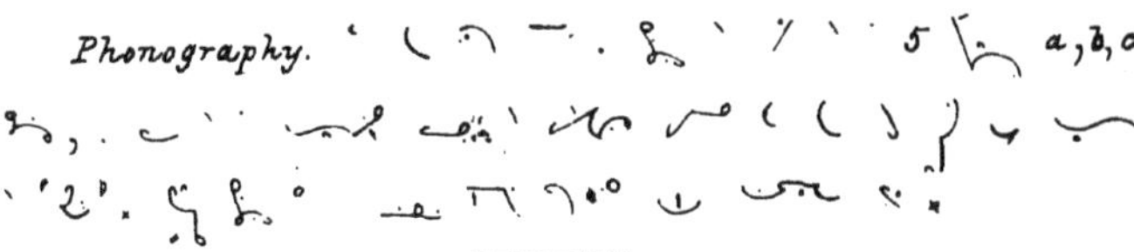

PHONETIC SHORTHAND ALPHABETS.

CONSONANTS.

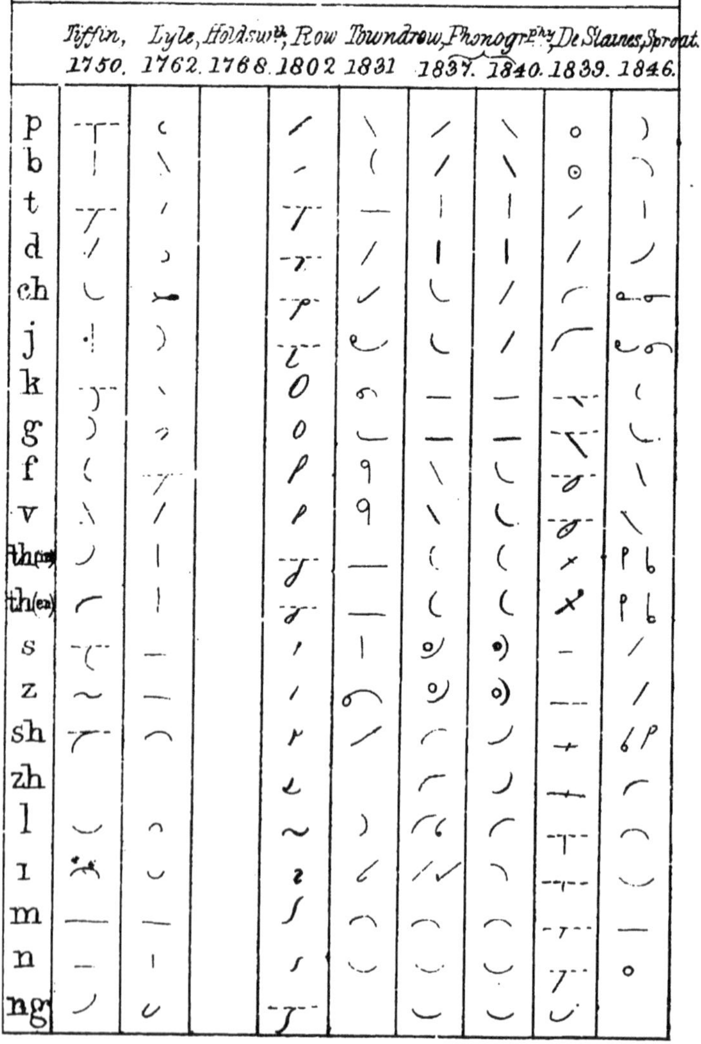

Tiffin, 1750.
Lyle, 1762.
Holdswth, 1768.
Row 1802
Towndrow, 1831
Phonogrphy, 1837. 1840.
De Stains, 1839.
Sproat. 1846.
p
b
t
d
ch
j
k
g
f
v
th(in)
th(en)
s
z
sh
zh
l
r
m
n
ng

PHONETIC SHORTHAND ALPHABETS.

VOWELS.

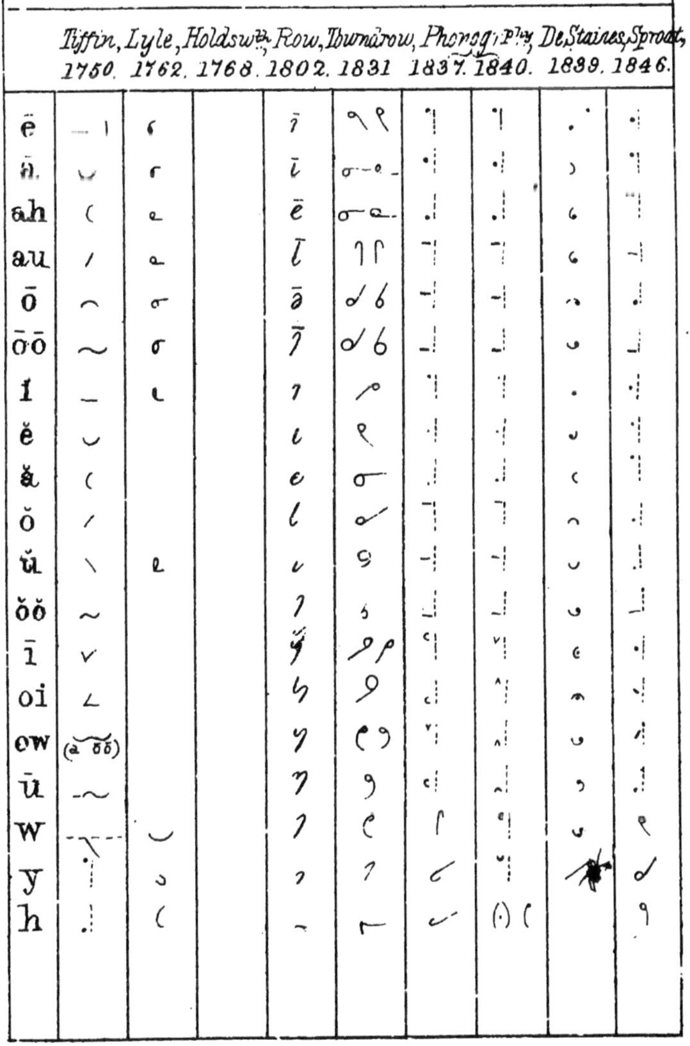

Tiffin, 1750.
Lyle, 1762.
Holdswth, 1768.
Row, 1802.
Ibunarow, 1831
Phonog^{phy}, 1837. 1840.
De Staines, 1839.
Sproat, 1846.
ē
ā
ah
au
ō
ōō
ĭ
ĕ
ă
ŏ
ŭ
ŏŏ
ī
oi
ow
(a ōō)
ū
w
y
h

SPECIMENS OF PHONETIC SYSTEMS.

TIFFIN 1750.

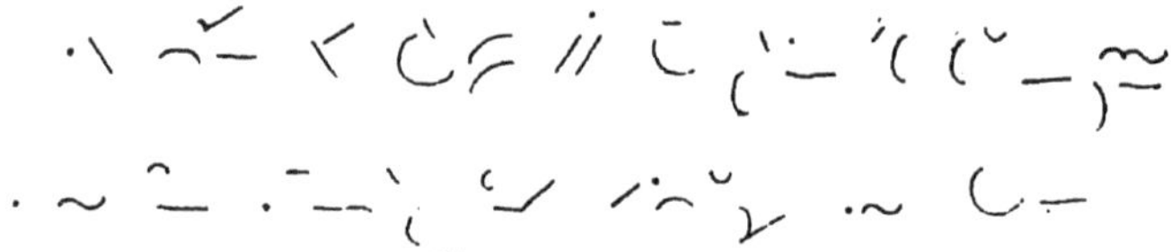

Transcription.

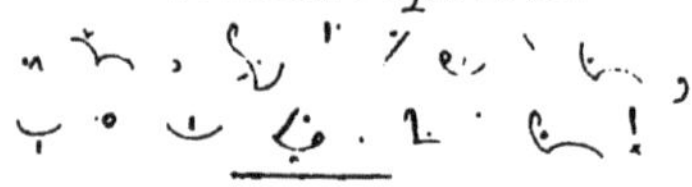

LYLE, 1762.

Transcription.

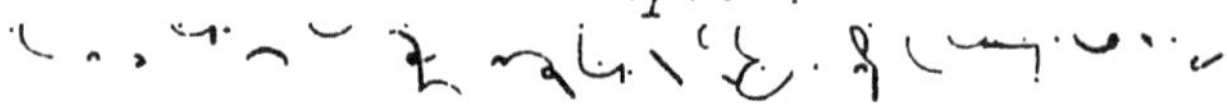

Note.

HOLDSWORTH, 1768.

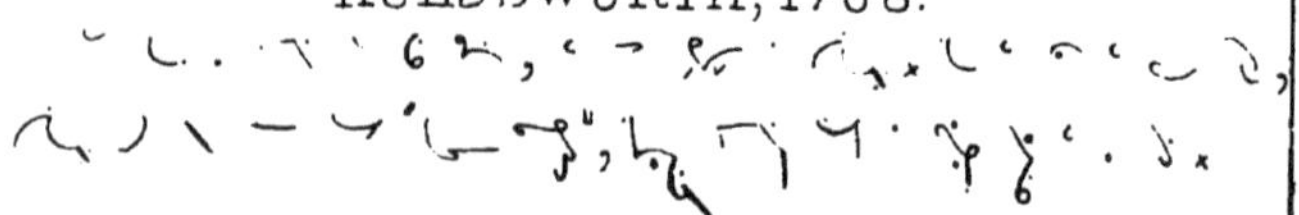

ROW, 1802.

The Lords Prayer.

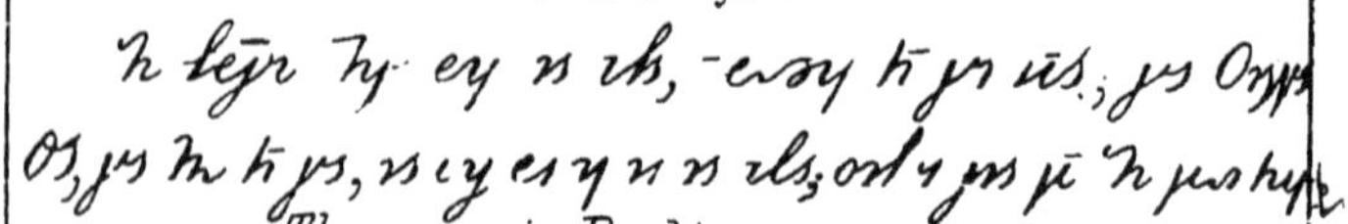

The same in Radiographic Shorthand.

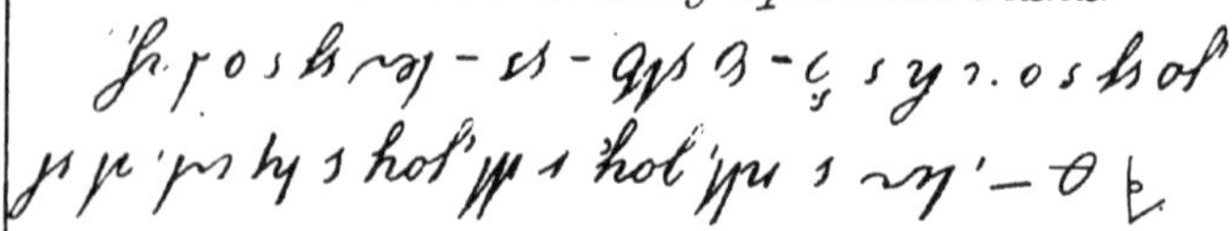

TOWNDROW, 1840,

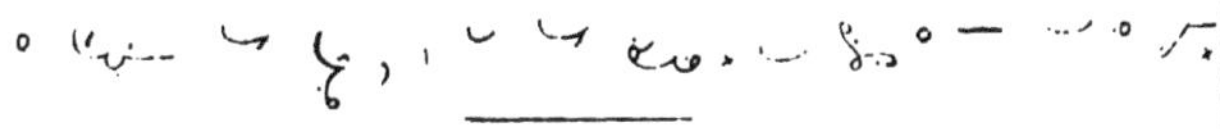

DE STAINES, 1839.

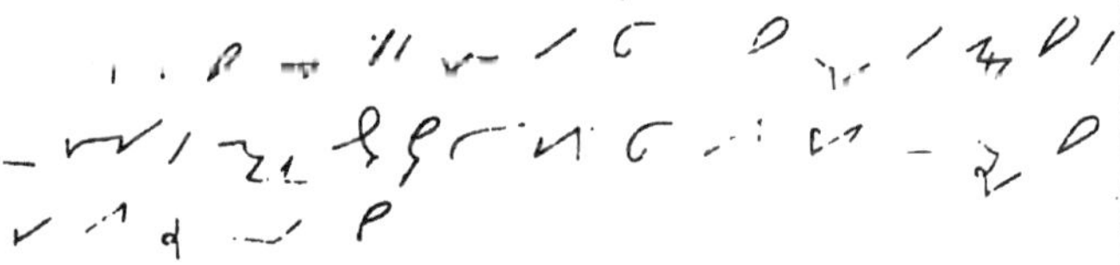

Transcription.

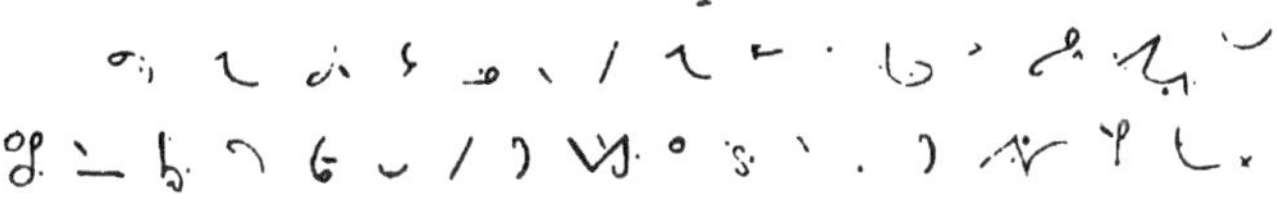

SPROAT, 1846.

Transcription.

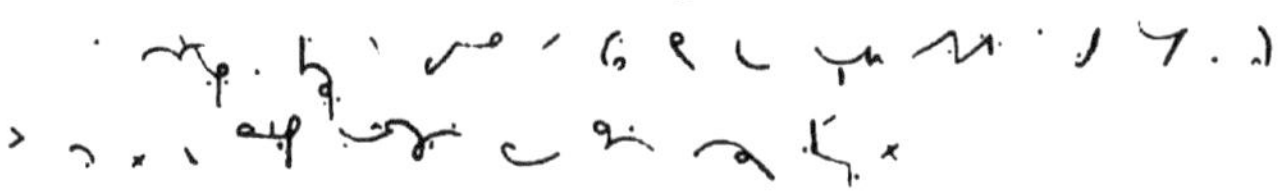

Printed in the USA
CPSIA information can be obtained
at www.ICGtesting.com
LVHW021316070524
779548LV00003B/543

9 781633 915367